What people are saying about
Pragmatic Thinking and Learning

This book will be the catalyst for your future.

► **Patrick Elder**
Agile Software Developer

By following Andy's concrete steps, you can make your most precious asset—your brain—more efficient and productive. Read this book, and do what Andy tells you to do. You'll think smarter, work better, and learn more than ever before.

► **Bert Bates**
Cocreator of Head First, Brain Friendly Books

I've always been looking for something to help me improve my learning skills, but I've never found anything as effective as this book. *Pragmatic Thinking and Learning* represents the best way to help you become an expert learner, improve your skills, and teach you how to improve your work efficiency by learning fast and easily.

► **Oscar Del Ben**
Software developer

I love books that explain that context matters. This book does—and helps you understand why. From the Dreyfus model (a source of many "aha's" for me) to explaining why experiential training works (the wall climbing story), Andy writes with humor and with tact so you can learn from reading and organize your own thinking and learning.

► **Johanna Rothman**
Consultant, author and speaker

This is an accessible and insightful book that will be useful to readers in many fields. I enjoyed reading it!

▶ **Dr. Patricia Benner**
Professor and Chair, Department of Social and Behavioral Sciences, University of California, San Francisco

Finished reading the beta last night. I loved this talk at NFJS (and the herding racehorses one), and to have it in book form— spectacular. All of this material has really changed my life!

▶ **Matt McKnight**
Software developer

This has been fun, and I've learned a lot—can't ask for more than that.

▶ **Linda Rising**
International speaker, consultant, and object-oriented expert

Pragmatic Thinking and Learning

Refactor Your "Wetware"

Pragmatic Thinking and Learning

Refactor Your "Wetware"

Andy Hunt

The Pragmatic Bookshelf

Raleigh, North Carolina   Dallas, Texas

Many of the designations used by manufacturers and sellers to distinguish their products are claimed as trademarks. Where those designations appear in this book, and The Pragmatic Programmers, LLC was aware of a trademark claim, the designations have been printed in initial capital letters or in all capitals. The Pragmatic Starter Kit, The Pragmatic Programmer, Pragmatic Programming, Pragmatic Bookshelf and the linking *g* device are trademarks of The Pragmatic Programmers, LLC.

Information contained in this book is intended as an educational aid only. Information is not intended as medical advice for any individual condition or treatment, and is not a substitute for professional medical care.

Every precaution was taken in the preparation of this book. However, the publisher assumes no responsibility for errors or omissions, or for damages that may result from the use of information (including program listings) contained herein.

Our Pragmatic courses, workshops, and other products can help you and your team create better software and have more fun. For more information, as well as the latest Pragmatic titles, please visit us at

http://www.pragprog.com

Printed in the United States of America.

ISBN-10: 1-934356-05-0

ISBN-13: 978-1-934356-05-0

Printed on acid-free paper.

P1.0 printing, October 2008

Version: 2008-9-15

For my wife and children,
and for everyone who becomes what they think.

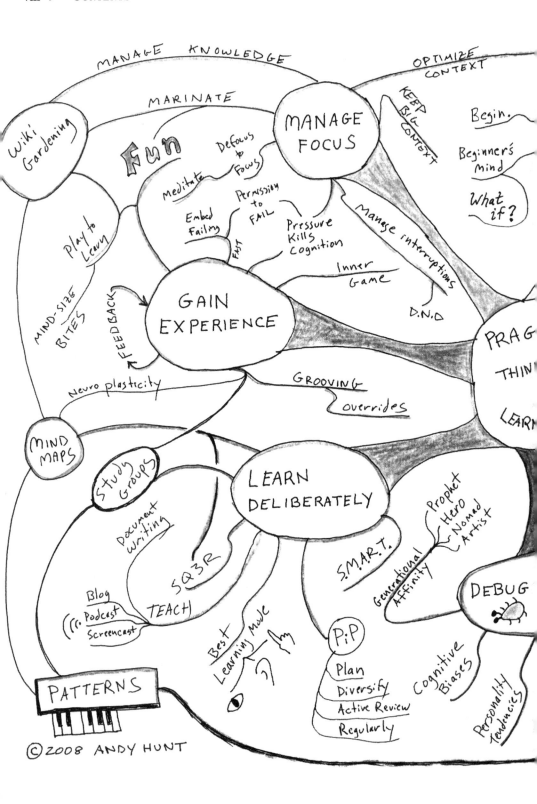

Contents

1 Introduction   **1**

   1.1   Again with the "Pragmatic"?   4

   1.2   Consider the Context   5

   1.3   Everyone Is Talking About This Stuff   6

   1.4   Where We're Going   7

   1.5   Grateful Acknowledgments 11

2 Journey from Novice to Expert   **13**

   2.1   Novices vs. Experts 15

   2.2   The Five Dreyfus Model Stages 17

   2.3   Dreyfus at Work: Herding Racehorses and Racing

         Sheep 25

   2.4   Using the Dreyfus Model Effectively 31

   2.5   Beware the Tool Trap 38

   2.6   Consider the Context, Again 41

   2.7   Day-to-Day Dreyfus 43

3 This Is Your Brain   **45**

   3.1   Your Dual-CPU Modes 46

   3.2   Capture Insight 24x7 51

   3.3   Linear and Rich Characteristics 55

   3.4   Rise of the $\mathcal{R}$-mode 63

   3.5 $\mathcal{R}$-mode Sees Forest; **L**-mode Sees Trees 68

   3.6   DIY Brain Surgery and Neuroplasticity 70

   3.7   How Do You Get There? 71

4 Get in Your Right Mind   **73**

   4.1   Turn Up the Sensory Input 73

   4.2   Draw on the Right Side 75

   4.3   Engage an $\mathcal{R}$-mode to **L**-mode Flow 80

   4.4   Harvest $\mathcal{R}$-mode Cues 92

   4.5   Harvesting Patterns 102

   4.6   Get It Right 110

5 Debug Your Mind **113**

5.1 Meet Your Cognitive Biases 115

5.2 Recognize Your Generational Affinity 123

5.3 Codifying Your Personality Tendencies 133

5.4 Exposing Hardware Bugs 136

5.5 Now I Don't Know What to Think 140

6 Learn Deliberately **145**

6.1 What Learning Is...and Isn't 145

6.2 Target SMART Objectives 149

6.3 Create a Pragmatic Investment Plan 154

6.4 Use Your Primary Learning Mode 158

6.5 Work Together, Study Together 164

6.6 Use Enhanced Learning Techniques 166

6.7 Read Deliberately with SQ3R 167

6.8 Visualize Insight with Mind Maps 171

6.9 Harness the Real Power of Documenting 178

6.10 Learn by Teaching 180

6.11 Take It to the Streets 182

7 Gain Experience **183**

7.1 Play in Order to Learn 183

7.2 Leverage Existing Knowledge 187

7.3 Embed Failing in Practice 189

7.4 Learn About the Inner Game 193

7.5 Pressure Kills Cognition 198

7.6 Imagination Overrides Senses 202

7.7 Learn It like an Expert 206

8 Manage Focus **209**

8.1 Increase Focus and Attention 210

8.2 Defocus to Focus 216

8.3 Manage Your Knowledge 219

8.4 Optimize Your Current Context 226

8.5 Manage Interruptions Deliberately 232

8.6 Keep a Big Enough Context 239

8.7 How to Stay Sharp 243

9   Beyond Expertise   245
    9.1   Effective Change 245
    9.2   What to Do Tomorrow Morning 247
    9.3   Beyond Expertise 248

A   Photo Credits   253

B   Bibliography   255

    Index   265

Chapter 1

Introduction

Welcome!

Thanks for picking up this book. Together, we're going to journey through bits of cognitive science, neuroscience, and learning and behavioral theory. You'll see surprising aspects of how our brains work and see how you can beat the system to improve your own learning and thinking skills.

We're going to begin to refactor your wetware—redesign and rewire your brain—to make you more effective at your job. Whether you're a programmer, manager, "knowledge worker," technogeek, or deep thinker, or if you just happen to have a human brain you'd like to crank up, this book will help.

I'm a programmer, so my examples and rants will be directed at the world of software development. If you're not a programmer, don't worry; programming really has little to do with writing software in arcane, cryptic languages (although we have a curious attachment to that habit).

Programming is all about problem solving. It requires creativity, ingenuity, and invention. Regardless of your profession, you probably also have to solve problems creatively. However, for programmers, combining rich, flexible human thought with the rigid constraints of a digital computer exposes the power and the deepest flaws of both.

Whether you're a programmer or frustrated user, you may have already suspected that software development must be the most difficult endeavor ever envisioned and practiced by humans. Its complexity strains our best abilities daily, and failures can often be spectacular—and newsworthy. We've smashed spaceships into distant planets, blown up expensive rockets filled with irreplaceable experiments, plagued consumers with automated collection letters for $0.00, and stranded airline travelers on a semiregular basis.

But now the good news (sort of): it's all our fault. We tend to make programming much harder on ourselves than we need. Because of the way the industry has evolved over time, it seems we've lost track of some of the most fundamental, most important skills needed by a software developer.

The good news is that we can fix that right here and right now. This book will help show you how.

The number of bugs programmers introduce into programs has remained constant for the past forty years. Despite advances in programming languages, techniques, project methodologies, and so on, the defect density has remained fairly constant.[1]

Maybe that's because we've been focusing on the wrong things. Despite all these obvious changes in technology, one thing has remained constant: us. Developers. People.

Software isn't designed in an IDE or other tool. It's imagined and created in our heads.

Software is created in your head.

Ideas and concepts are shared and communicated among a team, including the folks who are paying our organization to develop this software. We've spent the time investing in basic technology—in languages, tools, methodologies. That was time well spent, but now it's time to move on.

Now we need to look at the really hard problems of social interaction in and between teams and even at the harder issues of just plain old thinking. No project is an island; software can't be built or perform in isolation.

Frederick Brooks, in his landmark paper "No Silver Bullet–Essence and Accident in Software Engineering" [Bro86], claimed that "the software product is embedded in a cultural matrix of applications,

---

1. Based on research by Capers Jones via Bob Binder.

users, laws, and machine vehicles.[2] These all change continually, and their changes inexorably force change upon the software product."

Brooks' observation puts us squarely at the center of the maelstrom of society itself. Because of this complex interaction of many interested parties and forces and the constant evolution of change, it seems to me that the two most important modern skills are these:

- Communication skills
- Learning and thinking skills

Some improvement to communication skills is being addressed by our industry. Agile methods (see the sidebar on the following page), in particular, emphasize improved communications between team members and between the ultimate customer and the development team. Mass-media books such as *Presentation Zen: Simple Ideas on Presentation Design and Delivery* [Rey08] are suddenly best-sellers as more and more people realize the importance of simple, effective communication. It's a good start.

But then there's learning and thinking, which is a much harder nut to crack.

Programmers have to learn constantly—not just the stereotypical new technologies but also the problem domain of the application, the whims of the user community, the quirks of their teammates, the shifting sands of the industry, and the evolving characteristics of the project itself as it is built. We have to learn—and relearn— constantly. Then we have to apply this learning to the daily barrage of both old and new problems.

It sounds easy enough in principle perhaps, but learning, critical thinking, creativity, and invention—all those mind-expanding skills—are all up to you. You don't get taught; you have to learn. We tend to look at the teacher/learner relationship the wrong way around: it's not that the teacher *teaches*; it's that the student *learns*. The learning is always up to you.

It's my hope that *Pragmatic Thinking and Learning* can help guide you through accelerated and enhanced learning and more pragmatic thinking.

---

2. That is, platforms.

> ### What Are Agile Methods?
>
> The term *agile methods* was coined at a summit meeting in February 2001 by seventeen leaders in software development, including the founders of various development methodologies such Extreme Programming, Scrum, Crystal, and, of course, our own pragmatic programming.
>
> Agile methods differ from traditional plan-based methods in a number of significant ways, most notably in eschewing rigid rules and discarding dusty old schedules in favor of adapting to real-time feedback.
>
> I'll talk about agile methods often throughout the book, because many of the agile ideas and practices fit in well with good cognitive habits.

1.1 Again with the "Pragmatic"?

From the original *The Pragmatic Programmer: From Journeyman to Master* [HT00] to our Pragmatic Bookshelf publishing imprint, you will notice that we have a certain preoccupation with the word *pragmatic*. The essence of *pragmatism* is to do what works—for you.

So before we begin, please bear in mind that every individual is different. Although many of the studies that I'll reference have been conducted on large populations, some have not. I'm going to draw on a large variety of material ranging from hard scientific fact proven with functional MRI scans of the brain to conceptual theories, as well as material ranging from old wives' tales to "Hey, Fred tried it, and it worked for him."

In many cases—especially when discussing the brain—the underlying scientific reasons are unknown or unknowable. But do not let that worry you: if it works, then it's pragmatic, and I will offer it here for your consideration. I hope many of these ideas will work for you.

Only dead fish go with the flow.

But some folks are just plain wired differently; you may be one of them. And that's OK; you shouldn't follow any advice blindly. Even mine. Instead, read with an open mind. Try the suggestions, and decide what works for you.

What Is Wetware?

wet•ware |'wet,we(ə)r| : etymology: wet + software

Noun, humorous. Human brain cells or thought processes regarded as analogous to, or in contrast with, computer systems.

That is, using the model of a computer as an analogy to human thought processes.

As you grow and adapt, you may need to modify your habits and approaches as well. Nothing in life is ever static; only dead fish go with the flow. So, please take this book as just the beginning.

I'll share the pragmatic ideas and techniques I've found in my journey; the rest is up to you.

1.2 Consider the Context

Everything is interconnected: the physical world, social systems, your innermost thoughts, the unrelenting logic of the computer—everything forms one immense, interconnected system of reality. Nothing exists in isolation; everything is part of the system and part of a larger context.

Because of that inconvenient fact of reality, small things can have unexpectedly large effects. That disproportionate effect is the hallmark of nonlinear systems, and in case you hadn't noticed, the real world is decidedly nonlinear.

> *When we try to pick out anything by itself, we find it hitched to everything else in the universe.*
> ▶ John Muir, 1911, *My First Summer in the Sierra*

Throughout this book, you'll find activities or differences that seem to be so subtle or inconsequential that they couldn't *possibly* make a difference. These are activities such as thinking a thought to yourself vs. speaking it out loud or such as writing a sentence on a piece of paper vs. typing it into an editor on the computer. Abstractly, these things should be perfectly equivalent.

But they aren't.

These kinds of activities utilize very different pathways in the brain—pathways that are affected by your very thoughts and how you think them. Your thoughts are not disconnected from the rest of the brain machinery or your body; *it's all connected.* This is just one example (and we'll talk more about the brain later in the book), but it helps illustrate the importance of thinking about interacting systems.

Everything is interconnected.

In his seminal book *The Fifth Discipline: The Art and Practice of the Learning Organization* [Sen90], Peter Senge popularized the term *systems thinking* to describe a different approach of viewing the world. In systems thinking, one tries to envision an object as a connection point of several systems, rather than as a discrete object unto itself.

For instance, you might consider a tree to be a single, discrete object sitting on the visible ground. But in fact, a tree is a connection of at least two major systems: the processing cycle of leaves and air and of roots and earth. It's not static; it's not isolated. And even more interesting, you'll rarely be a simple observer of a system. More likely, you'll be part of it, whether you know it or not.[3]

> TIP 1
>
> Always consider the context.

Put a copy of that up on your wall or your desktop, in your conference room, on your whiteboard, or anywhere you think alone or with others. We'll be returning to it.

1.3 Everyone Is Talking About This Stuff

As I was mulling over the idea of writing this book, I started to notice that a *lot* of people in different disciplines were talking about the topics in which I was interested. But these were in very different and diverse areas, including the following:

- MBA and executive-level training
- Cognitive science research

---

3. Suggested by our old buddy Heisenberg and his quantum uncertainty principle, the more general *observer effect* posits that you can't observe a system without altering it.

- Learning theory
- Nursing, health care, aviation, and other professions and industries
- Yoga and meditative practices
- Programming, abstraction, and problem solving
- Artificial intelligence research

When you start to find the same set of ideas—the same common threads—showing up in different guises in these very different areas, that's usually a sign. **There's something fundamental here.** There must be something fundamental and very important lurking under the covers for these similar ideas to be present in so many different contexts.

Yoga and meditative techniques seem to be enjoying quite a bit of mainstream popularity these days, and not always for obvious reasons. I noticed an article in an in-flight magazine around October 2005 that trumpeted the headline "Companies Now Offering Yoga and Meditation to Help Fight Rising Health-Care Costs."

Large companies have not historically embraced such warm-and-fuzzy activities. But the meteoric rise of health-care costs has forced them to take *any* course of action that might help. Clearly, they believe the studies showing that practitioners of yoga and meditative techniques enjoy greater overall health than the general population. In this book, we're more interested in the areas related to cognition, but greater overall health is a nice side benefit.

I also noticed that a number of MBA and executive-level courses promote various meditative, creative, and intuitive techniques—stuff that fits in perfectly with the available research but that has not yet been passed down to the employees in the trenches, including us knowledge-worker types.

But not to worry, we'll be covering these topics here for you. No MBA required.

1.4 Where We're Going

Every good journey begins with a map, and ours appears in the front portion of this book. Despite the linear flow of a book, these topics are entwined and interrelated, as the map shows.

After all, everything is connected to everything else. But it's somewhat difficult to appreciate that idea with a linear read of a book. You can't always get a sense of what's related when faced with countless "see also" references in the text. By presenting the map graphically, I hope you get the opportunity to see what's related to what a little more clearly.

With that in mind, the following is roughly where we are headed, despite a few side trips, tangents, and excursions on the way.

Journey from Novice to Expert

In the first part of the book, we'll look at *why* your brain works as it does, beginning with a popular model of expertise.

The Dreyfus model of skill acquisition provides a powerful way of looking at how you move beyond beginner-level performance and begin the journey to mastery of a skill. We'll take a look at the Dreyfus model and in particular look at the keys to becoming an expert: harnessing and applying your own experience, understanding *context*, and harnessing *intuition*.

This Is Your Brain

The most important tool in software development is, of course, your own brain. We'll take a look at some of the basics of cognitive science and neuroscience as they relate to our interests as software developers, including a model of the brain that looks a lot like a dual-CPU, shared-bus design and how to do your own brain surgery of a sort.

Get in Your Right Mind

Once we have a better understanding of the brain, we will find ways to exploit underutilized facets of thinking to help encourage better creativity and problem solving, as well as harvest and process experiences more effectively.

We'll also take a look at where *intuition* comes from. Intuition, the hallmark of the expert, turns out to be a tricky beast. You need it, you rely on it, but you also probably fight against using it constantly, without knowing why. You may also be actively suspicious of your own and others' intuition, mistakenly thinking that it's "not scientific."

We'll see how to fix that and give your intuition freer reign.

Debug Your Mind

Intuition is a fantastic skill, except when it's wrong. There are a large number of "known bugs" in human thinking. You have built-in biases in your cognition, influences from when you're born and from your cohort (those born about the same time as you), your innate personality, and even hardware wiring problems.

These bugs in the system often mislead you by clouding your judgment and steering you toward bad, even disastrous, decisions.

Knowing these common bugs is the first step to mitigating them.

Learn Deliberately

Now that we've gotten a good look at how the brain works, we'll start taking a more deliberate look at *how* to take advantage of the system, beginning with learning.

Note that I mean *learning* in the broadest sense, covering not only new technologies, programming languages, and the like, but also your learning of the dynamics of the team you're on, the character-istics of the evolving software you're building, and so on. In these times, we have to learn all the time.

But most of us have never been taught how, so we sort of wing it as best we can. I'll show you some specific techniques to help improve your learning ability. We'll look at planning techniques, mind maps, a reading technique known as SQ3R, and the cognitive importance of teaching and writing. Armed with these techniques, you can absorb new information faster and easier, gain more insights, and retain this new knowledge better.

Gain Experience

Gaining experience is key to your learning and growth—we learn best by doing. However, just "doing" alone is no guarantee of success; you have to learn from the doing for it to count, and it turns out that some common obstacles make this hard.

You can't force experience either; trying too hard can be just as bad (if not worse) than slogging through the same old motions. We'll take a look at what you need to create an efficient learning environment using feedback, fun, and failure; see the dangers of deadlines; and see how to gain experience virtually with mental grooving.

Manage Focus

Managing your attention and focus is the next critical step in your journey. I'll share with you some tricks, tips, and pointers to help you manage the flood of knowledge, information, and insights that you need to gain experience and learn. We live in information-rich times, and it's easy to get so swamped under the daily demands of our jobs that we have no chance to advance our careers. Let's try to fix that and increase your attention and focus.

We'll take a look at how to optimize your current context, manage those pesky interruptions better, and see why interruptions are such cognitive train wrecks. We'll look at why you need to defocus in order to focus better in the mental marinade and manage your knowledge in a more deliberate manner.

Beyond Expertise

Finally, we'll take a quick look at why change is harder than it looks, and I'll offer suggestions for what you can do tomorrow morning to get started.

I'll share what I think lies beyond expertise and how to get there.

So, sit back, grab your favorite beverage, and let's take a look at what's under the hood.

Next Actions ⬇

Throughout the book, I'll suggest "next actions" that you can take to help reinforce and make this material real for you. These might include exercises to do, experiments to try, or habits to start. I'll list these using checkboxes so you can check the items you've done, like this:

- ☐ Take a hard look at current problems on your project. Can you spot the different systems involved? Where do they interact? Are these interaction points related to the problems you're seeing?
- ☐ Find three things you've analyzed out of context that caused you problems later.
- ☐ Put up a sign somewhere near your monitor that reads "Consider the context."

About the Figures

You may notice that figures in this book don't look like the typical shiny, mechanically perfect drawings you'd expect from Adobe Illustrator or something similar. That's quite deliberate.

From the electronics books by Forrest M. Mims III to the back-of-the-napkin design documents favored by agile developers, hand-drawn figures have certain unique properties, and we'll see why a bit later in the book.

1.5 Grateful Acknowledgments

Very special thanks to Ellie Hunt for introducing me to the Dreyfus model and related nursing research, suffering through my disjointed and rambling prose, keeping me on track, and keeping our domestic enterprises running like a well-oiled machine. A regular editor's job is often difficult and thankless, and mere appreciation in a preface really doesn't do it justice. To be editor, mom, and business manager all at once truly takes skill and patience.

Thanks to my friends on the Pragmatic Wetware mailing list and reviewers, including Bert Bates, Don Gray, Ron Green, Shawn Hartstock, Dierk Koenig, Niclas Nilsson, Paul Oakes, Jared Richardson, Linda Rising, Johanna Rothman, Jeremy Sydik, Steph Thompson, and everyone else who posted their thoughts, experiences, and readings. Their combined experiences are invaluable.

Special thanks to June Kim for his many contributions throughout the book, including pointers to far-flung research and stories of his own experiences, as well as his feedback throughout the stages of birthing this book.

Special thanks also to Dr. Patricia Benner, who introduced the Dreyfus model of skills acquisition to the nursing profession, for her support and permission to quote from her works and for her enthusiasm for learning.

Thanks go to Dr. Betty Edwards, who pioneered the practical applications of lateral specialization in the brain, for her kind support and permission to quote from her works.

Thanks to Sara Lynn Eastler for the index, to Kim Wimpsett for correcting my many typos and often haphazard grammar, and to Steve Peter for implementing a plethora of typesetting tricks.

And finally, thanks to *you* for purchasing this book and beginning the journey with me.

Let's move our profession forward in the right direction, harness our experience and intuition, and create new environments where learning matters.

We can't solve problems by using the same kind of thinking we used when we created them.

▶ Albert Einstein

Chapter 2

Journey from Novice to Expert

Wouldn't you like to be the expert? To intuitively *know* the right answer? This is the first step of our journey together along that road. In this chapter, we'll look at what it means to be a novice and what it means to be an expert—and all the stages in between. Here's where our story begins.

Once upon a time, two researchers (brothers) wanted to advance the state of the art in artificial intelligence. They wanted to write software that would learn and attain skills in the same manner that humans learn and gain skill (or prove that it couldn't be done). To do that, they first had to study how humans learn.

They developed the *Dreyfus model* of skill acquisition,[1] which outlines five discrete stages through which one must pass on the journey from novice to expert. We'll take a look at this concept in depth; as it turns out, we're not the first ones to use it effectively.

Back in the early 1980s, the nursing profession in the United States used the lessons of the Dreyfus model to correct their approach and help advance their profession. At the time, the problems faced by nurses mirrored many of the same problems programmers and engineers face today. Their profession has made great progress, and in the meantime we still have some work to do with ours.

---

1. Described in *Mind Over Machine: The Power of Human Intuition and Expertise in the Era of the Computer* [DD86].

Event Theories vs. Construct Theories

The Dreyfus model is what's called a *construct* theory. There are two types of theories: *event* theories and *construct* theories.* Both are used to explain some phenomenon that you've observed.

Event theories can be measured; these types of theories can be verified and proven. You can judge the accuracy of an event theory.

Construct theories are intangible abstractions; it makes no sense to speak of "proving them." Instead, construct theories are evaluated in terms of their usefulness. You can't judge a construct theory to be accurate or not. That's mixing apples and existentialism. An apple is a thing; existentialism is an abstraction.

For instance, I can prove all sorts of things about your brain using simple electricity or complex medical imaging devices. But I can't even prove you have a mind. *Mind* is an abstraction; there's really no such thing. It's just an idea, a concept. But it's a very useful one.

The Dreyfus model is a construct theory. It's an abstraction, and as we'll see, it's a very useful one.

---
*. See *Tools of Critical Thinking: Metathoughts for Psychology* (Lev97).

Here are some observations that ring true for both nurses and programmers, and probably other professions as well:

- Expert staff members working in the trenches aren't always recognized as experts or paid accordingly.
- Not all expert staff want to end up as managers.
- There's a huge variance in staff members' abilities.
- There's a huge variance in managers' abilities.
- Any given team likely has members at widely different skill levels and can't be treated as a homogeneous set of replaceable resources.

There's more to skill levels than just being better, smarter, or faster. The Dreyfus model describes how and why our abilities, attitudes, capabilities, and perspectives change according to skill level.

Figure 2.1: A UNIX WIZARD

It helps explain why many of the past approaches to software development improvement have failed. It suggests a course of action that we can pursue in order to meaningfully improve the software development profession—both as individual practitioners and for the industry as a whole.

Let's take a look.

2.1 Novices vs. Experts

What do you call an expert software developer? A *wizard*. We work with magic numbers, things in hex, zombie processes, and mystical incantations such as tar -xzvf plugh.tgz and sudo gem install --include-dependencies rails.

We can even change our identity to become someone else or transform into the root user—the epitome of supreme power in the Unix world. Wizards make it look effortless. A dash of eye of newt, a little bat-wing dust, some incantations, and poof! The job is done.

<u>**Making It Look Easy**</u>

I once was in a position to interview professional organists. For an audition piece, I chose Charles-Marie Widor's "Toccata" (from Symphony No. 5 in F Minor, Op. 42 No. 1, for those who care about such things), a frenetic piece that sounded suitably difficult to my amateur ears.

One candidate really worked it—both feet flying on the pedals, hands running up and down both ranks of the organ in a blur, a stern look of intense concentration across her brow. She was practically sweating. It was a terrific performance, and I was suitably impressed.

But then came along the true expert. She played this difficult piece a little bit better, a little bit faster, but was smiling and *talking* to us while her hands and feet flew in an octopus-like blur.

She made it look easy, and she got the job.

Despite the mythological overtones, this vision is fairly common when considering an expert in any particular field (ours is just arcane enough to make it a really compelling image).

Consider the expert chef, for instance. Awash in a haze of flour, spices, and a growing pile of soiled pans left for an apprentice to clean, the expert chef may have trouble articulating just *how* this dish is made. "Well, you take a bit of this and a dash of that—not too much—and cook until done."

Chef Claude is not being deliberately obtuse; he knows what "cook until done" means. He knows the subtle difference between just enough and "too much" depending on the humidity, where the meat was purchased, and how fresh the vegetables are.

It's hard to articulate expertise.

It's often difficult for experts to explain their actions to a fine level of detail; many of their responses are so well practiced that they become preconscious actions. Their vast experience is mined by nonverbal, preconscious areas of the brain, which makes it hard for us to observe and hard for them to articulate.

When experts do their thing, it appears almost magical to the rest of us—strange incantations, insight that seems to appear out of nowhere, and a seemingly uncanny ability to know the right answer when the rest of us aren't even all that sure about the question.

It's not magic, of course, but the way that experts perceive the world, how they problem solve, the mental models they use, and so on, are all markedly different from nonexperts.

A novice cook, on the other hand, coming home after a long day at the office is probably not even interested in the subtle nuances of humidity and parsnips. The novice wants to know *exactly* how much saffron to put in the recipe (not just because saffron is ridiculously expensive).

The novice wants to know *exactly* how long to set the timer on the oven given the weight of the meat, and so on. It's not that the novice is being pedantic or stupid; it's just that novices need clear, context-free rules by which they can operate, just as the expert would be rendered ineffective if he were constrained to operate under those same rules.

Novices and experts are fundamentally different. They see the world in different ways, and they react in different ways. Let's look at the details.

2.2 The Five Dreyfus Model Stages

In the 1970s, the brothers Dreyfus (Hubert and Stuart) began doing their seminal research on how people attain and master skills.

The Dreyfus brothers looked at highly skilled practitioners, including commercial airline pilots and world-renowned chess masters.[2] Their research showed

Dreyfus is applicable per skill.

that quite a bit changes as you move from novice to expert. You don't just "know more" or gain skill. Instead, you experience fundamental differences in how you perceive the world, how you approach problem solving, and the mental models you form and use. How you go about acquiring new skills changes. External factors that help your performance—or hinder it—change as well.

---

2. Cited in *From Novice to Expert: Excellence and Power in Clinical Nursing Practice* [Ben01].

Unlike other models or assessments that rate the whole person, the Dreyfus model is applicable per skill. In other words, it's a situational model and not a trait or talent model.

You are neither "expert" nor "novice" at all things; rather, you are at one of these stages in some particular skill domain. You might be a novice cook but an expert sky diver, or vice versa. Most nondisabled adults are experts at walking—we do so without planning or thinking. It has become instinct. Most of us are novices at tax preparation. We can get through it given a sufficient number of clear rules to follow, but we really don't know what's going on (and wonder why on Earth those rules are so arcane).

The following are the five stages on the journey from novice to expert.

Stage 1: Novices

Expert
Proficient
Competent
Advanced Beginner
→ Novice

Novices, by definition, have little or no previous experience in this skill area. By "experience," I mean specifically that performing this skill results in a change of thinking. As a counterexample, consider the case of the developer who claims ten years of experience, but in reality it was one year of experience repeated nine times. That doesn't count as *experience*.

Novices are very concerned about their ability to succeed; with little experience to guide them, they really don't know whether their actions will all turn out OK. Novices don't particularly want to learn; they just want to accomplish an immediate goal. They do not know how to respond to mistakes and so are fairly vulnerable to confusion when things go awry.

They can, however, be somewhat effective if they are given context-free rules to follow, that is, rules of the form "Whenever X happens, do Y." In other words, they need a recipe.

Novices need recipes.

This is why call centers work. You can hire a large number of folks who don't have a lot of experience in the subject matter at hand and let them navigate a decision tree.

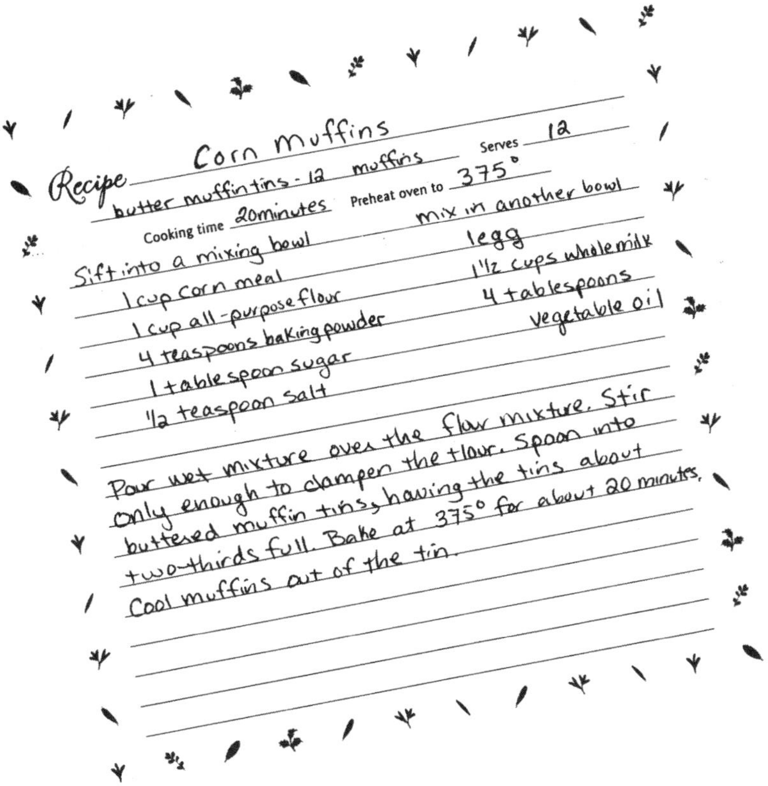

Figure 2.2: RECIPE FOR CORN MUFFINS. BUT HOW LONG DO YOU COOK IT?

A giant computer hardware company might use a script like this:

1. Ask the user whether the computer is plugged in.
2. If yes, ask whether the computer is powered on.
3. If no, ask them to plug it in and wait.
4. *and so on...*

It's tedious, but fixed rules such as these can give novices some measure of capability. Of course, novices face the problem of not knowing *which* rules are most relevant in a given situation. And when something unexpected comes up, they will be completely flummoxed.

As with most people, I am a novice when it comes to doing my taxes. I have little experience; despite having filed taxes for more than twenty-five years, I haven't learned anything or changed my thinking about it. I don't want to learn; I just want to accomplish the goal—to get them filed this year. I don't know how to respond to mistakes; when the IRS sends me a terse and rather arrogant form letter, I usually have no idea what they're on about or what to do to fix it.[3]

There is a solution, of course. A context-free rule to the rescue! Perhaps it's something such as the following:

- Enter the amount of money you earned last year.
- Send it in to the government.

That's simple and unambiguous.

The problem with recipes—with context-free rules—is that you can never specify everything fully. For instance, in the corn muffin recipe, it says to cook for "about 20 minutes." When do I cook longer? Or shorter? How do I know when it's done? You can set up more rules to explain, and then more rules to explain those, but there's a practical limit to how much you can effectively specify without running into a Clinton-esque "It depends upon what the meaning of the word *is* is." This phenomenon is known as *infinite regression*. At some point, you have to stop defining explicitly.

Rules can get you started, but they won't carry you further.

Stage 2: Advanced Beginners

Expert
Proficient
Competent
→Advanced Beginner
Novice

Once past the hurdles of the novice, one begins to see the problems from the viewpoint of the *advanced beginner.* Advanced beginners can start to break away from the fixed rule set a little bit. They can try tasks on their own, but they still have difficulty troubleshooting.

They want information fast. For instance, you may feel like this when you're learning a new language or API and you find yourself scanning the documentation quickly looking for that one method signature or set of arguments. You don't want to be bogged down with lengthy theory at this point or spoon-fed the basics yet again.

---

3. I forward it with my compliments and a large check to my accountant, who is expert in these matters. I hope.

Advanced beginners can start using advice in the correct context, based on similar situations they've experienced in the recent past but just barely. And although they can start formulating some

Advanced beginners don't want the big picture.

overall principles, there is no "big picture." They have no holistic understanding and really don't want it yet. If you tried to force the larger context on an advanced beginner, they would probably dismiss it as irrelevant.

You might see this sort of reaction when the CEO calls an all-hands meeting and presents charts and figures showing sales projections and such. Many of the less experienced staff will tend to dismiss it as not being relevant to their individual job.

Of course, it is very relevant and can help determine whether you'll still *have* a job with this company next year. But you won't see the connection while you're at the lower skill levels.

Stage 3: Competent

At the third stage, practitioners can now develop conceptual models of the problem domain and work with those models effectively. They can troubleshoot prob-

Expert
Proficient
→Competent
Advanced Beginner
Novice

lems on their own and begin to figure out how to solve novel problems—ones they haven't faced before. They can begin to seek out and apply advice from experts and use it effectively.

Instead of following the sort of knee-jerk response of the previous levels, the *competent* practitioner will seek out and solve problems; their work is based more on

Competents can troubleshoot.

deliberate planning and past experience. Without more experience, they'll still have trouble trying to determine which details to focus on when problem solving.

You might see folks at this level typically described as "having initiative" and being "resourceful." They tend to be in a leadership role in the team (whether it's formal or not).[4] These are great folks to have on your team. They can mentor the novices and don't annoy the experts overly much.

---

4. See *Teaching and Learning Generic Skills for the Workplace* [SMLR90].

In the field of software development, we're getting there, but even at this level, practitioners can't apply agile methods the way we would like—there isn't yet enough ability for reflection and self-correction. For that, we need to make a breakthrough to the next level: proficient.

Stage 4: Proficient

Expert
→ Proficient
Competent
Advanced Beginner
Novice

Proficient practitioners need the big picture. They will seek out and want to understand the larger conceptual framework around this skill. They will be very frustrated by oversimplified information.

For instance, someone at the proficient stage will not react well when they call the tech support hotline and are asked whether it's plugged in. (Personally, I want to reach through the phone and remove the first vital organ that presents itself in these situations.)

Proficient practitioners can self-correct.

Proficient practitioners make a major breakthrough on the Dreyfus model: they can correct previous poor task performance. They can reflect on how they've done and revise their approach to perform better the next time. Up until this stage, that sort of self-improvement is simply not available.

Also, they can learn from the experience of others. As a proficient practitioner, you can read case studies, listen to water-cooler gossip of failed projects, see what others have done, and learn effectively from the story, even though you didn't participate in it firsthand.

Along with the capacity to learn from others comes the ability to understand and apply *maxims*, which are proverbial, fundamental truths that can be applied to the situation at hand.[5] Maxims are not recipes; they have to be applied within a certain context.

For instance, a well-known maxim from the extreme programming methodology tells you to "test everything that can possibly break."

---

5. See *Personal Knowledge* [Pol58].

Pragmatic Tips

When Dave Thomas and I wrote the original *The Pragmatic Programmer*, we were trying to convey some of the advice we thought was most relevant to our profession.

These tips—these maxims—were a reflection of our collective years of expertise. From the mind-expanding practice of learning a new language every year to the hard-won principles of Don't Repeat Yourself (DRY) and No Broken Windows, maxims such as these are key to transferring expertise.

To the novice, this is a recipe. What do I test? All the setter and getter methods? Simple print statements? They'll end up testing irrelevant things.

But the proficient practitioner knows what can possibly break—or more correctly, what is likely to break. They have the experience and the judgment to understand what this maxim means *in context*. And context, as it turns out, is key to becoming an expert.

Proficient practitioners have enough experience that they know— from experience—what's likely to happen next; and when it doesn't work out that way, they know what needs to change. It becomes apparent to them which plans need to be discarded and what needs to be done instead.

Similarly, software Patterns (as espoused in *Design Patterns: Elements of Reusable Object-Oriented Software* [GHJV95], also known as the Gang of Four book) can be effectively applied by proficient-level practitioners (but not necessarily at lower skill levels; see the sidebar on the next page).

Now we're getting somewhere. Proficient practitioners can take full advantage of the reflection and feedback that is core to agile methods. This is a big leap from the earlier stages; someone at the proficient stage is much more like a junior expert than a really advanced competent.

Misapplied Patterns and Fragile Methods

As you may realize by now, some of the most exciting new movements in the software development community are targeted at proficient and expert developers.

Agile development relies on feedback; in fact, my definition of *agile development* from *Practices of an Agile Developer: Working in the Real World* (SH06) says this: "Agile development uses feedback to make constant adjustments in a highly collaborative environment." But being able to self-correct based on previous performance is possible only at the higher skill levels.

Advanced beginners and competent practitioners often confuse software design patterns with recipes, sometimes with disastrous results. For instance, I once knew a developer on a project who had just been exposed to the Gang of Four (GoF) book. In his enthusiasm, he wanted to start using design patterns. All of them. At once. In a small piece of report-writing code.

He managed to jam in about seventeen of the twenty-three GoF patterns into this hapless piece of code before someone noticed.

Stage 5: Expert

Finally, at the fifth stage, we come to the end of the line: the expert.

→Expert
Proficient
Competent
Advanced Beginner
Novice

Experts are the primary sources of knowledge and information in any field. They are the ones who continually look for better methods and better ways of doing things. They have a vast body of experience that they can tap into and apply in just the right context. These are the folks who write the books, write the articles, and do the lecture circuit. These are the modern wizards.

Statistically, there aren't very many experts—probably something on the order of 1 to 5 percent of the population.[6]

---

6. See *Standards for Online Communication* [HS97].

Experts work from *intuition*, not from reason. This has some very interesting ramifications and raises some key questions— what is intuition, anyway? (We'll delve more into the details of intuition throughout the book.)

> Experts work from intuition.

Although experts can be amazingly intuitive—to the point that it looks like magic to the rest of us—they may be completely inarticulate as to how they arrived at a conclusion. They genuinely don't know; it just "felt right."

For instance, suppose a physician looks in at a patient. At a glance, the doctor says, "I think this patient has Blosen-Platt syndrome; better run these tests." The staff runs the tests, and indeed, the doctor is correct. How did she know? Well, you could ask, but the doctor may well reply with "He didn't look right."

Indeed, the patient just didn't look "right." Somehow, in the vast array of experiences, distilled judgment, memories, and all the rest of the mental effluvia in the doctor's brain, a particular combination of subtle clues in the patient came together and suggested a diagnosis. Maybe it was the skin pallor or the way the patient was slumped over—who knows?

The expert does. The expert knows the difference between irrelevant details and the very important details, perhaps not on a conscious level, but the expert knows which details to focus on and which details can be safely ignored. The expert is very good at targeted, focused pattern matching.

2.3 Dreyfus at Work: Herding Racehorses and Racing Sheep

Now that we've looked at the Dreyfus model in detail, let's see how to apply the Dreyfus lessons at work. In software development at least, it turns out that we tend to apply them pretty poorly.

Experts aren't perfect. They can make mistakes just like anyone else, they are subject to the same cognitive and other biases that we'll look at later (in Chapter 5, *Debug Your Mind*, on page 113), and they will also likely disagree with one another on topics within their field.

But worse than that, by misunderstanding the Dreyfus model, we can rob them of their expertise. It's actually easy to derail an expert

Unskilled and Unaware of It

When you are not very skilled in some area, you are more likely to think you're actually pretty expert at it.

In the paper "Unskilled and Unaware of It: How Difficulties in Recognizing One's Own Incompetence Lead to Inflated Self-Assessments" (KD99), psychologists Kruger and Dunning relate the unfortunate story of a would-be thief who robbed a bank in broad daylight. He was incredulous at his prompt arrest, because he was under the impression that wearing lemon juice on your face would make you invisible to security cameras.

The "lemon juice man" never suspected that his hypothesis was, er, suspect. This lack of accurate self-assessment is referred to as *second-order incompetence*, that is, the condition of being unskilled and unaware of it.

This condition is a huge problem in software development, because many programmers and managers aren't aware that better methods and practices even exist. I've met many younger programmers (one to five years of experience) who *never* have been on a successful project. They have already succumbed to the notion that a normal project should be painful and should fail.

Charles Darwin pegged it when he said, "Ignorance more frequently begets confidence than does knowledge."

The converse seems to be true as well; once you truly become an expert, you become painfully aware of just how little you really know.

and ruin their performance. All you have to do is force them to follow the rules.

In one of the Dreyfus studies, the researchers did exactly that. They took seasoned airline pilots and had them draw

Rules ruin experts.

up a set of rules for the novices, representing their best practices. They did, and the novices were able to improve their performance based on those rules.

But then they made the experts follow their own rules.

It degraded their measured performance significantly.[7]

This has ramifications for teamwork as well. Consider any development methodology or corporate culture that dictates iron-clad rules. What impact will that have on the experts in the team? It will drag their performance down to the level of the novice. You lose all competitive advantage of their expertise.

But the software industry as a whole tries to "ruin" experts in this fashion all the time. You might say that we're trying to herd racehorses. That's not how you get a good return on investment in a racehorse; you need to let them run.[8]

Intuition is the tool of the expert in all fields, but organizations tend to discount it because they mistakenly feel that intuition "isn't scientific" or "isn't repeatable." So, we tend to throw out the baby with the bathwater and don't listen to the experts to whom we pay so much.

 Conversely, we also tend to take novices and throw them in the deep end of the development pool—far over their heads. You might say we're trying to race sheep, in this case. Again, it's not an effective way to use novices. They need to be "herded," that is, given unambiguous direction, quick successes, and so on. Agile development is a very effective tool, but it won't work on a team composed solely of novices and advanced beginners.

But forces in the industry conspire against us in both directions. A misguided sense of political correctness dictates that we treat

---

7. Cited in *The Scope, Limits, and Training Implications of Three Models of Aircraft Pilot Emergency Response Behavior* [DD79].
8. Like thoroughbreds, not mustangs.

> **Work to Rule**
>
> In industries or situations where one is not allowed a full-blown strike, a work slowdown is often used as a means of demonstration.
>
> Often this is called *work to rule* or *malicious obedience*, and the idea is that the employees do *exactly* what their job description calls for—no more, no less—and follow the rule book to the letter.
>
> The result is massive delays and confusion—and an effective labor demonstration. No one with expertise in the real world follows the rules to the letter; doing so is demonstrably inefficient.
>
> According to Benner (in *From Novice to Expert: Excellence and Power in Clinical Nursing Practice* (Ben01)), "Practices can never be completely objectified or formalized because they must ever be worked out anew in particular relationships and in real time."

all developers the same, regardless of ability. This does a disservice to both novices and experts (and ignores the reality that there is anywhere from a 20:1 to 40:1 difference in productivity among developers, depending on whose study you believe).[9]

> TIP 2
>
> Use rules for novices, intuition for experts.

The journey from novice to expert involves more than just rules and intuition, of course. Many characteristics change as you move up the skill levels. But the three most important changes along the way are the following:[10]

- Moving away from reliance on rules to intuition

---

9. In 1968, a difference of 10:1 in productivity among programmers was noted in *Exploratory Experimental Studies Comparing Online and Offline* [Sac68]. The gulf seems to have widened since then.

10. Identified in *From Novice to Expert: Excellence and Power in Clinical Nursing Practice* [Ben01]; more on this landmark book in just a bit.

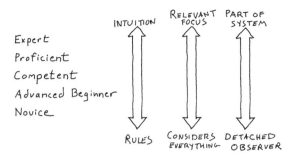

Figure 2.3: DREYFUS MODEL OF SKILL ACQUISITION

- A change in perception, where a problem is no longer a collection of equally relevant bits but a complete and unique whole where only certain bits are relevant
- Finally, a change from being a detached observer of the problem to an involved part of the system itself

This is the progression from novice to expert, away from detached and absolute rules and into intuition and (remember systems thinking?) eventually part of the system itself (see Figure 2.3).

The Sad Fact of Skill Distribution

Now at this point you're probably thinking that the great bulk of people fall smack in the middle—that the Dreyfus model follows a standard distribution, which is a typical bell curve.

It does not.

Sadly, studies seem to indicate that most people, for most skills, for most of their lives, never get any higher than the second stage, advanced beginner, "performing the

> Most people are advanced beginners.

tasks they need and learning new tasks as the need arises but never acquiring a more broad-based, conceptual understanding of the task environment."[11] A more accurate distribution is shown in Figure 2.4, on the following page.

Anecdotal evidence for the phenomenon abounds, from the rise of copy-and-paste coding (now using Google as part of the IDE) to the widespread misapplication of software design patterns.

---

11. Described in *Standards for Online Communication* [HS97].

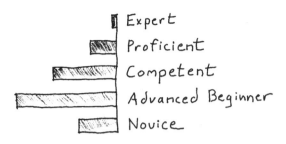

Figure 2.4: SKILL DISTRIBUTION

Also, *metacognitive* abilities, or the ability of being self-aware, tends to be possible only at the higher skill levels. Unfortunately, this means practitioners at the lower skill levels have a marked tendency to overestimate their own abilities—by as much as 50 percent, as it turns out. According to a study in *Unskilled and Unaware of It: How Difficulties in Recognizing One's Own Incompetence Lead to Inflated Self-Assessments* [KD99], the only path to a more correct self-assessment is to improve the individual's skill level, which in turn increases metacognitive ability.

You may see this referred to as *second-order incompetence*, not knowing just how much it is that you don't know. The beginner is confident despite the odds; the expert will be far more cautious when the going gets weird. Experts will show much more self-doubt.

> TIP 3
>
> Know what you don't know.

Unfortunately, we'll always have more advanced beginners than experts. But even though it is weighted at the bottom, it's still a distribution. If you're lucky enough to have an expert on your team, you need to accommodate them. Similarly, you need to accommodate the few novices, the many advanced beginners, and the small but powerful number of competent and proficient practitioners.

Expert != Teacher

Experts aren't always the best teachers. Teaching is an expertise in its own right; just because you are expert in some subject is no guarantee that you can teach it to others.

Also, given the phenomenon that experts are often unable to articulate why they reached a particular decision, you may find that someone at a competent level might be in a better position to teach a novice than an expert would be. When pairing or mentoring within the team, you might try using mentors who are closer in skill level to the trainee.

The hallmark of the expert is their use of intuition and the ability to recognize patterns in context. That's not to say that novices have zero intuition or that competents can't recognize patterns at all but

> Intuition and pattern matching replace explicit knowledge.

that the expert's intuition and pattern recognition now take the place of explicit knowledge.

This transition from the novice's context-free rules to the expert's context-dependent intuition is one of the most interesting parts of the Dreyfus model; so our goal, for most of the rest of this book, is to see how we might better harness intuition and get better at recognizing and applying patterns.[12]

2.4 Using the Dreyfus Model Effectively

By the late 1970s or so, the nursing profession was in dire straits. In a nutshell, these were their problems, which I've drawn from several case studies and narratives:[13]

- Nurses themselves were often disregarded as a mere commodity; they just carried out the highly trained doctor's orders and weren't expected to have any input on patient care.

---

12. That's *patterns* in the usual English sense, not software design patterns.
13. Described in *From Novice to Expert: Excellence and Power in Clinical Nursing Practice* [Ben01].

Ten Years to Expertise?

So, you want to be an expert? You need to budget about ten years of effort, regardless of the subject area. Researchers* have studied chess playing, music composition, painting, piano playing, swimming, tennis, and other skills and disciplines. In virtually every case, from Mozart to the Beatles, you find evidence of a minimum of a decade of hard work before world-class expertise shows up.

The Beatles, for instance, took the world by storm in 1964 with a landmark appearance on the *Ed Sullivan Show*. Their first critically successful album, *Sgt. Pepper's Lonely Hearts Club Band*, was released shortly after, in 1967. But the band didn't just magically form for a tour in 1964—they had been playing in clubs since 1957. Ten years before *Sgt. Pepper's*.

And hard work it is—merely working at a subject for ten years isn't enough. You need to *practice*. Deliberate practice, according to noted cognitive scientist Dr. K. Anderson Ericsson, requires four conditions:

- You need a well-defined task.
- The task needs to be appropriately difficult—challenging but doable.
- The environment needs to supply informative feedback that you can act on.
- It should also provide opportunities for repetition and correction of errors.

Do that sort of practice, steadily, for ten years, and you've got it made. As we noted in *The Pragmatic Programmer: From Journeyman to Master* (HT00), even Chaucer complained that "the lyfe so short, the craft so long to lerne."

However, there is some good news. Once you become an expert in one field, it becomes much easier to gain expertise in another. At least you already have the acquisition skills and model-building abilities in place.

Thanks to June Kim for the reference to Dr. Ericsson.

---

*. See *The Complete Problem Solver* (Hay81) and *Developing Talent in Young People* (BS85).

- Because of pay-scale inequities, expert nurses were leaving direct patient care in droves. There was more money to be made in management, teaching, or the lecture circuit.
- Nursing education began to falter; many thought that formal models of practice were the best way to teach. An overreliance on formal methods and tools eroded real experience in practice.
- Finally, they had lost sight of the real goal—patient outcomes. Despite whatever process and methodology you followed, despite who worked on this patient, what was the outcome? Did the patient live and thrive? Or not?

If you read that list carefully, you may have noticed that these problems sound eerily familiar. Allow me to slightly edit this bullet list to reflect software development:

- Coders themselves were often disregarded as a mere commodity; they just carried out the highly trained analysts' orders and weren't expected to have any input on the design and architecture of the project.
- Because of pay-scale inequities, expert programmers were leaving hands-on coding in droves. There was more money to be made in management, teaching, or the lecture circuit.
- Software engineering education began to falter; many thought that formal models of practice were the best way to teach. An overreliance on formal methods and tools eroded real experience in practice.
- Finally, they had lost sight of the real goal—project outcomes. Despite whatever process and methodology you followed, despite who worked on this project, what was the outcome? Did the project succeed and thrive? Or not?

Huh. It sounds a little more familiar that way; indeed, these are serious problems that our industry now faces.

Back in the early 1980s, nursing professionals began to apply the lessons of the Dreyfus model to their industry with remarkable results. Dr. Benner's landmark book exposed and explained the Dreyfus model so that all involved parties had a better understanding of their own skills and roles and those of their co-workers. It laid out specific guidelines to try to improve the profession as a whole.

Over the course of the next twenty-five years or so, Benner and subsequent authors and researchers turned their profession around.

So in the best spirit of R&D (which stands for "Rip off and Duplicate"), we can borrow many lessons from their work and apply them to software development. Let's take a closer look at how they did it and what we can do in our own profession.

Accepting Responsibility

Twenty-five years ago, nurses were expected to follow orders without question, even vehemently—and proudly—maintaining that they "never veer from doctor's orders," despite obvious changes in patients' needs or conditions.

This attitude was enculturated in part by the doctors, who weren't in a position to see the constant, low-level changes in patients' conditions, and in part by the nurses themselves, who willingly abdicated responsibility for decision making in the course of practice to the authority of the doctors. It was professionally safer for them that way, and indeed there is some psychological basis for their position.

In one experiment,[14] a researcher calls a hospital ward posing as a doctor and orders the nurse to give a particular medication to a given patient. The order was rigged to trigger several alarm bells:

- The prescription was given over the phone, not in writing.
- The particular medication was not on the ward's usual approved list.
- According to labels on the medication itself, the prescribed dosage was double the maximum amount.
- The "doctor" on the phone was a stranger, not known to the nurse or staff.

But despite these clear warning signs, 95 percent of the nurses fell for it and went straight to the medicine cabinet, en route to the patient's room to dose 'em up.

---

14. Described in *Influence: Science and Practice* [Cia01].

Fortunately, they were stopped by an accomplice who explained the experiment—and stopped them from carrying out the bogus order.[15]

We see very much the same problems with programmers and their project managers or project architects. Feedback from coders to those who define architecture, requirements, and even business process has traditionally been either lacking entirely, brutally rejected, or simply lost in the noise of the project. Programmers often implement something they *know* is wrong, ignoring the obvious warning signs much as the nurses did in this example. Agile methods help promote feedback from all members of the team and utilize it effectively, but that's only half the battle.

Individual nurses had to accept responsibility in order to make in-the-field decisions according to the unfolding dynamics of a particular situation; individual programmers must accept the same responsibility. The Nuremberg-style defense "I was only following orders" did not work in WWII, it did not work for the nursing profession, and it does not work in software development.

> "I was just following orders!" doesn't work.

But in order to accomplish this change in attitude, we *do* need to raise the bar. Advanced beginners aren't capable of making these sorts of decision by themselves. We must take the advanced beginners we have and help them raise their skill levels to competent.

A major way to help achieve that is to have good exemplars in the environment; people are natural mimics (see Section 7.4, *Learn About the Inner Game*, on page 193). We learn best by example. In fact, if you have children, you may have noticed that they rarely do as you say but will always copy what you do.

Tip 4

Learn by watching and imitating.

---

15. This was an older study; don't go calling the hospital up now with bogus orders, or the feds may well come a knockin'.

> ### No Expertise Without Experience
>
> Jazz is an art form that relies heavily on real-world experience. You may learn all the chords and techniques required to play jazz, but you have to *play* it in order to get the "feel." The famous trumpet player and vocalist Louis "Satchmo" Armstrong said of jazz, "Man, if ya gotta ask, you'll never know."
>
> There's no expertise without experience, and there's no substitute for experience—but we can work to make the experience you have more efficient and more effective.

Trumpeter Clark Terry used to tell students the secret to learning music was to go through three phases:

- Imitate
- Assimilate
- Innovate

That is, first you imitate existing practice and then slowly assimilate the tacit knowledge and experience over time. Finally you'll be in a position to go beyond imitation and innovate. This echoes the cycle of training in the martial arts known as Shu Ha Ri.

In the *Shu* phase, the student copies the techniques as taught—from a single instructor—without modifications. In the *Ha* stage, the student must reflect on the meaning and purpose and come to a deeper understanding. *Ri* means to go beyond or transcend; no longer a student, the practitioner now offers original thought.

So, among other things, we need to look at ways to keep as much existing expertise as we can in the project itself; none of this progression will help if practitioners don't stay in the field.

Keeping Expertise in Practice

The nursing profession was losing expertise rapidly; because of the limits of pay scales and career development, nurses with high skill levels would reach a point in their careers where they were forced to move out of direct clinical practice and into areas of management or education or move out of the field entirely.

This largely remains the case in software development as well. Programmers (aka "coders") are paid only so much; salespeople, consultants, upper management, and so on, might be compensated more than twice the amount of the best programmer on a team.

Companies need to take a much closer, much more informed look at the value that these star developers bring to an organization.

For instance, many project teams use a sports metaphor to describe positive aspects of teamwork, a common goal, and so on. But in reality, our idealized view

> Winners don't carry losers.

of teamwork doesn't match what really happens on professional sports teams.

Two men may both play the position of pitcher for a baseball team, yet one may earn $25 million a year, and the other may earn only $50,000. The question isn't the position they play, or even their years of experience; the question is, what is the value they bring to the organization?

An article by Geoffrey Colvin[16] expands on this idea by noting that real teams have stars: not everyone on the team is a star; some are rookies (novices and advanced beginners), and some are merely competent. Rookies move up the ladder, but winners don't carry losers—losers get cut from the team. Finally, he notes that the top 2 percent isn't considered world-class. The top 0.2 percent is.

And it's not just high-pressure sports teams; even churches recognize difference in talent and try to use it effectively. Recently I was shown a national church's newsletter that offered advice on how to grow and maintain a music program. Their advice sounds very familiar:

- A group is only as good as its weakest link. Put the best performers together to perform for the main service, and create "farm teams" for other services.
- Keep a steady group with the same performers every week. You want the group to jell; rotating players in and out is counterproductive.

---

16. *Fortune Magazine*, March 18, 2002, p.50.

- Timing is everything: the drummer (for a band) or accompanist (for choral groups) has to be solid. Better to use a prerecorded accompaniment than a flaky drummer or organist.
- Make your group a safe place for talented musicians, and watch what happens.

That's exactly the same thing you want on a software team.[17] This idea of providing the right environment for skilled developers is critical.

Given that the highest-skilled developers are orders of magnitude more productive than the least-skilled developers, the current common salary structures for developers is simply inadequate. Like the nursing profession years ago, we continually face the risk of losing a critical mass of expertise to management, competitors, or other fields.

This tendency is made worse by the recent increases in outsourcing and offshoring development to cheaper countries. It's an unfortunate development in that it further cements the idea in people's minds that coding is just a mechanical activity and can be sent away to the lowest bidder. It doesn't quite work that way, of course.

As in the nursing profession, experts at coding must continue to code and find a meaningful and rewarding career there. Setting a pay scale and a career ladder that reflects a top coder's value to the organization is the first step toward making this a reality.

> **Tip 5**
>
> Keep practicing in order to remain expert.

2.5 Beware the Tool Trap

There has been much written on the role of tools, formal models, modeling, and so on, in software development. Many people claim that UML and model-driven architecture (MDA) are the future, just

---

17. The drummer analogy is stretching it a bit, but I do talk more about the rhythm of development projects in *Practices of an Agile Developer: Working in the Real World* [SH06].

as many people claimed that RUP and CMM process models were the salvation of the industry.

But as with all silver-bullet scenarios, people soon found out that it just ain't that easy. Although these tools and models have their place and can be useful in the right environments, *none* of them has become the hoped-for universal panacea. Worse yet, the misapplication of these approaches has probably done far more damage than good.

Interestingly enough, the nursing profession had similar problems with regard to the use of tools and formal models. They had fallen into the same trap that many architects and designers fall for: forgetting that the model is a tool, not a mirror.

> The model is a tool, not a mirror.

Rules cannot tell you the most relevant activities to perform in a given situation or the correct path to take. They are at best "training wheels"—helpful to get started but limiting and actively detrimental to performance later.

Dr. Deborah Gordon contributed a chapter to Benner's book, in which she outlines some of the dangers of overreliance on formal models for the nursing profession. I've reinterpreted her sentiments with the particulars of our profession, but even the original version will sound pretty familiar to you.

Confusing the model with reality

A model is not reality, but it's easy to confuse the two. There's the old story of the young project manager, where his senior programmer announced she was pregnant and going to deliver during the project, and he protested that this "wasn't on the project plan."

Devaluing traits that cannot be formalized

Good problem-solving skills are critical to our jobs, but problem solving is a very hard thing to formalize. For instance, how long can you just sit and think about a problem? Ten minutes? A day? A week? You can't put creativity and invention on a time clock, and you can't prescribe a particular technique or set of techniques. Even though you *want* these traits on your team, you may find that management will stop valuing them simply because they cannot be formalized.

Legislating behavior that contradicts individual autonomy
You don't want a bunch of monkeys banging on typewriters to churn out code. You want thinking, responsible developers. Overreliance on formal models will tend to reward herd behavior and devalue individual creativity.[18]

Alienating experienced practitioners in favor of novices
This is a particularly dangerous side effect. By targeting your methodology to novices, you will create a poor working environment for the experienced team members, and they'll simply leave your team and/or organization.

Spelling out too much detail
Spelling out the particulars in too much detail can be overwhelming. This leads to a problem called *infinite regress*: as soon as you make one set of assumptions explicit, you've exposed the next level of assumptions that you must now address. And so on, and so on.

Oversimplification of complex situations
Early proponents of the Rational Unified Process (and some recent ones) cling to the notion that all you have to do is "just follow the process." Some advocates of Extreme Programming insist all you need to do is "just follow these twelve—no wait, maybe thirteen—practices" and everything will work out. Neither camp is correct. Every project, every situation, is more complex than that. Any time someone starts a sentence with "All you need to do is..." or "Just do this...," the odds are they are wrong.

Demand for excessive conformity
The same standard may not always apply equally in all situations. What worked great on your last project may be a disaster on this one. If Bob and Alice are hugely productive with Eclipse, it might wreck Carol and Ted. They prefer IntelliJ or TextMate or vi.[19]

---

18. Of course, there's a balance here—you do not want a "cowboy coder" who ignores the team and common sense to strike out on his own.
19. OK, I have to confess that over the course of time, I wrote this book using vi, XEmacs in vi mode, and TextMate.

Insensitivity to contextual nuances

Formal methods are geared to the typical, not the particular. But when does the "typical" really ever happen? Context is critical to expert performance, and formal methods tend to lose any nuances of context in their formulations (they have to; otherwise, it would take thousands of pages just to describe how to get coffee in the morning).

Confusion between following rules and exercising judgment

When is it OK to break the rules? All the time? Never? Somewhere in between? How do you know?

Mystification

Speech becomes so sloganized that it becomes trivial and eventually loses meaning entirely (for example, "We're a customer-focused organization!"). Agile methods are fast losing effectiveness because of this very problem.

Formal methods have other advantages and uses but are not helpful in achieving these goals. Although it may be advantageous to establish baseline rules for the lower skill levels, even then rules are no substitute for judgment. As ability to judge increases, reliance on rules must be relaxed—along with any rigid institutional enforcement.

TIP 6

Avoid formal methods if you need creativity, intuition, or inventiveness.

Don't succumb to the false authority of a tool or a model. There is no substitute for thinking.

2.6 Consider the Context, Again

One of the most important lessons from the Dreyfus model is the realization that although the novice needs context-free rules, the expert uses context-dependent intuition.

The man with his pickled fish has set down one truth and has recorded in his experience many lies. The fish is not that color, that texture, that dead, nor does he smell that way.

▶ John Steinbeck, *The Sea of Cortez*

In *The Sea of Cortez*, Steinbeck muses on the interplay of context and truth. You can describe a Mexican Sierra fish in the laboratory. All you have to do is "open an evil smelling jar, remove a stiff colorless fish from formalin solution, count the spines, and write the truth 'D. XVII-15-IX.'" That's a scientific truth, but it's devoid of context. It's not the same as the living fish, "its colors pulsing and tail beating in the air." The living fish, in the context of its habitat, is a fundamentally different reality from the preserved fish in the jar in the lab. Context matters.

You may have noticed that the high-priced consultant's favorite answer is "It depends." They're right, of course. Their analysis depends on a great many things—all those critical details that the expert knows to look for, while ignoring the irrelevant details. Context matters.

 You might ask the expert to open a locked door. Fair enough, but consider the difference context might make: opening the door to rescue the baby on the other side in a burning house is quite a different exercise than picking the lock and leaving no traces at the Watergate Hotel, for instance. Context matters.[20]

Beware decontextualized objectivity. There is an inherent danger in *decontextualized objectivity*, that is, in trying to be objective about something after taking it out of its context. For instance, in the previous Steinbeck quote, a preserved fish—perhaps dissected for study—is quite a different thing from the silvery flashing beast gliding though a cresting wave.

For the breaking-and-entering example, "I want to open this locked door" really isn't sufficient. What's the context? Why does the door need to be opened? Is it appropriate to use an axe, a chainsaw, or lock-picking tools, or can we just go around back and use the other door?

In systems thinking, as in object-oriented programming, it's often the relationships between things that are interesting, not the things themselves. These relationships help form the context that makes all the difference.

---

20. For more on expertise in lock picking, see *How to Open Locks with Improvised Tools* [Con01].

Context matters, but the lower several stages on the Dreyfus model aren't skilled enough to know it. So once again, we have to look at ways of climbing the Dreyfus ladder.

2.7 Day-to-Day Dreyfus

Well, this has been all fun and fascinating, but what good is the Dreyfus model really? Armed with knowledge of it, what can you do with it? How can you use this to your advantage?

First, remember that one size does not fit all, either for yourself or for others. As you can see from the model, your needs will

One size does not fit all.

be different depending on what level you are on. What you need for your own learning and personal growth will change over time. And of course, how you listen and react to others on the team needs to take into account their own skill levels as well.

Novices need quick successes and context-free rules. You can't expect them to be able to handle novel situations on their own. Given a problem space, they'll stop to consider everything, whether it's relevant or not. They don't see themselves as part of the system, so they won't be aware of the impact they're having—positive or negative. Give them the support they need, and don't confuse them unnecessarily with the big picture.

At the other end of the spectrum, experts need to have access to the big picture; don't cripple them with restrictive, bureaucratic rules that aim to replace judgment. You *want* the benefit of their expert judgment. Remember they think they're part of the system itself, for better or for worse, and may take things more personally than you would expect.

Ideally you want a mix of skills on a team: having an all-expert team is fraught with its own difficulties; you need some people to worry about the trees while everyone is pondering the forest.

Since the Dreyfus model is probably new to you from reading about it here, you're probably still a novice at understanding and using it. Understanding the Dreyfus model and skills acquisition is a skill itself; learning to learn is subject to the Dreyfus model.

Tip 7

Learn the skill of learning.

Going Forward

We will use these lessons of the Dreyfus model to guide the rest of the book. To embark on this path to expertise, we'll need to do the following:

- Cultivate more intuition
- Realize the increasing importance of context and of observing situational patterns
- Better harness our own experience

To see how to accomplish these goals, we'll start the next chapter by taking a closer look at how the brain works.

Next Actions ⬇

☐ Rate yourself. Where do you see yourself in the Dreyfus model for the primary skills you use at work? List the ways your current skill level impacts you.

☐ Identify other skills where you are a novice, advanced beginner, and so on. Be aware of the possibility of second-order incompetence when making these evaluations.

☐ For each of these skills, decide what you need to advance to the next level. Keep these examples in mind as you read the remainder of this book.

☐ Think back to problems you've experienced on a project team. Could any of them have been avoided if the team had been aware of the Dreyfus model? What can you do differently going forward?

☐ Think of your teammates: Where are they on their journey? How can that be helpful to you?

The human brain starts working the moment you are born and never stops until you stand up to speak in public.

▶ Sir George Jessel

Chapter 3

This Is Your Brain

Your brain is the most powerful computer in existence. But it's not at all like the computers we're familiar with, and in fact it has some really odd peculiarities that can either trip you up or propel you to greatness. So in this chapter, we're going to take a quick look at how your brain works.

We'll see where intuition comes from, begin to look at harnessing it better to become more expert, and learn why a lot of things that perhaps you think "don't matter" turn out to be absolutely critical to your success.

Since we're pretty familiar with computers, it seems useful to talk about the brain and its cognitive processes as if they were designed as a computer system.

But that's *just a metaphor*. The brain is not a mechanical device; it's not a computer. You aren't programmable. Unlike a computer, you can't even perform the same action exactly the same way twice.

That's not just a hardware problem; it has nothing to do with muscles. It's a software problem. The brain actually plans out your motion slightly differently each and every time, much to the chagrin of golfers, pitchers, and bowlers.[1]

The brain is a horrifically complicated squishy lump of stuff. It's so complicated that it has a very hard time analyzing and studying itself. So, please remember that this is *just an analogy*—but I hope a helpful one.

---

1. *A Central Source of Movement Variability* [CAS06].

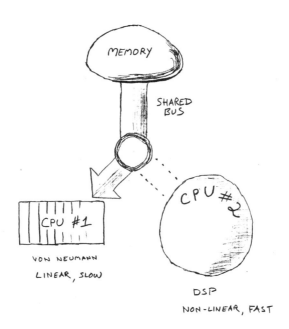

Figure 3.1: THIS IS YOUR BRAIN.

With that said: Your brain is configured as a dual-CPU, single-master bus design, as shown in Figure 3.1.

As we'll see in this chapter and the next, this dual design presents some problems, but it also presents some terrific opportunities that you might not be aware of.

3.1 Your Dual-CPU Modes

CPU #1 is probably the most familiar to you: it is chiefly responsible for linear, logical thought, and language processing. It's like a traditional von Neumann–style CPU that processes instructions step-by-step, in order. CPU #1 is relatively slow and uses a relatively small amount of overall brain real estate.

It's programmed with an "idle loop" routine as well. If CPU #1 is not processing anything else, it will simply generate an internal stream of verbal chatter. It's that little voice in your head.[2]

---

2. Let's hope you have just the one.

CPU #2, however, is very different. Instead of the linear, step-by-step approach of CPU #1, CPU #2 is more like a magic digital signal processor. It's your brain's answer to Google: think of it like a super regular-expression search engine, responsible for searching and pattern matching. As such, it might grab matching patterns that aren't obviously related. It can go off searching while you are "thinking" of something else and return a result set asynchronously—and possibly days later. Since CPU #2 doesn't do any verbal processing, that means its results aren't verbal, either.

Notice that both CPUs share the bus to the memory core; only one CPU can access the memory banks at a time. That means if CPU #1 is hogging the bus, CPU #2 can't get at memory to perform searches. Similarly, if CPU #2 is cranking away on a high-priority search, CPU #1 cannot get at memory either. They interfere with each other.

These two CPUs correspond to two different kinds of processing in your brain. We'll call the linear processing style of CPU #1 *linear mode*, or just **L**-mode. We'll refer to the asynchronous, holistic style of CPU #2 as *rich mode*, or $\mathcal{R}$-mode for short.

> Two CPUs provide
> $\mathcal{R}$-mode and **L**-mode.

You need both: $\mathcal{R}$-mode is critical for intuition, problem solving, and creativity. **L**-mode gives you the power to work through the details and make it happen. Each mode contributes to your mental engine, and for best performance, you need these two modes to work together. Let's start looking at the details of each of these vital cognitive modes.

Memory and Bus Contention

$\mathcal{R}$-mode is very important to your day-to-day work: it acts as your search and retrieval engine for long-term memory and ideas that are "in process." But as I mentioned, $\mathcal{R}$-mode *doesn't* do any verbal processing. It can retrieve and recognize verbal elements, but it can't do anything with them by itself because of that memory bus contention between **L**-mode and $\mathcal{R}$-mode.

For instance, have you ever had the experience of trying to describe a dream when you first wake up? Many times it seems that a crystal-clear, vivid dream evaporates from your memory as soon as you try to describe it in words. That's because the images, feelings, and overall experience are $\mathcal{R}$-mode things: your dream was

<hr>

Holographic Memory

Memory is stored holographically, in the sense that your memory has certain properties of a hologram.[*]

In a real hologram (made using a laser), every piece of the film contains the entire image. That is, if you cut the film in half, each half will still have the entire image—but with lower fidelity or resolution. You can continue to cut the film in half indefinitely, and smaller and smaller pieces will continue to contain a representation of the whole image. That's because the whole image is stored scattered across the whole film; each small part contains a representation of the whole.

Scientists have studied this phenomenon in mice. Researchers start by training a bunch of mice in a maze. Then they scoop out half of their brains with a melon baller (what better to do on a lonely Saturday night in the lab?).

The mice can still navigate the whole maze (although I imagine somewhat spastically), but with less and less precision as the researchers scoop out more and more.[†]

---

[*]. See *Hare Brain, Tortoise Mind: How Intelligence Increases When You Think Less* (Cla00).
[†]. See *Shufflebrain: The Quest for the Hologramic Mind* (Pie81).

<hr>

generated in $\mathcal{R}$-mode. As you try to put your dream into words, you experience a sort of bus contention. **L**-mode takes over the bus, and now you can't get at those memories anymore. In effect, they aren't verbalizable.[3]

You have amazing perceptual powers, many of which *can't* be effectively put into words. For instance, you can instantly recognize the faces of a large number of familiar people. It doesn't matter whether they've changed their hairstyle, changed their manner of dress, or put on ten pounds or twenty years.

But try to describe the face of even your closest loved one. How do you put that recognition ability into words? Can you make a

---

3. *Verbal Overshadowing of Visual Memories; Some Things Are Better Left Unsaid* [SES90].

Memory Must Be Refreshed

Remember the movie *Total Recall*? Well, if you can't, maybe your memories were suppressed by a secret spy agency as well. It turns out that this sort of mental manipulation isn't science fiction after all. Memories can be erased by simply repressing a specific enzyme.*

An enzyme located in the synapses called PKMzeta acts as a miniature memory engine that keeps memory up and running by changing some facets of the structure of synaptic contacts. If the PKMzeta process in an area of the brain stops for some reason, you lose that memory—no matter what it is.

It had long been thought that memory was somewhat like flash RAM; memory was somehow recorded by neuron configuration with a physical persistence. Instead, it is actively maintained by an executing loop.

Even with volatile static RAM, data sticks around as long as power is applied. It turns out your brain doesn't have static RAM, but instead it has dynamic RAM that needs constant refreshing or it fades. That means even riding a bicycle isn't something you can take for granted. It means you can unlearn anything. It means no matter how horrible or wonderful some experience is, you *can* lose it.

So, your brain is not like software. Software never ages and never degrades. But wetware must be refreshed, must be used, or it is lost.

If your brain stops running, it forgets everything.

Thanks to Shawn Harstock for this tidbit and write-up.

---

*. http://pressesc.com/news/1088/16082007/memories-can-be-erased-scientists-find

database describing the faces of the people you know in such a way that you could recognize them based on that description? No. It's a great ability, but it isn't rooted in the verbal, linguistic, L-mode.

R-mode isn't directly controllable. And to compound problems, the R-mode search engine isn't under your direct conscious control. It's a bit like your peripheral vision. Peripheral vision is much more sensitive to light than your central vision. That's why if you see something faint out of the corner of your eye (such as a ship on the horizon or a star), it can disappear if you look at it head-on. R-mode is the "peripheral vision" of your mind.

Have you ever had the solution to a vexing problem (a bug, a design problem, the name of a long-forgotten band) come to you while you're in the shower? Or sometime the next day, when you aren't thinking about it? That's because R-mode is asynchronous. It's running as a background process, churning through old inputs, trying to dig up the information you need. And there's a lot for it to look through.

R-mode is quite diligent at storing input. In fact, it's possible that every experience you have, no matter how mundane, is stored. But it is not necessarily indexed. Your brain saves it (writes it to disk, if you will) but doesn't create a pointer to it or an index for it.[4]

Have you ever driven to work in the morning and realized with a start that you have no memory of actually driving the last ten minutes? Your brain recognizes that this isn't terribly useful data, so it doesn't bother to index it. That makes remembering it a little difficult.

However, when you're trying hard to solve a problem, R-mode processes will search *all* your memory for matches that might aid in the solution. Including all this unindexed material (and perhaps that lecture in school that you half-dozed through). That might really come in handy.

We'll see how to take advantage of that and look at particular techniques to help get around some of the other problems with R-mode

---

4. Technically, of course, there is no indexing going on, so it's more like being at the end of a very long hash bucket with decreasing activation energy at each link. But metaphorically, just think of it as an index.

> ### Who's in Charge Here?
>
> You might think that the narrative voice in your head is in control and that the voice is your consciousness, or the real "you." It is not. In fact, by the time the words are formed in your head, the thought behind them is very old. Some considerable time later those words might actually be formed by your mouth.
>
> Not only is there a time delay from the original thought to your awareness of it, but there is no central locus of thought in the brain. Thoughts rise up and compete in clouds, and the winner at any point in time is your *consciousness*. We'll look at this in more depth in Section 8.2, *Defocus to Focus*, on page 216.

in the next chapter. But first, let's take a look at a hugely valuable but very simple technique to deal with the fact that R-mode is asynchronous.

3.2 Capture Insight 24x7

R-mode is unpredictable at best, and you need to be prepared for that. Answers and insights pop up independently of your conscious activities, and not always at a convenient time. You may well get that million-dollar idea when you are nowhere near your computer (in fact, you're probably much more likely to get that great idea precisely *because* you are away from the computer, but more on that later).

That means you need to be ready to capture any insight or idea twenty-four hours a day, seven days a week, no matter what else you might be involved in. You might want to try these techniques:

Pen and notepad

I carry around a Fisher Space Pen and small notepad. The pen is great; it's the kind that can write even upside down in a boiling toilet, should that need arise.[5] The notepad is a

---

5. Folks also recommend the Zebra T3 series; see http://www.jetpens.com for both a pen and mechanical pencil version.

cheap 69-cent affair from the grocery store—skinny, not spiral bound, like an oversize book of matches. I can carry these with me almost everywhere.

Index cards

Some folks prefer having separate cards to make notes on. That way you can more easily toss out the dead ends and stick the very important ones on your desk blotter, corkboard, refrigerator, and so on.

PDA

You can use your Apple iPod or Touch or Palm OS or Pocket PC device along with note-taking software or a wiki (see Section 8.3, *Manage Your Knowledge*, on page 219 for more on this idea).

Voice memos

You can use your cell phone, iPod/iPhone, or other device to record voice memos. This technique is especially handy if you have a long commute, where it might be awkward to try to take notes while driving.[6] Some voicemail services now offer voice-to-text (called *visual voicemail*), which can be emailed to you along with the audio file of your message. This means you can just call your voicemail hands-free from wherever you are, leave yourself a message, and then just copy and paste the text from your email into your to-do list, your source code, your blog, or whatever. Pretty slick.

Pocket Mod

The free Flash application available at http://www.pocketmod.com cleverly prints a small booklet using a regular, single-sided piece of paper. You can select ruled pages, tables, to-do lists, music staves, and all sorts of other templates (see Figure 3.2, on the next page). A sheet of paper and one of those stubby pencils from miniature golf, and you've got yourself a dirt cheap, disposable PDA.

Notebook

For larger thoughts and wanderings, I carry a Moleskine notebook (see the sidebar on page 54). There's something about the heavyweight, cream-colored, unlined pages that invites

---

6. Remember to use your hands-free device per local laws :-).

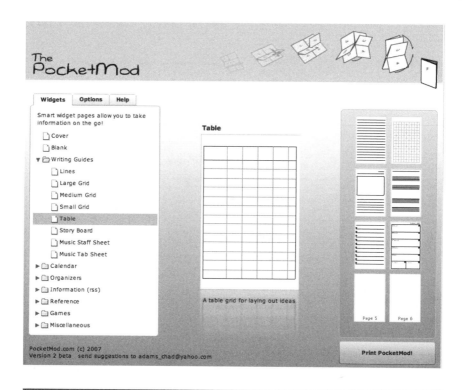

Figure 3.2: DISPOSABLE POCKET ORGANIZER FROM POCKETMOD.COM

invention. Because it feels more permanent than the cheap disposable notepad, I noticed a tendency to *not* write in it until a thought had gelled for a while, so I wouldn't fill it up prematurely. That's bad, so I started making sure I always had a backup Moleskine at the ready. That made a big difference.

The important part is to use something that you *always* have with you. Whether it's paper, a cell phone, an MP3 player, or a PDA doesn't matter, as long as you always have it.

TIP 8

Capture all ideas to get more of them.

If you don't keep track of great ideas, you will stop noticing you have them.

> ### Moleskine Notebooks
>
> A very popular style of notebook these days is made by Moleskine (see http://www.moleskine.com). These come in a variety of sizes and styles, ruled or not, thicker or thinner paper. There's a certain mystique to these notebooks, which have been favored by well-known artists and writers for more than 200 years, including van Gogh, Picasso, Hemingway, and even your humble author.
>
> The makers of Moleskine call it "a reservoir of ideas and feelings, a battery that stores discoveries and perceptions, and whose energy can be tapped over time."
>
> I like to think of it as my *exocortex*—cheap external mental storage for stuff that doesn't fit in my brain. Not bad for ten bucks.

The corollary is also true—once you start keeping track of ideas, *you'll get more of them*. Your brain will stop supplying you with stuff if you aren't using it. But it will quite happily churn out more of what you want if you start using it.

Everyone has good ideas.

Everyone—no matter their education, economic status, day job, or age—has good ideas. But of this large number of people with good ideas, far fewer bother to keep track of them. Of those, even fewer ever bother to act on those ideas. Fewer still then have the resources to make a good idea a success.[7] To make it into the top of the pyramid shown in Figure 3.3, on the next page, you have to at least keep track of your good ideas.

But that's not enough, of course. Just capturing ideas is only the first step; you then need to work with the idea, and there are some special ways we can go about doing that to be more effective. We'll talk about this in depth a bit later (see Section 8.3, *Manage Your Knowledge*, on page 219).

Get something to take notes on, and keep it with you....

---

7. If you doubt this, just ask any venture capitalist.

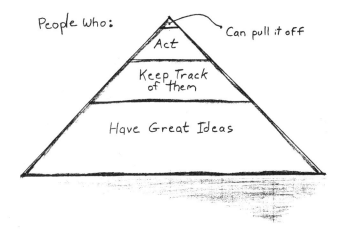

Figure 3.3: EVERYONE HAS GOOD IDEAS; FEWER GO FURTHER.

3.3 Linear and Rich Characteristics

Of course, there are quite a few differences between $\mathcal{R}$-mode and L-mode beyond $\mathcal{R}$-mode's unpredictability.

If you've ever said, "I'm of two minds about that," you were probably more literally correct than you thought at the time. You actually have a number of different processing modes in the brain. Each one has unique characteristics that can help you just when you need it most.

The fastest processing modes are the muscle-memory sorts of responses that don't even travel up to the cortex itself.[8] Piano players don't think about each and every note and chord in a fast passage; there isn't time. Instead, the muscles involved more or less just tackle the problem on their own without much conscious involvement or direction.

Similarly, that instinctive slam on the brakes or quick dodge on the bicycle doesn't involve any CPU processing—it's all in the peripherals. Since lightning-fast typing and similar physical skills aren't of too much interest to us as programmers, I'm not going to talk too much about these non-CPU modes and responses.

---

8. The *cortex*, which comes from the Latin word for tree bark, is the outer layer of folded gray matter and is key to conscious thinking.

There is of course plenty to talk about with these two major modes of thinking and consciousness, R-mode and L-mode, and what they can do for you.

In the 1970s, psychobiologist Roger W. Sperry pioneered the famous "split-brain" studies, where he discovered that the left and right hemispheres process information quite differently from each other (and just to add a little street credibility, he won the Nobel Prize for this work in 1981).

First, here's a little something to try. While seated, lift your right foot off the floor, and make clockwise circles. Now, while doing this, draw the number six (6) in the air with your right hand.

Notice that your foot will change direction. It's how you're wired. Cut the wiring, and two things happen: you'll have some very odd experiences, and famous researchers get a chance to learn a lot about the brain.

Sperry's research took patients who had an operation such that their left and right hemispheres could no longer communicate or coordinate with each other. The connections were simply cut right out. This made it relatively easy to see which hemisphere was uniquely responsible for specific behaviors and capabilities.

For instance, in one experiment, these split-brain patients were shown a different image in each eye at the same time. If asked to *name* the object they saw, they'd report the image seen in the right eye (using the primarily verbal left hemisphere). But if asked to identify it by touch, they'd report the image found in the left eye (which is attached to the nonverbal right hemisphere). Figure 3.4, on the next page, shows what was going on.

It was Sperry who originally assigned these different capabilities purely on a hemispheric basis and added the terms *left brain* and *right brain* to the modern lexicon. As it turns out, that's not entirely true, as described in the sidebar on page 58, so I'll refer to these modes as *linear mode* (L-mode) and *rich mode* (R-mode).

Sperry, Jerre Levy, and subsequent researchers identified the following characteristics as being associated with each mode.[9]

---

9. As described in *The New Drawing on the Right Side of the Brain* [Edw01].

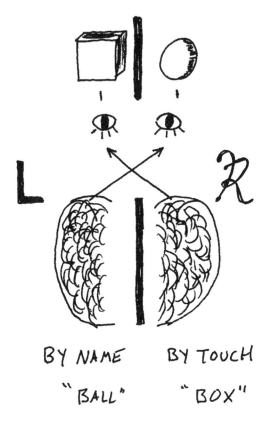

Figure 3.4: SPLIT-BRAIN SUBJECTS SHOWING SENSORY PREFERENCE

Left Brain vs. Right Brain

There's really no such thing as left brain and right brain thinking per se; the various lobes of the brain and structures at different levels cooperate in a highly distributed fashion, from the older, reptilian-like mechanisms up to the more recently added neocortex. But despite that cooperation, you still have these two different cognitive styles—our CPU #1 and CPU #2.

These different cognitive styles are known by many names. In the pop psychology lexicon, they are still simply known as *left-brain* and *right-brain* thinking. But that's a misnomer, because the dance of neurons is quite a bit more complicated than that, so various other terms have emerged.

Guy Claxton, in *Hare Brain, Tortoise Mind: How Intelligence Increases When You Think Less* (Cla00), refers to these as *d-mode* and the *undermind*. The *d* in d-mode stands for "deliberate," and *undermind* emphasizes that the CPU #2 processing occurs at a preconscious level.

Dan Pink, author of *A Whole New Mind: Moving from the Information Age to the Conceptual Age* (Pin05), refers to these two as *l-directed* and *r-directed*.

Dr. Betty Edwards, of *Drawing on the Right Side of the Brain* (Edw01) fame, was the first to break out of the right/left brain mold and referred to these simply as *L mode* and *R mode*.

To help clarify the nature of each of these cognitive modes, I will refer to them in this book as *linear mode* and *rich mode*, abbreviated as **L**-mode and $\mathcal{R}$-mode.

Characteristics of L-mode Processing

L-mode processing is comfortable, familiar, geek turf. L-mode gives you these abilities:

Verbal

Using words to name, describe, and define

Analytic

Figuring things out step-by-step and part-by-part

Symbolic

Using a symbol to stand for something

Abstract

Taking out a small bit of information and using it to represent the whole thing

Temporal

Keeping track of time and sequencing one thing after another

Rational

Drawing conclusions based on reason and facts

Digital

Using numbers as in counting

Logical

Drawing conclusions based on logic (theorems, well-stated arguments)

Linear

Thinking in terms of linked ideas, one thought directly following another, often leading to a convergent conclusion

This is clearly the motherhood-and-apple-pie of the white-collar, information-worker, engineering kind of life. These are the abilities we are tested on in school, use on the job, and fit in nicely with the sort of computer systems we've enjoyed up to now.

But as Pablo Picasso famously observed, "Computers are useless. They only give you answers." What would make him say such a heretical statement?

If "answers" are useless, then that would imply that the *question* is more important. In fact, that sort of opposite view of things seems to be a hallmark of $\mathcal{R}$-mode thinking. To those of us firmly entrenched in the **L**-mode way, the $\mathcal{R}$-mode traits may sound a little strange, fuzzy, or even acutely uncomfortable.

Characteristics of $\mathcal{R}$-mode Processing

In comparison to **L**-mode, $\mathcal{R}$-mode gives you the abilities shown in Figure 3.5, on the next page. These are all important, as we'll see, but note right off the bat that *intuition*—the hallmark of the expert—is over here.

This side of the house is nonverbal. It can retrieve language but can't create it. It favors learning by synthesis: putting things together to form wholes. It's very concrete, in the sense of relating to things just as they are, in the present moment. It uses analogies to evaluate relationships between things. It likes a good story and doesn't bother with timekeeping. It's not bound by rationality in that it does not require a basis of reason or known facts in order to process input—it's perfectly willing to suspend judgment.

The $\mathcal{R}$-mode is decidedly holistic and wants to see the whole thing at once, perceiving the overall patterns and structures. It works spatially and likes to see where things are in relation to other things and how parts go together to form a whole. Most important, it's intuitive, making leaps of insight, often based on incomplete patterns, hunches, feelings, or visual images.

Overall, though, this is far less comfortable territory. These traits seem more appropriate for artists or other *weirdos*. Not engineers. Not us.[10]

And what about "nonrational"? That borders on insulting. Many programmers would rather be accused of murder than be accused of being anything less than completely rational.

But many very valid thought processes are *not* rational, including intuition, and that's OK. Are you married? Was that a rational decision; that is, did you list the pros and cons or make a decision tree or matrix to make that decision in a logical, rational manner? Didn't think so.

---

10. They aren't even measurable. HR can't measure or reward most of these skills, at least not as easily as they can the **L**-mode traits.

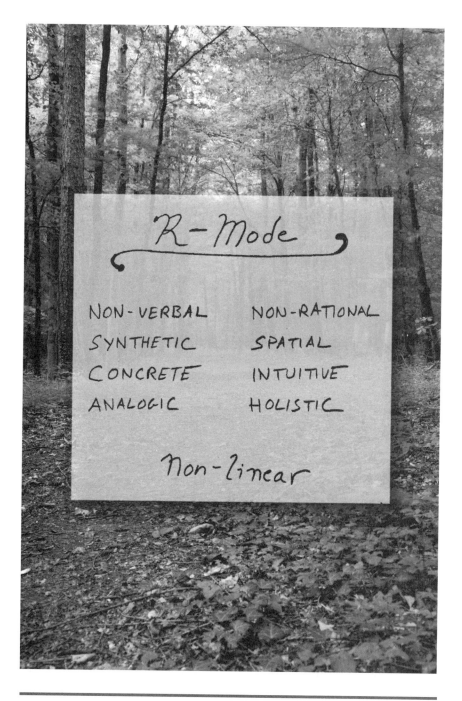

Figure 3.5: R-MODE ATTRIBUTES

There's nothing wrong with that; just because a thought process is nonrational or nonrepeatable doesn't mean it is unscientific, irresponsible, or inappropriate in any way.

Did the discussion of the Dreyfus model make you uncomfortable because it's not an event-style theory that can be proven? If so, that's your **L**-mode bias showing.

There's a lot of value in $\mathcal{R}$-mode processes

Power is going to waste.

that we're not using; a lot of power is going to waste. I don't know about you, but frankly, I can use all the brain power I can get. And there's a lot of interesting, underutilized power over on the $\mathcal{R}$-mode.

Why Emphasize $\mathcal{R}$-mode?

We want to use $\mathcal{R}$-mode more than we have because the $\mathcal{R}$-mode provides intuition, and that's something we desperately need in order to become experts. We cannot be expert without it. The Dreyfus model emphasizes the expert's reliance on tacit knowledge; that's over here in the $\mathcal{R}$-mode as well. Experts rely on seeing and discriminating patterns; pattern matching is here too.

$\mathcal{R}$-mode's analogic and holistic thinking styles are very valuable to software architecture and design—that's the stuff that good designs are made of.

And you might already be reaching for synthetic learning more often than you think. When faced with a difficult design problem, or an elusive bug, good programmers generally have an urge to reach for code and build something that they can learn from. That's $\mathcal{R}$-mode *synthesis*, as opposed to the **L**-mode *analysis*. That's why we like prototypes and independent unit tests. These give us the opportunity to learn by synthesis—by building.

In fact, synthesis is such a powerful learning technique that Nicholas Negroponte of the MIT Media Lab suggested in *Don't Dissect the Frog, Build It* [Neg94] that to really learn about a frog, traditional dissection is not the way to go. The better way to learn about a frog is to build one.

That is, task the students with building a being that has froglike characteristics. It's a great way to really learn what makes a frog a frog and how frogs are adapted to their particular environment. It's a perfect example of learning by *synthesis*.

TIP 9

> Learn by synthesis as well as by analysis.

But embracing synthesis as a learning technique is just the beginning. In fact, you can do a lot of things to increase the amount of brain power you can bring to bear on a problem, by leveraging both modes of thinking as appropriate—from simple techniques such as fiddling with something with your hand while you think to doodling while on the phone to some really interesting—and exotic—techniques.

We'll take a look at all of these as we see just how we can put you in your right mind (pun intended). But first, I'll digress to point out a slightly bigger picture that's afoot here and hint at why this $\mathcal{R}$-mode thing might be even more important than you think.

3.4 Rise of the $\mathcal{R}$-mode

As you may have felt from looking at the characteristics of **L**-mode and $\mathcal{R}$-mode, we have a bit of cultural bias toward **L**-mode thinking and related activities, and we might tend to dismiss $\mathcal{R}$-mode thinking as being the province of lesser mortals. $\mathcal{R}$-mode seems like a quaint leftover, a vestigial appendage from some previous age when people believed the world was flat and thunder was the result of unseen gods at war.

And indeed, it was the strengths of **L**-mode that differentiated humankind from common beasts; it brought humanity out of the forests and jungles and into villages and towns, out of the fields and into the factories, finally to land behind a desk and a copy of Microsoft Word.

But although the analytical and verbal capabilities of **L**-mode thinking have brought us this far, we've lost some key capabilities from an overreliance on **L**-mode at the expense of $\mathcal{R}$-mode. To progress, in order to move on to the next revolution in human development, we need to learn to reintegrate our largely neglected $\mathcal{R}$-mode processing with **L**-mode.

> **L**-mode is necessary but not sufficient.

Now before you toss the book down in disgust, afraid I might ask you to get in touch with your inner child or some other lame, weenie-sounding thing, let me tell you about Robert A. Lutz.

Mr. Lutz is a former Marine and pilot. The picture of him in the *New York Times* shows a no-nonsense, square-jawed fellow with a crew cut. As I write this, he's the chairman of General Motors North America. Pretty serious business.

And yet, when interviewed in the *Times* about the future direction of GM under his leadership, Mr. Lutz was quoted as saying, "It's more right brain...I see us being in the art business. Art, entertainment and mobile sculpture, which, coincidentally, also happens to provide transportation."

He's not talking about engineering or features. Everyone has those pop-up cup holders and iPod connectors these days. Instead, he's talking about *aesthetics*.

But this is not some artist holed up in a loft or researcher espousing some crackpot theory. This is the chairman of the third-largest corporation in America.[11] Lutz thinks this focus on aesthetics is the right course of action at this point in history.

Author Dan Pink agrees. In his popular book *A Whole New Mind: Moving from the Information Age to the Conceptual Age* [Pin05], Dan makes the case that economic and societal forces have taken us to the point where these artistic, aesthetic, R-mode attributes aren't a neat luxury for Martha Stewart types who want to craft their own greeting cards; instead, they are positively required for plain old, mainstream business.

Design Trumps Features

> Commoditization means you compete on aesthetics.

For example, consider the effects of commoditization. Suppose you are a large retailer, and you need to sell some common item, such as a toilet brush. You can't compete on price; anyone can get toilet brushes made in China for fractions of a cent. So, how do you differentiate your product?

Well, giant retailer Target decided to address this problem by featuring toilet brushes created by the famous designer and architect

---

11. That was in 2006. The automotive business remains tough, however.

Michael Graves. Since you can't compete on price, you have to compete on aesthetics.

Beyond toilet brushes, look at something closer to our hearts and ears: the iPod. Is the market-leading iPod feature-for-feature better than any alternative? Or is it just better designed and more aesthetically pleasing?

Start with the package itself. The iPod package isn't very verbose; it says how many songs and videos it will hold. And it has a nice picture. It's stark but elegant.

By comparison, there's a parody floating around on YouTube that shows what the iPod would look like if Microsoft had designed it. The parody is pretty brutal—the box is far from simple. It's packed with a dense assortment of text, branding, icons, disclaimers, and so on.

The box is replete with a multipage foldout of legal disclaimers, third-party endorsements, and, in big print, the fact that it's a 30GB model* (complete with an asterisk explaining that a gigabyte ain't exactly a billion bytes, your mileage will vary, and you don't actually get all that space anyway. I think it also mentions that you'll burn in eternal torment if you rip your own MP3s, but I digress…).

That's an important point: the iPod says *how many songs* it holds.

The Microsoft-flavored parody (and many real competing devices) say *how many gigabytes* it will hold. Consumers don't care about gigabytes; only we geeks do. Real people want to know *how many songs* it will hold or how many photos or videos.[12]

> It's about the songs, not gigabytes.

The iPod is well-designed and attractive, from the packaging to the user interface. And as it turns out, that's not just marketing sugarcoating. Attractive things actually do work better.

---

12. Rumor has it that this parody was in fact created by a design group within Microsoft, possibly to complain about the constraints they were operating under.

Attractive Works Better

Several studies[13,14,15] have conclusively shown that *attractive* user interfaces are easier to use than *unattractive* (or to use the scientific term, *ugly*) interfaces.

Researchers in Japan did a study of a bank's ATM interfaces; subjects found the aesthetically pleasing button layouts much easier to use than the ugly ones, even though the functionality and workflow was the same.

 Thinking that maybe there was a cultural bias at work, researchers repeated the experiment in Israel. The results were even stronger, even in a completely different culture. But how could this be? Aesthetic considerations are merely an emotional response. That couldn't possibly affect cognitive processing. Could it?

Yes, it can. In fact, additional studies[16] have shown exactly that: positive emotions are essential to learning and creative thinking. Being "happy" broadens your thought processes and brings more of the brain's hardware online.

Even corporate logos can affect your cognition. One study at Duke University[17] showed that brief exposure to the Apple logo made people more creative. Once you're primed with a stereotypical image of some sort, your behavior becomes influenced according to those behaviors you associate with the stereotype. In this case, the Apple logo, which many associate with nonconformity, innovation, and creativity, influences you to be creative and innovate.

The converse has been well-established. When you are fearful or angry—filled with negative emotions—your brain starts shutting down extra resources in preparation for the inevitable fight or flight (we'll look at that side of the reaction in Section 7.5, *Pressure Kills*

---

13. *Emotional Design: Why We Love (or Hate) Everyday Things* [Nor04].

14. *Apparent Usability vs. Inherent Usability: Experimental Analysis on the Determinants of the Apparent Usability* [KK95].

15. *Aesthetics and Apparent Usability: Empirically Assessing Cultural and Methodological Issues* [Tra97].

16. *A Neuropsychological Theory of Positive Affect and Its Influence on Cognition* [AIT99].

17. *Automatic Effects of Brand Exposure on Motivated Behavior: How Apple Makes You "Think Different"* [FCF07].

Cubicles Kill Neurons

You may have always heard that you start off with a certain number of brain cells, and that's all you get. These brain cells might die off, but you'll never get any new ones. Alcohol and aging can kill brain cells, which makes old age look pretty unappetizing, because you'd be left with a lot less brain cells than when you started.

Fortunately, professor Elizabeth Gould thought otherwise. In a discovery that turned the field on its ear, she discovered neurogenesis—the continued birth of new brain cells throughout adulthood. But here's the funny part. The reason researchers had never witnessed neurogenesis previously was because of the environment of their test subjects.

If you're a lab animal stuck in a cage, you will never grow new neurons.

If you're a programmer stuck in a drab cubicle, you will never grow new neurons.

On the other hand, in a rich environment with things to learn, observe, and interact with, you will grow plenty of new neurons and new connections between them.

For decades, scientists were misled because an artificial environment (sterile lab cages) created artificial data. Once again, context is key. Your working environment needs to be rich in sensory opportunities, or else it will literally cause brain damage.

Cognition, on page 198). For that matter, things in the environment that are obviously broken can create havoc as well. We've seen the Broken Windows theory (see *The Pragmatic Programmer: From Journeyman to Master* [HT00]) in action for years. Known problems (such as bugs in code, bad process in an organization, poor interfaces, or lame management) that are left uncorrected have a debilitating, viral effect that ends up causing even more damage.

Aesthetics make a difference, whether it's in a user interface, the layout of your code and comments, the choices of variable names, the arrangement of your desktop, or whatever.

> ### TIP 10
> Strive for good design; it really works better.

But we're slipping into some ill-defined waters here; what makes something "attractive" or not? How do you design something to be beautiful? What does that even mean?

One of the foremost building architects of the twentieth century, Louis Kahn, offers a useful explanation of the relationship between beauty and design: "Design is not making beauty; beauty emerges from selection, affinities, integration, love."

Beauty emerges from selection.

Kahn explains that beauty emerges from *selection*. That is, art comes not so much from the act of creation itself but rather from selecting among a near infinite supply of choices.

The musician has a near-infinite palette combining different instruments, rhythms, scale modes, tempo, and the hard-to-define but easy-to-sense "groove." The painter starts with some 24 million distinguishable colors to choose from. The writer has the full breadth of the Oxford English Dictionary (all 20 volumes; some 300,000 main entries) from which to select the perfect word.

Creativity comes from the selection and assembly of just the right components in just the right presentation to create the work. And selection—knowing what to select and in what context—comes from *pattern matching*, and that's a topic to which we'll keep returning.

3.5 $\mathcal{R}$-mode Sees Forest; L-mode Sees Trees

Pattern matching is a key ability demonstrated by experts. It's how they can narrow their choices and focus on just the relevant parts of a problem.

And for the most part, the pattern matching we've been interested in lies in the neglected $\mathcal{R}$-mode activity. But both L-mode and $\mathcal{R}$-mode have their separate approaches to pattern matching, and in the end you need both.

Consider the following figure:[18]

```
        I                 I
        I                 I
        I                 I
        I                 I
        I I I I I I I
        I                 I
        I                 I
        I                 I
        I                 I
```

Here we have an *H* character made up of individual *I* characters. This kind of pattern is known as a *hierarchical letter*. Psychologists present this sort of figure to subjects one eye at a time—quickly— and ask them to identify the big and small letters.

The hemispheres in your brain tackle this problem of identification differently; one hemisphere is better at identifying the local criteria (the small letters), and the other is better at the global criteria (the big letter).

Subjects do very well when asked about the global pattern using their left eye, which uses mostly $\mathcal{R}$-mode. They also do very well when asked about the local criteria (the parts) using their right eye, which uses mostly L-mode. But when asked the other way around, the results are considerably poorer. There looks to be some significant lateral specialization going on here.

This experiment seems to amplify the fact that if you're looking for global, holistic patterns, you need $\mathcal{R}$-mode. If you need to analyze parts and look into the detail, then you need a more L-mode approach. For most of us, this level of specialization is how it is. $\mathcal{R}$-mode sees the forest; L-mode sees the trees.

But for some fortunate few, the hemispheric differences are not as profound. Math prodigies, in particular, do not show these differences; their brain parts are much more cooperative.[19] When they see the *I* characters or the *H*s, both hemispheres are more equally involved.

---

18. Thanks to June Kim for this one.
19. *Interhemispheric Interaction During Global/Local Processing in Mathematically Gifted Adolescents, Average Ability Youth and College Students* [SO04].

If by chance you *aren't* a math prodigy, then we need to take a look at some other way to get the $\mathcal{R}$-mode and L-mode to cooperate: to better integrate L-mode and $\mathcal{R}$-mode processing. We'll take a look at how to do that in the next chapter.

3.6 DIY Brain Surgery and Neuroplasticity

You can physically rewire your brain. Want more capability in some area? You can wire yourself that way. You can repurpose areas of the brain to perform different functions. You can dedicate more neurons and interconnections to specific skills. You can build the brain you want.

Before you get carried away, put away the Dremel tool and dental pick; there's an easier way to do brain surgery. No tools required.

Until recently, it was believed that brain capacity and internal "wiring" were fixed from birth. That is, certain localized areas of the brain were specialized to perform certain functions according to a fixed map. One patch of cortical real estate was devoted to processing visual input, another to taste, and so on. This also meant that the capacity for whatever abilities and intelligence you were born with were largely fixed and that no additional training or development would get you past some fixed maximum.

Fortunately for us and the rest of the race, it turns out that isn't true.

Instead, the human brain is wonderfully plastic—so much so that researchers have been able to teach a blind man to see with his tongue.[20] They took a video camera chip and wired its output to the patient's tongue in a small 16x16-pixel arrangement. His brain circuits rearranged themselves to perform visual processing based on the neural input from his tongue, and the patient was able to see well enough to drive around cones in a parking lot! Also notice that the input device isn't particularly high resolution: a mere 256 pixels. But the brain fills in enough details that even this sort of low-res input is enough.

---

20. Described in *The Brain That Changes Itself: Stories of Personal Triumph from the Frontiers of Brain Science* [Doi07].

> **Tip 11**
>
> Rewire your brain with belief and constant practice.

Neuroplasticity (the plastic nature of the brain) also means that the maximum amount you can learn, or the number of skills you attain, is not fixed. There is no upper limit—as long as you believe that. According to Stanford University research psychologist Carol Dweck, author of *Mindset: The New Psychology of Success* [Dwe08], students who believed they could not increase their intelligence in fact couldn't. Those who believed in the plasticity of their brains increased their abilities easily.

In either case, what you think about the brain's capacities physically affects the "wiring" of the brain itself. That's a pretty **Thinking makes it so.** profound observation. Just *thinking* that your brain has more capacity for learning makes it so.

It's do-it-yourself brain surgery.

Cortical competition

And it's not just your beliefs that can rewire your brain; there is always an ongoing competition for cortical real estate in your brain.

Skills and abilities that you constantly use and constantly practice will begin to dominate, and more of your brain will become wired for those purposes.

At the same time, lesser-used skills will lose ground. "Use it or lose it" is perfectly accurate in this case, because your brain will dedicate more resources to whatever you are doing the most.

Perhaps this is why musicians practice scales incessantly; it's sort of like refreshing dynamic RAM. Want to be a better coder? Practice coding more. Engage in deliberate, focused practice as described in the sidebar on page 32. Want to learn a foreign language? Immerse yourself in it. Speak it all the time. Think in it. Your brain will soon catch on and adapt itself to better facilitate this new usage.

3.7 How Do You Get There?

In this chapter, we've looked at features of your brain, including the L-mode and R-mode cognitive processes, and at rewiring your brain through practice. You should also begin to appreciate the underutilized power of $\mathcal{R}$-mode.

So if this $\mathcal{R}$-mode thing is so great—or at least so necessary at this particular point in time—what can you do to experience more $\mathcal{R}$-mode processing yourself? What can you do to cultivate $\mathcal{R}$-mode and better integrate L-mode and $\mathcal{R}$-mode?

We'll look at some specifics of how to achieve better cultivation and integration in the next chapter.

Next Actions ⬇

- ☐ Make a short list of your favorite software applications and a list of the ones you just despise. How much does aesthetics play a role in your choices?
- ☐ Consider what aspects of your work and home life target L-mode. What aspects of your work and home life target $\mathcal{R}$-mode? Do you feel they are in balance? If not, what will you do differently?
- ☐ Keep a doodle pad on your desk (and in your car, with your laptop, by your bed), and use it.
- ☐ In addition, keep something on your person for 24×7 note taking (which may or may not be paper/pen based).

Try This

- ☐ Make a conscious effort to learn something new primarily by synthesis, instead of analysis.
- ☐ Try creating your next software design *away* from your keyboard and monitor (and we'll talk more about this in detail a bit later in the book).

A man should learn to detect and foster that gleam of light which flashes across his mind from within far more than the lustre of the whole firmament without. Yet he dismisses without notice his peculiar thought because it is peculiar.

▶ Ralph Waldo Emerson

Chapter 4

Get in Your Right Mind

In this chapter, we'll look at a whole bunch of techniques to help bring more mental processing power online for you. Some may be familiar to you, and others will definitely be more exotic; don't shy away from the "odd" ones. If you are repelled and don't want to try something, that's probably *exactly* what you should try first.

Emerson points out in the opening epigraph that we tend to dismiss unusual or uncomfortable thoughts—and that's a bad thing. You might miss out on that million-dollar idea of a lifetime. Instead, you need to pay attention to all that your mind has to offer. Sure, some of what you find will be the intellectual equivalent of a *Gilligan's Island* rerun, but you may also find that one idea that makes all the difference in the world. So, we're going to look at it all, be it good, bad, or ugly.

You probably know what **L**-mode processing feels like; it's that little voice in your head that makes **L**-mode very noticeable. But what does $\mathcal{R}$-mode feel like? You'll do an exercise that will let you experience a *cognitive shift* to $\mathcal{R}$-mode, and we'll see different ways to help engage more $\mathcal{R}$-mode processing.

We'll also look at ways of integrating **L**-mode and $\mathcal{R}$-mode more effectively, and I'll show you a variety of techniques to help harvest the fruits of your $\mathcal{R}$-mode's hidden labor.

4.1 Turn Up the Sensory Input

The simplest thing you can do to begin to involve more of your brain in problem solving and creativity is to activate more neural pathways than usual.

That means expanding sensory involvement—using different senses than usual. It's not a small effect; one study showed a 500 percent improvement for students using multisensory techniques.[1] Even surprisingly simple things can help.

For instance, try fiddling with a paper clip or some sort of tactile puzzle while stuck on a tedious conference call or while pondering a tricky problem.

> TIP 12
>
> Add sensory experience to engage more of your brain.

I've seen development teams have good success using *tactile enhancement*. Instead of trying to create and document a design or architecture directly in a commercial tool (using UML or something similar), use building blocks. Toy blocks. In assorted colors. Or Lego bricks.

Object-oriented design with Lego bricks is quite effective with a group of people: everyone can participate without fighting for the keyboard or the whiteboard marker; you can animate the actions and behaviors easily, and it encourages multisensory involvement. It helps you visualize—and generate imagery of—the proposed workings of the system. CRC cards[2] also have good cross-sensory, tactile properties.

Use cross-sensory feedback.

The next step is to emphasize cross-sensory feedback. Involving one extra sense is a good first step; now involve several other senses and allow them to interact. Suppose you take the design and do a couple of things to it:

- Write it down in your usual form.
- Draw a picture (not UML or an official diagram; just a *picture*). What visual metaphor is appropriate?
- Describe it verbally.
- Engage in open discussion with your teammates; respond to questions and criticisms, and so on.

---

1. *Improving Vocabulary Acquisition with Multisensory Instruction* [DSZ07].
2. Invented by Kent Beck and Ward Cunningham, each index card describes a *class*, its *responsibility*, and any *collaborators*. CRC cards are a good start at looking at the dynamic properties of a system, not the static (as in a UML class diagram).

- Act out the roles involved. (Any physical metaphors come to mind? We'll talk a lot about metaphors shortly.)

That last idea is quite powerful (and we'll see it again a bit later); see the sidebar on page 77 for a real-life example.

Notice that these activities begin to involve additional senses and styles of interaction. When you involve an additional input mode, you are activating more areas of the brain—you're bringing more processing power online, as it were.

Primary school educators have known for a long time that cross-sensory feedback is a very effective way of increasing understanding and retention. It's a pretty well-established pedagogical technique. That's probably why you were forced to create that dreaded diorama of ancient Rome or the papier-mâché model of Pompeii in grade school.

Your brain is always hungry for this kind of additional, novel stimulus. It's built to constantly adapt to a changing environ- **Feed your brain.** ment. So, change your environment regularly, and feed your brain. Any sort of extrasensory involvement is probably helpful, whether it's a long walk though crunchy leaves with your dog, opening your window and listening to the day's weather (and actually smelling some fresh air!), or just walking to the break room or down to the gym (the air there is less fresh, but exercise is also very helpful for better brain function).

4.2 Draw on the Right Side

I've claimed a number of times that we're not using our R-mode facilities as well as we might. Well, we're going to do a little experiment now to prove that and see how to deliberately get into a pure R-mode cognitive state.

I've given many talks across the United States and Europe based on the material that became this book. One of my favorite bits from the talks is a simple survey question I ask the audience: tell me how well you can draw. The results are *always* the same.

In a crowd of 100 technical types (programmers, testers, and managers), maybe one or two folks claim to be able to draw very well. Maybe another five to eight or so claim somewhat competent drawing skills but nothing suitable for framing. The vast majority in every case agrees with my own self-assessment: we suck at drawing. Just plain stink. There's a reason for that.

> "Drawing" is really about seeing.

Drawing is an $\mathcal{R}$-mode activity. Actually, let me back up a moment and describe what I mean by *drawing*. Drawing really isn't about making marks on paper. Anyone with normal physical abilities can put the appropriate marks on paper as required for drawing and sketching. The hard part isn't the drawing end; it's the *seeing*. And this sort of visual perception is very much an $\mathcal{R}$-mode task.

The essence of the problem is that shared bus I showed you a while back (in Chapter 3, *This Is Your Brain*, on page 45). The L-mode is sitting there chatting away, actively blocking the $\mathcal{R}$-mode from doing its job. And interestingly enough, many popular leisure-time activities can engage an $\mathcal{R}$-mode flow that shuts down the chatter of the L-mode: listening to music, drawing, meditation, jogging, needlework, rock climbing, and so on.

To access the perceptual $\mathcal{R}$-mode of the brain, it's necessary to present the brain with a job that the verbal, analytic L-mode will turn down. Or as Jerre Levy (prominent Cal Tech student of Sperry) says, you want to look at "setting up conditions that cause you to make a mental shift to a different mode of information processing—the slightly altered state of consciousness—that enables you to see well."

> Limit cognitive interference.

In the late 1970s, art teacher Dr. Betty Edwards wrote the seminal work *Drawing on the Right Side of the Brain*. It quickly became a very popular technique to teach drawing and sketching to those of us who weren't quite getting it. Expanding on the work of Sperry, Edwards realized that the reason many people have difficulty drawing is because of the cognitive interference from the dominant L-mode.

The L-mode is a symbolic machine; it rushes in quickly to provide a symbolic representation for some sensory input. That's great for symbolic activities such as reading and writing but is not appropriate for other activities.

Role-Playing

Johanna Rothman describes her experience using roles to work through some design issues:

"The team was working on *the* project to save the company. They had a new way of dealing with queued requests into the system. I suggested we assign everyone a role. The scheduler would have a whistle, the requests would stand in their appropriate queue, the director would tell the request where to go, and so on.

"A couple of people thought it was stupid, but everyone was tired and ready for a change. We made signs for ourselves. I had a stopwatch and clipboard so I could observe by timing and taking notes. We started.

"The first people collided (oh, it was so funny to watch their faces). We made a design change. Reroled. Got through a few of the normal scenarios. We realized as we got ready for one scenario that we would have another timing issue.

"That was enough for people to realize the thirty to sixty minutes we'd spent role-playing was more valuable than any of the design review meetings.

"Role-playing a design is not open discussion; it's participating in and watching the design in action."

Linda Rising describes another use of acting out: training a team. After several experiences introducing a new framework to teams that didn't quite get it, she and colleague David DeLano had the next team act out the framework as a play. This time, instead of complaining they didn't get it, the developers complained the play was a waste of a time because the material was "soooo easy!"

Ah, the curse of effectiveness.

For instance, here's a quick quiz for you. Get a piece of paper and a pencil. In five seconds, draw your house.

Take five seconds and try this....

Figure 4.1: IS THIS YOUR HOUSE?

I'm guessing you drew something like Figure 4.1. Now tell me truthfully, does your house *really* look like that? Unless you live in Flatland,[3] that is not an accurate picture of your house. Your ever-helpful L-mode is rushing in and screaming, "House! I know that one! It's a box with a triangle on top."

It's not your house any more than a stick figure looks like a person. It's a symbol, a convenient shorthand representation for the real thing. But oftentimes you don't want the trite symbol; you want to perceive the real thing—when drawing or perhaps when interviewing users to gather requirements.

Feel $\mathcal{R}$-mode with a Cognitive Shift

It was Dr. Edwards who first suggested that to get at the real perception you need to shut down the L-mode and let the $\mathcal{R}$-mode do the task for which it is best suited. To accomplish this, she recommends an exercise similar to the following to help you experience a cognitive shift.

This exercise will show you what $\mathcal{R}$-mode feels like. There are only a few rules:

1. Allow thirty to forty minutes of quiet, uninterrupted time.
2. Copy the image shown Figure 4.2, on the next page.
3. *Do not* reorient the page.

---

3. Seen any good shrinking circles lately? (See *Flatland: A Romance of Many Dimensions* [SQU84].)

Figure 4.2: DRAW THIS PICTURE.

4. *Do not* name any parts you recognize; just say to yourself up, over, this goes that way a little bit, and so on.

It's very important that you not name any features you think you see—that's the hard part. Try to just focus on the lines and their relationships.

When you're done, turn the picture right-side up and you might be quite surprised at the result.

Try this before reading on....

Why does this work?

It works because you've given your L-mode a job it doesn't want. By consistently refusing to name the parts you see, the L-mode finally gives up. This isn't a task it can handle, so it gets out of the way and lets the R-mode processing handle it instead—which is exactly what you want.

That's the whole point of *Drawing on the Right Side of the Brain*. It's all about using the correct tool for the job.

How did you feel during this exercise? Did it feel "different"? Did you get a sense of losing track of time and being immersed in flow? Did the drawing turn out better than had you tried to just copy it normally?

If not, don't be discouraged. You may need to try this exercise a few times before it works for you. Once you experience the cognitive shift, you'll better know what pure R-mode processing feels like, and it will become easier over time.

4.3 Engage an R-mode to L-mode Flow

Although I've been extolling the virtues of the R-mode, that's not the complete story. There was a spate of self-help books a few years ago that promised all manner of benefits based on the right side of the brain. I think there was even a *Right Brain Cookbook*.

That's nonsense, of course. Half-witted, even.

Although we can take advantage of R-mode processing that we have traditionally neglected, it's not a silver bullet or panacea. By itself, it won't solve all our problems—it can't even process language, after all.

Instead, what we need is a better way of synchronizing our L-mode and R-mode processing so that the whole mind can work better and more efficiently.

There's a particular technique that will let you accomplish this, and I found out about it quite by accident. I didn't exactly stumble on it; I sort of climbed over it.

Go Climb a Wall

Once upon a time, my wife thought it would be fun for us to try rock climbing. Many of the participants looked a little uncertain—none of us had ever attempted anything like this before, but we were determined to soldier on.

The instructor came out and made sure everyone was properly fitted in their safety gear. Once we were all fitted up and checked out, he stood in front of the group; we fell silent, ready for the lecture.

But there wasn't going to be a lecture. Instead, he told us to go start climbing. Just like that. For thirty minutes; then we'd all meet back here. There was some grumbling in the crowd—we had paid good money for this introductory package, and here the instructor was just throwing us to the wolves (or to the rocks, as the case may be). He went and got a coffee.

So, we cavorted on the rocks for a while, not really knowing what we were doing. And after a half hour, the instructor reappeared and *then* began the lecture, explaining to us how to climb. Now, having had some experience (however brief), his explanations made much more sense. We had some context in which to place his instruction: when he talked about shifting your weight in a certain way, it made sense—much more sense than if he had simply begun with the lecture.

In fact, thinking back on it, this instructor really did the correct thing: he provided us with a safe environment in which to explore (remember, he made sure everyone's safety gear was correctly fitted and adjusted before turning us loose). He first presented us with a multisensory, experiential context so that we could "get our heads around it," as it were. Then he followed up with a more traditional, fact-filled lecture.

What he did here was create a sort of $\mathcal{R}$-mode to L-mode flow. As it turns out, that's exactly what you want to do to facilitate learning.

Engage an $\mathcal{R}$-mode to L-mode flow.

The Lozanov Seance

In the late 1970s, Bulgarian psychologist Georgi Lozanov began experimenting with what he termed a *seance*.[4] The idea was to create a learning environment that would help create an $\mathcal{R}$-mode to L-mode flow, in this case, specifically for foreign language training.

Prof. Lozanov took his students into a darkened room, with gentle baroque music playing in the background (because this was the 1970s, no lawsuits were imminent). By using yoga-inspired breathing techniques and rhythmic exercises in this relaxed, comfortable environment, he hoped to improve the student's ability to concentrate and assimilate the new material.

While the students were in this state, the professor bombarded them with foreign language examples. No lecture, no footnotes, no explanations—just exposure. In other sessions, they would follow up with more traditional skills and drills.

It worked well, and the students who followed this intensive regimen outperformed those who participated in the normal classroom regime. In the years since, many educators have seized this idea of leveraging the $\mathcal{R}$-mode for its acquisition capabilities.[5]

As with any exciting new technique, some folks took it too far in one direction and advocated pure $\mathcal{R}$-mode techniques that completely ignored the L-mode. There were faddish books pushing right-brain bowling and a host of other ill-conceived ideas.

That's throwing the baby out with the bathwater. You can't ignore either mode of thinking; you need both working in concert. You want to let the $\mathcal{R}$-mode lead and then switch to L-mode to "productize" it, if you will.

> **Tip 13**
>
> Lead with $\mathcal{R}$-mode; follow with L-mode.

Both ways of thinking work naturally together; for instance, start with the analogic processes for connections and theories, and then use the analytic processes to validate your thinking. But remember

---

4. See the Education Resources Information Center at http://eric.ed.gov.
5. See, for example, *The Neuroscientific Perspective in Second Language Acquisition Research* [Dan94].

it's not a one-way trip; you need to return to $\mathcal{R}$-mode to keep the ideas flowing. $\mathcal{R}$-mode is the source, and you want to give it free, uninhibited reign.

Write Drunk, Revise Sober

There's an old writer's adage that advises would-be authors to "write drunk; revise sober." Now before you go stock up on Patrón Silver or Guinness, let's take a look at what this means.

You want your creativity to have free reign, unrestricted by "common sense" or "practicality." There's plenty of time to reign it in or discard the absurd later, but to begin with, you want to let 'er rip.

Just as creativity can be stifled by trying to tie ideas down prematurely, learning can be impeded by trying to memorize minor facts when you don't yet grasp the whole.

Don't be in such a hurry. When problem solving, learn to be comfortable with **Get used to it.** uncertainty. When creating, be comfortable with the absurd and the impractical. When learning, don't try so hard to learn and memorize; just get "used to it" first. Try to understand the meaning first; get the overall gist of it.

Then follow up with traditional L-mode activities to get to the next step: an $\mathcal{R}$-mode to L-mode flow.

There's a bit of a push in educational circles along these same lines. Dr. David Galin is a noted researcher at the Langley Porter Neuropsychiatric Institute, University of California at San Francisco. He believes that teachers these days have three main responsibilities to the whole student:[6]

- Train both hemispheres, not only the verbal, symbolic, logical left mode (as is traditional) but also the spatial, relational, holistic right mode.
- Train students to use the cognitive style suited to the task at hand.
- Train students to bring both styles to bear on a problem in an integrated manner.

---

6. See http://www.rogerr.com/galin/.

Shitty First Drafts

Part of being comfortable with uncertainty means being comfortable with something that's incomplete and unfinished. You want to avoid the headlong rush to try to achieve "perfection." Author Anne Lamott is an advocate of purposefully creating a shitty first draft. That is, it's better to complete a shitty first draft than to never complete a perfect one. In her book *Bird by Bird: Some Instructions on Writing and Life*, Lamott explains the dangers of perfectionism:

"Perfectionism is the voice of the oppressor, the enemy of the people. It will keep you cramped and insane your whole life, and it is the main obstacle between you and a shitty first draft. I think perfectionism is based on the obsessive belief that if you run carefully enough, hitting each stepping-stone just right, you won't have to die. The truth is that you will die anyway and that a lot of people who aren't even looking at their feet are going to do a whole lot better than you, and have a lot more fun while they're doing it."

You have the same responsibility to yourself. You want to end up using both L-mode and R-mode in concert, as needed, effectively.

But those of us in the learned, white-collar, technical professions are at a greater disadvantage than the general population. We have become *so* highly focused on (and rewarded for) the L-mode style of thinking and learning that we neglect the R-mode. We need to honor, respect, and foster attention to these largely ignored R-mode processes.

Let's look at a few other ways to get the L-mode and R-mode working well with each other.

Pair Programming

An interesting way to get L-mode to work with R-mode is to use another person for the other mode. In other words, have your L-mode work with another person's R-mode or their R-mode work with your L-mode.

One of the more effective—and controversial—practices espoused by Extreme Programming is *pair programming*. In pair programming, you have two programmers working at a single keyboard and monitor. One person types code in the IDE (the *driver*), while the other (the *navigator*) sits back and offers suggestions, advice, and kibitzes in general.

One reason this might work so well is that while the driver is locked in verbal mode at a particular level of detail, the navigator is free to engage more nonverbal centers. It's a way of using $\mathcal{R}$-mode and L-mode

> Work with one person in L-mode, one in $\mathcal{R}$-mode.

together at the same time, using two people. Reader Dierk Koenig describes the experience:

"While pair programming, I often experience that the navigator falls into a kind of 'pattern-matching' mode when the driver cannot. This is sometimes a source of disagreement; the navigator says: 'All that code over here is exactly the same as that other thing over there, I mean—beside all the words....' And the driver disagrees, because he just cannot see it while driving."

The navigator is free to see these larger relationships and the larger picture. And most of the time, you *cannot* see these relationships if you're driving. So if you aren't pair programming, you definitely need to stop every so often and *step away from the keyboard*.

When you talk to another person or work hand in hand with someone at a whiteboard or a paper, your thinking tends to get more abstract. You are more likely to discover new abstract patterns, which is what all of us programmers are trying to achieve.

This phenomenon of increased abstract awareness was demonstrated in a study[7] of secondary-school students who were given the following problem: five meshing gears are arranged in a horizontal line much like a row of quarters on a table. If you turn the gear on the far left clockwise, what will the gear on the far right do?

Some students were selected to work alone, others in pairs, as the researchers steadily increased the number of gears. By 131 gears, it was easy to see who had discovered the abstract pattern (in

---

7. *The Emergence of Abstract Representations in Dyad Problem Solving* [Sch95]. Thanks to June Kim for this pointer and summary.

this case, the well-known computer-science *parity rule*) and who hadn't. Only 14 percent of the solo workers discovered the rule, but a whopping 58 percent of the pairs did.

In another experiment, one pair of students came up with an abstract matrix representation based on a very concrete problem statement. The researchers reported the following:

> *...The experimenter asked the members how they came up with the matrix. One member stated, 'He wanted to make columns and I wanted to make rows.' To negotiate their two perspectives on the problem, they managed to come up with the matrix formalism that included both columns and rows.*
>
> ▶ Schwartz, et al.

Working together is a provably effective way to discover helpful and interesting abstractions.

Meeting in Metaphor

As we've seen, L-mode and R-mode processing are radically different, and yet there may be a common meeting ground between them in your own mind, a place where creativity gives birth to new ideas. L-mode and R-mode meet in *metaphor*—in the act of creating analogies.

"Metaphor, a common ground for both verbalizations and images, is a way to voyage back and forth between the subconscious and conscious, between right and left hemispheres."[8]

The use of metaphor is a powerful technique to open up creativity.

> **TIP 14**
>
> Use metaphor as the meeting place between L-mode and R-mode.

Now, when you hear *metaphor* and *analogy*, you might have a flashback to some horrid English class in grade school. But in fact, we use metaphors all the time. What we call *windows* on the computer screen aren't really windows at all. The mouse isn't actually a

---

8. See *Conscious/Subconscious Interaction in a Creative Act* [GP81].

rodent. A folder on your hard disk isn't a real folder, and the trash can isn't a real can.

When you write a concurrent program using *threads*, you're not sewing. It's just a metaphor. Don't even get me started on *zombie* processes in Unix or the typographic flotsam of *widows* and *orphans*.

We use metaphors constantly; in fact, cognitive linguist George Lakoff (*Women, Fire, and Dangerous Things: What Categories Reveal About the Mind* [Lak87]) maintains that we can't even think at all without the use of metaphor. Most humans aren't particularly good at dealing with the abstract; using a metaphor to relate some abstract notion to something concrete, something found in everyday life, makes it much easier for people to grasp.

But metaphors have differing potency. Common, everyday ones seem to be more like the symbolic representation of L-mode. Grander metaphors, on the other hand, are much more powerful. They can change our thinking and generate their own answers. What makes the difference?

Juxtaposing Frames of Reference

Metaphor comes from the Greek meaning "to transfer," with the idea that you are transferring the properties of one object to another in a way that is not literally possible.

This notion of combining two different, incompatible ideas is the very definition of creativity according to researcher/philosopher Arthur Koestler.[9] In his model, some particular topic area forms a particular frame of reference. The sudden switch from one self-consistent frame of reference to a different, unexpected, incompatible frame of reference is the basis of a strong metaphor. That junction of the two different frames is called a *bisociation.*

The more unlikely the association—the further apart the frames of reference—the greater the creative achievement when bisociated. This idea is the basis of Edward de Bono's Po technique.[10] *Po* is

---

9. See his article "Bisociation in Creation" included in *The Creativity Question* [RH76]. Thanks to Steph Thompson for this information. Koestler had some other unsettling beliefs and was accused of violent crimes against women. Genius and madness are often close companions it seems.

10. See *PO: A Device for Successful Thinking* [DB72] for more.

an invented word that tries to go beyond the binary notion of "yes" and "no." Several techniques involve Po; for now, you might think of it as a super-powerful version of *suppose*.

Use random juxtaposition to create metaphor.

One of the Po techniques is *random juxta-position*. You take a word from your subject area and combine it with a completely random, unrelated word. For instance, consider the words *cigarette* and *traffic light*. The challenge is to form a bisociation from these completely unrelated ideas. For example, cigarette and traffic light might meld into the concept of using a red band on the cigarette as a stop-smoking aid.

The further away the ideas are, the harder it is to join them in a metaphor that works. When we come across a particularly inventive metaphor, one where the frames of reference are suitably distant, we praise the author for centuries:

> *But soft! What light through yonder window breaks? It is the East, and Juliet is the sun!*
>
> *Love is a smoke made with the fume of sighs.*
>
> *Adversity's sweet milk, philosophy.*
>   ▶ William Shakespeare

What is that bright light in the window? It's not a celestial object; it's this girl Romeo just met at a masquerade ball.[11] Love is an emotion; it has nothing to do with smoke, fumes, or sighs in a literal sense, but what a fantastic image that conjures up. You can almost see the wisps of smoke from a young lover's obsessive desire building into a cloudy, potent fog.

The characteristics of the "smoky" frame of reference joins with the frame of reference for emotion (love); it begins to impart many of its known (but unstated) features onto the emotional frame. That sort of imprinting from one frame of reference to another is very powerful and something we can use to our advantage.

There's metaphor, and then there's metaphor.

---

11. Modern greeting cards have probably inured us to this sort of comparison; it likely had far greater impact in Shakespeare's day.

System Metaphor

The original published version of Extreme Programming (described in *Extreme Programming Explained: Embrace Change* [Bec00]) featured a fascinating practice: system metaphor. The idea is that any software system should be able to be guided by an appropriate metaphor. For instance, a payroll system might be considered analogous to a post office, with discrete mailboxes, delivery schedules, and so on. Or maybe a scientific measuring system could be thought of as a manufacturing system with conveyor belts, storage buckets, and so on.

All metaphors break down eventually, but the idea was that a sufficiently rich metaphor could help guide the design of a system and help answer questions that come up during development (this idea is somewhat similar to our discussion of system invariants in *The Pragmatic Programmer: From Journeyman to Master* [HT00]).

The features of the metaphorical frame of reference can imprint themselves onto the software system; implicit, well-understood properties of the real world start to transfer into the software itself.

But coming up with good metaphors—ones that help answer questions instead of causing more—can be hard. System metaphor, as a practice, is not as widely accepted as, say, test-first development or pair programming.

I was talking to Kent Beck, the father of XP, about metaphors in general, and he said this:

"Metaphorical thinking is fundamental in programming, as it is in all abstract thought. When we aren't aware of our metaphors, we can lead ourselves astray. Mixing metaphors negates much of their power. Why do we **over**ride a method in a **sub**class? Clear metaphors make it easier to learn, reason about, and extend code."

Clear metaphors are a powerful tool, but we don't always get it right. Kent goes on: "Why is it that we mess up metaphors? Why is the converse of add() not always delete()? Why do we insert() something into a container instead of add() it? Programmers are sloppy in their use of metaphors—tables that aren't at all like tables, threads that aren't like threads, memory cells that aren't like memory or cells."

We use metaphors so much that we're not even aware of many of them (as with windows, mice, and so on). It's really easy to latch onto the first metaphor that presents itself without thinking too much about it. However, that's probably not the best metaphor you could use.

Generative metaphors are hard.	Coming up with a really good metaphor that has generative properties suitable for your context is much harder. There is no "metaphor compiler" that can tell you

whether it's right or not; you have to actually try it in practice. Use the metaphor to guide your design, and be aware of how it helps— or not. You won't know immediately; the outcome will be uncertain. And as we saw in Section 4.3, *Engage an R-mode to L-mode Flow*, on page 80, you need to be OK with uncertainty. Don't force the issue; just be aware of it.

After some experience, you might suddenly realize that the metaphor you started out with was wrong, but this other idea really fits more closely (and that's of course fine; it will just take some code refactoring).

If you're not used to deliberately creating metaphors, you might find the practice of a system-level metaphor difficult.[12] But there is a way you can improve your ability to create metaphor and analogy, funnily enough.

So, This Duck Walks into a Bar...

Humor is neither a waste of time nor a harmless diversion; instead, it reflects an important ability necessary for thinking, learning, and creativity. It's all about connections.

Humor arises from making novel connections across disparate ideas. It may be absurd, but humor is often based on identifying relationships and distorting them. For instance, "My best friend ran away with my wife. I'm sure going to miss him." You assume the primary relationship is between the man and his wife, but instead it turns out that his relationship with his best friend is more impor-tant to him; the skewed connection makes it funny.

---

12. Personally, I suspect that's the driving reason why it hasn't been adopted as widely.

Or the all-time classic line from Henny Youngman: "Take my wife. Please." You initially think that "take my wife" is merely

Take my wife.

an idiom that means "Consider my wife's behavior, for example," only to realize it is a plaintive request instead. That sudden linguistic U-turn is the source of humor. The creativity comes from realizing that "take my wife" can have multiple meanings and from exploiting the potential for misunderstanding.

Comedian Steven Wright was famous for drawing interesting parallels, as with his friend the radio announcer who would disappear when driving under a bridge. That is, Wright drew the analogy that just as a radio signal can sometimes fade out under a bridge, so might the radio announcer himself. He also describes accidentally using his car keys on his apartment door and taking the building for a spin around the block.

Instead of drawing an analogy, you might also extend an existing idea past what's reasonable. For example, if an airplane's black box can survive a crash, then why can't they make the whole plane out of the stuff?

In either case, the talent for humor comes from drawing or extending relationships beyond the norm, truly seeing "out of the box." A quick wit—being able to draw connections between things that aren't related or to extend an idea past its breaking point—is a skill well worth practicing, honing, and encouraging in your team.

> **TIP 15**
>
> Cultivate humor to build stronger metaphors.

Have you seen my fishbowl? The implicit, habitual frame of reference would lead you to think I'm looking for the glass bowl in which my fish resides. But if the answer is, "Yes, he just got a strike!" then we're in a completely different, cartoon frame of reference where *bowl* was actually a verb.

By practicing making these far-flung connections, you'll become better at doing so. In fact, you'll actually begin to change the very fabric of your brain to accommodate this new activity.

Next Actions ⬇

☐ Make more metaphors. You can do this as part of software design or something more artistic—your own jokes, fables, or songs.

☐ If you're new to creating metaphors, start with something simple: a thesaurus (you know, that thick book that's sold next to the dictionaries in the bookstore or that "other" window in your online dictionary program).

☐ For more in-depth exploration, try playing with WordNet (available for all platforms from http://wordnet.princeton.edu). This gives you not only synonyms but also antonyms, hypernyms, hyponyms, and other derivations of various flavors.

4.4 Harvest $\mathcal{R}$-mode Cues

Despite years of being ignored, your $\mathcal{R}$-mode remains hard at work, toiling away in the background to match up disparate facts, make far-flung associations, and retrieve long-lost bits of important data from the morass of otherwise uninteresting memories.

In fact, it's entirely possible that your $\mathcal{R}$-mode already has exactly the answer to the most important problem that you're working on right now.

But how can you get at it? We'll spend the rest of this chapter looking at techniques to help invite, coax, ferment, and jiggle great ideas out of your head.

You Already Know

You may already have that great idea or know the solution to that impossibly vexing problem.

Every input gets stored.

Your brain stores every input it receives. However, even though stored, it does not necessarily index the memory (or if you prefer a more die-hard computer analogy, "store a pointer to it").

Just as you can arrive at work with no memory of how you got there (as we saw earlier), the same thing can happen while you're sitting in a lecture hall, sitting in a training seminar, or reading a book. Even this one.

But, all is not lost. It turns out that when you are trying to solve a hard problem, all of your memories are scanned—even the ones you cannot consciously recall. It's not the most efficient thing (I'm envisioning something like a SQL full-table scan on a large table with very long rows), but it does work.

Have you ever heard an old song on the radio and then several days later you suddenly remembered the title or artist? Your $\mathcal{R}$-mode was still working on the problem, asynchronously in the background, until it finally found the memory.

But many times the answer isn't so easily divulged: the $\mathcal{R}$-mode, after all, cannot *process* language. It can retrieve chunks of it from memory, but it can't do anything with it. This leads to some rather odd scenarios.

The Strange Case of Elias Howe

In 1845, one Elias Howe was struggling to invent a practical lock-stitch sewing machine. It wasn't going very well for him. One night, after a long, hard, unproductive day, he had a terrifying nightmare—the wake-up-screaming, projectile-sweating kind of nightmare.

In the nightmare, he was in Africa, abducted by hungry cannibals. About to be made into stew, he was quite literally in a lot of hot water. As he tried to escape, the headhunters kept poking at him with their funny-looking spears.

As he's describing the nightmare the next morning, his attention focuses on the "funny-looking spears." What made them odd was that they had holes in the end, in the barbed tip of the spear; it was almost like holes in a handheld sewing needle but up at the tip. Hey...

Elias went on to receive the first American-issued patent for an automatic sewing machine, based on his hard-won inspiration that the hole for the needle needed to be opposite the normal, handheld orientation.

It would seem that Elias already knew the answer to this difficult technical problem—at least, his $\mathcal{R}$-mode had retrieved an answer. But since the $\mathcal{R}$-mode is nonverbal, how can it be presented to the L-mode for processing?

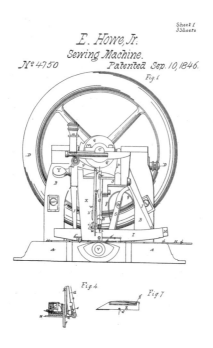

Figure 4.3: ELIAS HOWE'S PATENT

The $\mathcal{R}$-mode has to throw it over the fence visually, in this case wrapped up in the disturbing—and very memorable—imagery of an outlandish dream.

Many ideas are not verbalizable. And as it turns out, you have many excellent skills and ideas that are simply not verbalizable. As noted earlier (in Chapter 3, *This Is Your Brain*, on page 45), you can recognize thousands of faces, but try to describe even one face—that of a spouse, parent, or child—to any degree of accuracy. You don't have the words to describe it. That's because facial recognition (and indeed, most pattern-based recognition) is an $\mathcal{R}$-mode activity.

You might also notice that you can't read text that appears in dreams, such as road signs or headlines. Most people can't.

Let us now take a quick look at two different ways of harvesting some of this $\mathcal{R}$-mode recognition: image streaming and free-form journaling.

Inarticulate Ability

One group of researchers* experimented with showing students random numbers flashing on different quadrants of a computer screen. Some students were shown a jumping number before the main number; the control group was not. The jumping number appeared to jump around in different quadrants at random, but it wasn't random at all—there was a subtle pattern to it.

The students exposed to the jumping number could locate the main number much more quickly than the others. However, they couldn't explain why they could find the number on the screen so quickly. They thought they were guessing and just lucky, but in fact they had learned the pattern unconsciously and couldn't verbalize it.

Thanks to June Kim for this; also documented in Hare Brain, Tortoise Mind: How Intelligence Increases When You Think Less (Cla00).

---

*. *Acquisition of Procedural Knowledge About a Pattern of Stimuli That Cannot Be Articulated* (Lew88).

Harvesting with Image Streaming

In the case of Elias Howe, the answer he was seeking was being presented in the form of a dream. You might experience the same thing once you start paying more attention to the contents of your dreams. Not all dreams "mean something." Sometimes in a dream "a cigar is just a cigar," as Sigmund Freud reportedly said. But there are many times when your R-mode is trying to tell you something, something that you want to know.

Image streaming is a technique designed to help harvest R-mode imagery.[13] The basic idea is to deliberately observe mental imagery: pay close attention to it, and work it around in your mind a bit.

First, pose a problem to yourself, or ask yourself a question. Then close your eyes, and maybe put your feet up on the desk (this is perfect for doing at work) for about ten minutes or so.

---

13. Described in *The Einstein Factor: A Proven New Method for Increasing Your Intelligence* [WP96]; evidence that this technique works is largely anecdotal, but that's somewhat to be expected in this case.

For each image that crosses your mind, do the following:

1. Look at the image, and try to see all the details you can.

2. Describe it out loud (really use your voice; it makes a difference). Now you're sitting with feet up on the desk *and* talking to yourself.

3. Imagine the image using all five senses (or as many as practical).

4. Use present tense, even if the image was fleeting.

By explicitly paying attention to the fleeting image, you're engaging more pathways and strengthening connections to it. As you try to interpret the image, you're broadening the search parameters to the $\mathcal{R}$-mode, which may help coalesce related information. At any rate, by paying close attention to those "random" images that flit across your consciousness, you may begin to discover some fresh insights.

It's not magic, and it may or may not work for you, but it does seem to be a reasonable way of checking in with the rest of your brain.

A fair percentage of the population will not see any images in this fashion. If that's the case, you might try to artificially induce a random image by gently rubbing your eyes or briefly staring at a light source (this creates what is called a *phosphene*, the sensation of seeing light from some nonvisual source).

The source of the image is not that important; how you try to interpret it is. We'll talk more about this phenomenon in just a bit.

Harvesting with Free-Form Journaling

Another simple way of harvesting your $\mathcal{R}$-mode's preconscious treasures is to write.

Blogging has enjoyed tremendous popularity in recent years, and probably rightfully so. In previous eras, people wrote letters— sometimes a great many letters. We saved the best ones from famous people such as Voltaire, Ben Franklin, Thoreau, and other notables.

Letter writing is a great habit. Sometimes the material is relatively dull—what the weather was doing, how the prices at the market were up, how the scullery maid ran off with the stable boy, and so

Tools and Interference

When you try to start any creative endeavor, such as writing on a blog, an article, or (heaven help you) a full-length book, you *will* encounter massive resistance. Resistance can take many forms, from niggling self-doubt to wildly creative procrastination to a myriad assortment of other distractions and excuses (see *The War of Art: Break Through the Blocks and Win Your Inner Creative Battles* (Pre02) for a disturbingly complete catalog of the many manifestations of resistance).

With blogging in particular, the tool itself can get in the way and stop you from writing. For instance, if you use a third-party web service for blogging (such as TypePad or Blogspot), are you set up to write blog entries while offline? Or if inspiration strikes when you're away from the Net, does that become an excuse not to write? If you've written your own blogging software, do you spend more time tweaking the software or your blog design instead of creating new articles? Not to be too much of a Luddite, but writing on paper has worked well for many thousands of years. It can be a lot faster to capture ideas on paper first and then transcribe them into your blog editors.

Once you start writing, it's important to maintain the flow. Don't let technical issues distract you once you get going. Don't worry about what needs to be edited yet; get it all down first.

Famous letters were carefully saved and preserved; what about yours? Do you have backups? Once you've written a blog post, is it being archived anywhere other than Google's cache?

on. But in the detailed minutiae of everyday life were occasional philosophical gems. This sort of free-form journaling has a long pedigree, and those skillful thinkers from days gone by were eventually well regarded as "men of letters" for penning these missives.

Today, blogs are taking on this role. There's a lot of "what I had for breakfast" and the occasional virulent rant indicative of declining mental health, but there are also penetrating insights and germs of ideas that will change the world. Some already have.

But there are many ways to write your thoughts down, and some are more effective for our purposes than others. One of the best is a technique known as *morning pages.*

The Morning Pages Technique

 This is a technique that I first heard about in the context of a writer's workshop (also described in *The Artist's Way* [Cam02]); it's a common technique for authors. But I was surprised to also come across it in a popular MBA program and in other senior executive–level courses and workshops.

Here are the rules:

- Write your morning pages *first thing* in the morning—before your coffee, before the traffic report, before talking to Mr. Showerhead, before packing the kids off to school or letting the dog out.
- Write at least three pages, long hand. No typing, no computer.
- Do not censor what you write. Whether it's brilliant or banal, just let it out.
- Do not skip a day.

It's OK if you don't know what to write. One executive taking this program loudly proclaimed that this exercise was a *complete waste of time.* He defiantly wrote three pages of "I don't know what to write. Blah blah blah." And that's fine.

Because after a while, he noticed other stuff started appearing in his morning pages. Marketing plans. Product directions. Solutions. Germs of innovative ideas. He overcame his initial resistance to the idea and found it to be a very effective technique for harvesting thoughts.

Why does this work? I think it's because you're getting an unguarded brain dump. The first thing in the morning, you're not really as awake as you think. Your unconscious still has a prominent role to play. You haven't yet raised all the defenses and adapted to the limited world of reality. You have a pretty good line direct to your $\mathcal{R}$-mode, at least for a little while.

Thomas Edison had an interesting twist on this idea. He'd take a nap with a cup full of ball bearings in his hand. He knew that just as he started to drift off into sleep, his subconscious mind would take up the challenge of his problem and provide a solution. As he fell into a deep sleep, he'd drop the ball bearings, and the clatter would wake him up. He'd then write down whatever was on his mind.[14]

The "Just Write" Technique

And then there's blogging itself. Any chance to write is a good exercise. What do you *really* think about this topic? What do you actually know about it—not just what you think, but what can you defend? Writing for a public audience is a great way to clarify your own thoughts and beliefs.

But where to start? Unless you're burning with passion for some particular topic, it can be hard to sit down and just *write* about something. You might want to try using Jerry Weinberg's Fieldstone method, described in *Weinberg on Writing: The Fieldstone Method* [Wei06].[15]

This method takes its name from building fieldstone walls: you don't plan ahead to gather these particular stones for that wall. You just walk around and pick up a few good-looking stones for the future and make a pile. Then when you get around to building the wall, you look into the stone pile and find a nice match for the section you're working on at the moment.

Make a habit of gathering mental fieldstones. Once you have some piled up, the process of building walls becomes easy.

It's a good habit to get into.

Harvesting by Walking

You can harvest $\mathcal{R}$-mode cues just by walking, if you do it right. Do you know the difference between a labyrinth and a maze?

According to the Labyrinth Society,[16] a maze may have multiple entrances and exits, and it offers you choices along the way. Walls prevent you from seeing the way out; it's a puzzle.

---

14. Cited in *Why We Lie: The Evolutionary Roots of Deception and the Unconscious Mind* [Smi04]; thanks to Linda Rising for suggesting it.
15. Thanks to several readers for suggesting this and to June Kim for this summary.
16. On the Web at http://www.labyrinthsociety.org.

Figure 4.4: GRACE CATHEDRAL, SAN FRANCISCO

 A labyrinth is not a puzzle; it's a tool for meditation. Labyrinths offer a single path—there are no decisions to be made. You walk the path to sort of give the **L**-mode something to do and free up the $\mathcal{R}$-mode.

It's the same idea as taking a long walk in the woods or a long drive on a straight, lonely stretch of highway, just in a smaller more convenient space.

Labyrinths go back thousands of years; you'll find them today installed in churches, hospitals, cancer treatment centers and hospices, and other places of healing and reflection.

Have you ever noticed that great ideas or insights may come to you at the oddest times? Perhaps while taking a shower, mowing the yard, doing the dishes, or doing some other menial task.

That happens because the **L**-mode sort of gets bored with the routine, mundane task and tunes out—leaving the $\mathcal{R}$-mode free to present its findings. But you don't have to start washing a lot of dishes or compulsively mowing your yard in order to take advantage of this effect.

In fact, it's as easy as a walk on the beach.

 Henri Poincaré, the famous mathematician, used a variation of this idea as a problem-solving technique.[17] Faced with a difficult, complicated problem, he would pour everything he knew about the subject onto paper (I'll suggest something similar in a later section; see Section 6.8, *Visualize Insight with Mind Maps*, on page 171). Looking at the problems that this step revealed, Poincaré would then answer the easy ones right away.

Of the remaining "hard problems," he would choose the easiest one of those as a subproblem. Then he would leave his office and go for a walk, thinking *only* about that particular subproblem. As soon as an insight presented itself, he would break off in the middle of the walk and return to write the answer down.

Repeat this process until everything is solved. Poincaré described the sensation: "Ideas rose in crowds; I felt them collide until pairs interlocked, so to speak, making a stable combination."

If you don't have a labyrinth at hand, just go for a walk around the parking lot or down the hall. However, try to avoid just walking around the office because that might offer too many distractions: a co-worker's conversation, an impromptu meeting with the boss or client, or an assessment of the latest sports scores or political intrigue at the water cooler all will distract you from the problem in a negative way.

Now, I may have just misled you in the past several paragraphs. When you go for your "thinking walk," don't actually do any *thinking*. It's important to draw a vital distinction between $\mathcal{R}$-mode and L-mode processing. L-mode is deliberate: when you focus, when you concentrate, that's L-mode at work. $\mathcal{R}$-mode is different. It can't be commanded, only invited.

> $\mathcal{R}$-mode can be invited, not commanded.

---

17. Thanks to June Kim for suggesting this example.

You have to sort of defocus a bit. In the *Laws of Form* [SB72], mathematician George Spencer Brown refers to this not as thinking but as simply "*bearing in mind* what it is that one needs to know."

As soon as you focus on a goal, **L**-mode processes will dominate, and that's not what you want here. Instead, you want to cultivate a style of non-goal-directed thinking. As Poincaré did, dump everything out onto paper (or into an editor buffer, if you must), and then leave it be. Don't rehash it or go over it in your mind. Bear it in mind, as Brown suggests, but don't focus on it. Hold it ever so lightly in your thoughts. Let the stew of facts and problems marinate (we'll talk more about this in Section 8.2, *Defocus to Focus*, on page 216).

> TIP 16
>
> Step away from the keyboard to solve hard problems.

And then when you least expect it, you may find that the answer will emerge by itself.

Now put the book down. Go for a walk. I'll wait....

4.5 Harvesting Patterns

Although we've been talking a lot about harvesting great ideas, your ability to harvest thoughts and insights isn't limited to Great Ideas. Your $\mathcal{R}$-mode search engine can pattern match based on the merest fragment of a pattern to go on.

Cna yuo raed tihs?[18]

Aoccdrnig to rscheearch, it dseno't mtaetr in waht oerdr the ltteres in a wrod are; the olny iproamtnt tihng is taht the frsit and lsat ltteer be in the rghit pclae. The rset can be a taotl mses, and you can sitll raed it whotuit a pboerlm. Tihs is bcuseae the huamn mnid deos not raed ervey lteter by istlef but the wrod as a whloe. Azanmig...

---

18. *The Significance of Letter Position in Word Recognition* [Raw76] and *Reibadailty* [Raw99].

Using Martial Arts to Improve Focus

June Kim tells us the following story:

"After beginning martial arts, I recognized that my focus span (the period of time I can keep focusing on something) and control (such as getting focused in a poor environment) has improved. I have been continuously recommending my practice to software developers and other knowledge workers. It's called Ki-Chun; it has a martial arts aspect as well as tai chi, meditation, and breathing aspects.

"I have seen a recognizable difference in a friend of mine who started the practice. In less than a month you could see the difference clearly. He told me that he could more easily concentrate and the quality of his concentration improved."

Yoga, meditation, breathing techniques, and martial arts all affect how your brain processes information. We are complex systems, and as we saw with systems thinking, that means everything is connected. Even something as simple as breathing in a particular manner can profoundly affect how you think.

Your mind is quite adept at reconstructing reality based on fragmentary patterns. It can make associations based on incomplete data, and it does so all the time, even if you're not aware of it.

Patterns in Code

Here's an example of patterns that you've probably experienced if you're a programmer. Source code, even in its monospaced, fixed-width font, has typographic qualities to it that can help you understand the author's intent.

Remember: source code is read many, many more times than it's written, so it's usually worth some effort to help make the code more human-readable. In other

Code is write-once, read-many.

words, we should make the larger patterns in the code easier to see.

For instance, why do we use fixed-width fonts? The compiler doesn't care. But we tend to want to align text, braces, and code:

```
String foofoo = 10
int    bar    = 5
```

to make it easier to scan and recognize. Similarly, you might tend to separate code blocks with character graphics, like this:

```
/************************/
/** Something Important **/
/************************/
```

That catches your attention and, when done regularly, becomes part of a larger pattern that your mind recognizes and latches on to. Reader Dierk Koenig tells us that he deliberately takes the time to "typeset" his code in this way.

Novices will start off doing this—it's an easy rule to follow, after all. But advanced beginners may begin to push back, complaining that spending time on code layout is a waste of time. Proficients and experts will bristle at poor code if it's harder for them to see the patterns they're used to seeing, whatever those may be.

These visual cues may take many forms, such as alignment and header blocks as we've seen here, or even more subtle cues such as method size. Once you get used to seeing very small methods, with only a few lines of code, very long methods jump out at you as *wrong*.

Brace placement forms a visual pattern as well, which may explain why some folks will fight long and hard in favor of a particular style of brace placement in those languages that use curly braces. They aren't being argumentative for the sake of argument; this sort of pattern matching affects their perception.

There's a dark side to pattern matching in code, though. Consider this classic fragment from the venerable C language:

```
if (receivedHeartbeat())
    resetWatchdog();
else
    notifyPresident();
    launchNukes();
```

In this unfortunate case, launchNukes() will always be executed regardless of the value of receivedHeartbeat(). The indented code makes it nice and readable, but that's not how the compiler sees it:

only the first statement binds to the else; the indention is misleading. Typography has a powerful impact on perception—for better or for worse.

Try to aid visual perception by using consistent typographic cues. The compiler may not care, but we do. Be sensitive to this effect: if you're at the higher skill lev-

Accommodate different skill levels.

els and you're encountering resistance from the rest of the team, understand that they literally don't see it the same way you do. They won't automatically appreciate the value; you'll have to explain it to them.

If you don't see the value in these patterns but more expert folks on your team do, humor them. Realize it's not a waste of time on some foolish affectation but an important communication tool.

Using a Whack on the Side of Your Head

Many times it's hard to see things that are right in front of you, because you get used to seeing patterns in a certain way. It's easy to get stuck in a rut—to get stuck in certain thought patterns and accustomed

The only difference between a rut and a grave is the dimensions.

ways of thinking. The trick to gaining insight is to try to see a problem from a completely different viewpoint.

For instance, here's a question that might stump you (if you're older than six): what do John the Baptist and Winnie the Pooh have in common? The answer[19] isn't what you would normally think of. OK, it's a stupid joke, but the point is that it's an astoundingly literal answer in a context that you're probably not used to.

The key to creativity and problem solving lies in finding different ways of looking at a problem. Different associations force the $\mathcal{R}$-mode to initiate different searches; new material might now come up.

When faced with a thorny problem, Dave Thomas will often say, "Turn that on its head." That's one *mental whack*: a way to knock you out of your rut to make you look at a problem from a different point of view.

---

19. A middle name: "the."

For instance, sound engineers use a well-known technique when mixing a recording. To make the sound as good as possible, they first go through and make each instrument sound *as bad* as possible. Make the saxophone honk abrasively, turn up the fret noise from the guitar, hum from the electric bass, and so on. Now reverse the settings: everything that you emphasized to make things sound bad, turn down or cut out to get to clean, sparkling sound.

Turn the problem around. That simple change of viewpoint, looking at the problem from the other way around, is by itself a very powerful technique. You can use that when debugging: instead of trying to prevent a difficult-to-find bug, try coming up with three to four ways to deliberately cause it. Along the way, you might discover what's really happening. Or perhaps try the same thing with a user interface design: instead of trying to come up with the perfect layout or workflow, make the *worst* layout and workflow. That might help you hone in on what's really important.

> **TIP 17**
>
> Change your viewpoint to solve the problem.

In *A Whack on the Side of the Head* [vO98], Roger von Oech lists many different "whacks" such as these, including looking at something in reverse, exaggerating an idea, combining disparate ideas, and so on.

In addition to the whacks, he describes common mental locks that tend to block you from seeing alternatives. The locks include assuming there's only one right answer, thinking that a given solution is not logical, or dismissing *play* as frivolous.

These are dangerous assumptions because they aren't true, and they can actively impede your progress. Most problems have multiple solutions or multiple "right answers." The one-right-answer idea probably was true only for grade-school arithmetic. Afraid a solution isn't logical? Most of your brain processing isn't logical either, but that doesn't make it wrong. And the notion of "playing" with an idea is one of the most powerful tools we have. Non-goal-directed playing with an idea is where you'll make connections, see relationships, and gain insights. It helps change your viewpoint.

Necessity is the mother of invention. Play is the father of invention.
► Roger von Oech

A great example of insight gained from changing your viewpoint appears in T. H. White's *The Once and Future King* [Whi58]. In this story of Merlin the magician training the young King Arthur, Merlin transforms Arthur into different animals and birds so that he might experience the world in different ways.

At one point, young Arthur is learning to fly with the wild geese, flying high above the countryside. As a goose looking down on the landscape below, Arthur is struck with the insight that boundaries are artificial constructs: there are no painted lines on the ground showing kingdoms or countries. He begins to realize that all of England could be united under one king.

But you don't have to actually transform into a bird as Arthur did; just imagining yourself as a bird (for instance) would have the same effect. From this different vantage point, your brain's search engine will be forced to scrape up different ideas.

For example, imagine yourself as an integral component of the problem you're working on: suppose you *are* the database query or the packet on the network. When you get tired of waiting in line, what will you do? Who would you tell?

The Magic of an Oracular Whack

In classical times, high priests of the temples would often consult an oracle[20] for advice. As with most fortune tellers or newspaper horoscopes, the response or message given by an oracle would typically be ambiguous, almost a riddle. You have to "interpret" it for yourself. That's a whack on the side of your head.

It's the same idea as in a paradoxical Zen koan, such as "What is the sound of one hand clapping?" Rationally, that doesn't make any sense at all. The brain is forced

Reconcile unlike patterns.

to try to reconcile unlike patterns; this broadens the scope of material under consideration. On a more familiar note, think about playing the word game Scrabble. What do you do when you're stuck and don't see any obvious words to form? You rearrange the letters, hoping to see a new relationship.

---

20. Lowercase *o*, not the database vendor.

Composers Brian Eno and Peter Schmidt came up with a set of 100 oblique strategies[21] along these same lines. These questions and statements force you to draw analogies and to think more deeply about the problem. They are a great resource to draw on when you get stuck (and are available online, as a Dashboard Widget for Mac and iPhones, text versions for Palm OS, a command-line version for Linux, and so on). Here are some examples:

- What else is this like?
- Change nothing and continue consistently.
- Shut the door and listen from the outside.
- Your mistake was a hidden intention.

I particularly like that last one: perhaps your mistake wasn't such a mistake after all. Freud would like that one, too.

Go grab the oblique strategies or some other oracle and see what it means to you today.

Try that before reading on....

Shakespeare's Brain Teasers

Some patterns are so unusual that they "wake your brain up." That is, they actually overclock your brain (to use the CPU metaphor again) briefly to attend to this novel input.

For instance, kids make up awesome words. From active verb forms such as *imaginate*[22] to mash-ups such as *prettiful* and the curiously skewed *flavoring* (as in, "I'm not flavoring that food today"). It's a pity that we adults don't do more of this, because there's more to these shifting word forms than meets the ear.

William Shakespeare engaged in a lot of this sort of verbal reengineering. In fact, he's credited with coining quite a few phrases that we use to this day:[23]

- "Full circle"
- "Method to the maddness"

21. See http://www.rtqe.net/ObliqueStrategies.
22. See my IEEE article "Imaginate" [HT04].
23. Described in *Brush Up Your Shakespeare!* [Mac00].

Change Is Good

It's been said that *only wet babies like change*. We are creatures of habit. But ingrained habit isn't the best thing for the brain; you don't make new connections that way, and you'll become increasingly blind to other alternatives.

Think about your morning routine. The order you perform your daily preparations in is probably pretty consistent, right down to small details such as which tooth gets brushed first. You want to mix that up and get out of the rut.

Use a different hand. Park on the other side. Change the part of your hair. Use a different kind of towel. Start shaving. Stop shaving. Eat earlier or later.

These small changes are good for your brain; they help change the wiring and prevent neural ruts. Seriously. Your brain is tuned to be adaptive; if there's nothing to adapt to, it will get "flabby," metaphorically speaking.

- "Neither rhyme nor reason"
- "Eaten out of house and home"

In addition to adding new phrases to the lexicon, Shakespeare would repurpose certain key words to create a sense of wonder and surprise. For example, he might use a noun to serve as a verb (as in, "he godded me"). This technique, known as a *functional shift*, causes a sudden peak in brain activity.

Because it's an unexpected input, the brain has to do some work to figure out the full meaning. But interestingly, researchers discovered that you'll understand what the word *means* before understanding its *function* in the sentence.[24] This technique helps keep the text active and keeps the reader engaged—breaking the reader out of the usual rut of standard idioms and clichés. It's a verbal whack on the head.

---

24. See http://www.physorg.com/news85664210.html for details.

Although using a functional shift will create a brain burst in your readers, it will likely cause *agita* (that is, dyspepsia of the soul) on the part of one's copy editor. But it's still a very cleverful technique.

4.6 Get It Right

In this chapter, we've looked at some of the properties of *R*-mode thinking. Your *R*-mode processes are subtle and cannot be forced into action.

Yet these ways of thinking are vital to achieving a balanced, full-throttle approach to problem solving and creativity. You don't want to focus on *R*-mode at the exclusion of **L**-mode, and you don't want to continue to focus on **L**-mode to the exclusion of *R*-mode. Instead, you want to structure your learning and thinking to support an *R*-mode to **L**-mode flow.

Start to pick up on subtle clues, and begin to harvest your *R*-mode's existing output. Give your *R*-mode processes more of a chance to function using techniques such as morning pages, writing, and non-goal-directed thinking time (aka walking).

Finally, since memory is a frail and expensive mechanism, be prepared to write down the gems of insight that your *R*-mode may deliver, whenever—and wherever—that may be.

Next Actions ⬇

New Habits

- ☐ Do morning pages for at least two weeks.
- ☐ Hone a quick wit. Look for connections or analogies between unrelated things.
- ☐ Involve more senses when faced with a tricky problem. What works best for you?
- ☐ Read something different from your usual material, for example, fiction, not science fiction, and so on.
- ☐ Try a different genre of movie, vacation, music, or coffee.
- ☐ Order something you've never had at your favorite restaurant.
- ☐ Turn each problem around. What can you learn from the reverse?

Try This

☐ Deliberately vary your morning routine or other consistent habit.

☐ Hold a design session using Lego blocks or office supplies.[25]

☐ Take a class or start a hobby that involves more $\mathcal{R}$-mode processing. Work on it daily.

☐ Use the buddy system: have a buddy help keep you motivated, and discuss your progress.

☐ Think of a metaphor, or set of metaphors, that would largely describe your current project (it may be helpful to think in terms of something very tangible). Try to come up with a few jokes about it using metaphor or exaggeration.

☐ Look at experts you know. What "quirky" habits now make more sense to you?

☐ What words can you add to your workplace lexicon?

---

25. You get extra credit if you can use a red stapler.

I never set out to be weird. It was always the other people who called me weird.

▶ Frank Zappa

Chapter 5

Debug Your Mind

Intuition is great, except when it's not.

It's a popular vision that leaders are diligent, thoughtful decision makers. They gather all the relevant facts, weigh them, and come up with the logical, rational

We are not rational creatures.

decision. But in fact, that idealized process is basically *never* followed, even by expert, high-pressure decision makers.[1]

Instead, we make decisions and solve problems based on faulty memory and our emotional state at the time, ignoring crucial facts and fixating on irrelevant details because of where and when they occur or whether they are brightly colored. Especially if they are brightly colored.

We need to debug the system.

The modern idea of "debugging" a computer comes from a real bug—a moth trapped in a relay of the Mark II Aiken Relay Calculator (see Figure 5.1, on the following page). While running a series of cosine regression tests, the operators spotted an error. Looking into the matter, they found the moth. The operators removed the bug, dutifully taped it to the log book, and so truly debugged the system.[2]

---

1. This is pretty well-worn territory; see, for example, *The Power of Intuition: How to Use Your Gut Feelings to Make Better Decisions at Work* [Kle04].
2. The term itself has a long and rich history which has been strongly associated with a "bogeyman."

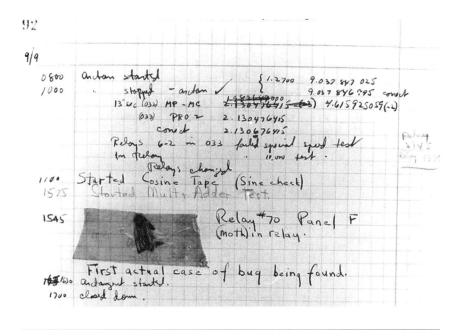

Figure 5.1: THE FIRST BUG IN THE SYSTEM (SEPT. 9, 1945)

Although that's a fine metaphor (and occasionally literal truth) in hardware systems, the idea of debugging your mind is, well, kind of gross. But we really do have "bugs" in the way we think—fundamental errors in how we process information, make decisions, and evaluate situations. James Noble and Charles Weir sum up the problem nicely:

"Development is always done by people; clients and users are people; and under strict genetic testing most managers can be shown to share at least 50% of their genetic code with *homo montipythonus*."[3]

Unfortunately, the human mind is not open source. None of us has ready access to the source code to fix these bugs, but I can help show you where they occur so that you can be more aware of the influence of these erroneous processes on your thinking. We'll look at four broad categories of problems:

- *Cognitive biases*: How your thinking can be led astray
- *Generational affinity*: How your peers influence you

---

3. *Process Patterns for Personal Practice: How to Succeed in Development Without Really Trying* [WN99].

- *Personality tendencies*: How your personality influences your thoughts
- *Hardware bugs*: How older portions of your brain can override the smarter portions

Being aware of these bugs is the first step to mitigating them.

5.1 Meet Your Cognitive Biases

Cognitive biases come in several flavors. These mental "bugs" can affect your decision making, memory, perception, rationality, and so on. There are a *lot* of them. Wikipedia lists some ninety common cognitive biases. I've met some folks who surely had a few more than that.

Here are some of my personal favorites:

Anchoring

Just seeing a number will affect how you then predict or decide some quantity. For instance, if I keep mentioning something about having 100 books for sale, I've primed you with that number. If I now offer you a book for $85, you'll tend to anchor on the 100, and the 85 sounds like a bargain.

Fundamental attribution error

We tend to ascribe *other* people's behavior to their personality, instead of looking at the situation and the context in which their behavior occurs. We might excuse our own actions more easily ("I was tired; I felt a cold coming on."). But people who are normal in all respects can be driven to extraordinary actions, including theft, murder, and mayhem, especially in time of war or personal crisis. It doesn't have to take such extreme conditions; as we saw earlier, context is everything. Remember that behavior is oftentimes more because of reaction to a context than because of fundamental personality traits.

Self-serving bias

This is the tendency to believe that if the project is a success, I'm responsible. If it tanked, then I'm not. This behavior is probably a protective mechanism, but remember that you're part of the system—whether it turns out well or not.

Need for closure

We are not comfortable with doubt and uncertainty—so much so that we'll go to great lengths to resolve open issues and to remove uncertainty and reach closure. But uncertainty can be a good thing: it leaves your choices open. Forcing premature closure, as in Big Design Up Front (BDUF),[4] cuts off your options and leaves you vulnerable to errors. Artificially declaring a decision, such as the end date of a project, doesn't remove the inherent uncertainty; it just masks it.

Confirmation bias

Everyone looks for choice facts to fit your own preconceptions and pet theories. You could argue that this entire book (and most books) are giant examples of confirmation biases of the author.

Exposure effect

We tend to prefer things just because they are familiar. This includes tools, techniques, or methods that aren't working well anymore or that are even actively causing harm.

Hawthorne effect

Researchers have noticed that people have a tendency to change their behaviors when they know they are being studied. You'll see this when you introduce a new practice or a new tool on a team. At first, while everyone is watching—and everyone knows they are being watched—results look great. Discipline is high, and the excitement of something new fuels the effort. But then the novelty wears off, the spotlight moves away, and everyone slides inexorably back to previous behaviors.

False memory

It's actually pretty easy for your brain to confuse imagined events with real memories. We're susceptible to the power of suggestion; as we saw earlier, memory isn't written to some static store in the brain. Instead, it's an active process—so much so that *every read is a write*. Your memories are constantly rewritten in light of your current context: age,

---

4. BDUF was a popular design technique that demanded heavy initial investment in design and architecture despite uncertainty and volatility in the details that often invalidated the design.

experience, worldview, focus, and so on. That incident at your sixth birthday party? It probably didn't happen that way, and it may not have happened at all.

Symbolic reduction fallacy

As we saw earlier, **L**-mode is anxious to provide a quick symbol to represent a complex object or system, which loses at least the nuances and sometimes even the truth of the matter.

Nominal fallacy

A kind of symbolic reduction problem; this is the idea that labeling a thing means you can explain it or understand it. But a label is just that; and naming alone does not offer any useful understanding. "Oh, he's ADHD" doesn't enhance understanding any more than "She's a Republican" or "They're from Elbonia."

And all this is just the beginning. Our irrational nature could take several books.[5]

Failure to Predict

It's tough to make predictions, especially about the future.

▶ Yogi Berra, Philosopher

Symbolic reduction is an especially pernicious problem because it's so deeply ingrained in our usual analytical, programmatic thinking. Indeed, the only way the brain can keep up with the complexity of reality is to reduce large, complex systems to simple, easily manipulated symbols. This is an essential mechanism in the brain and a very useful one in computer programming and knowledge-based work. But if you take it for granted, you fall into the symbolic reduction fallacy.

We've seen examples of the symbolic reduction fallacy before; for instance, when you're trying to draw a human hand, the **L**-mode reduces the complexity of light, shadow, and texture to "five lines and a stick." That reduction can be thought of as taking complex reality and treating it as if it were comprised of very basic, archetypical elements: *platonic solids*.

---

5. And it has; see the excellent *Predictably Irrational: The Hidden Forces That Shape Our Decisions* [Ari08] for more.

Named for Plato, these ideal forms supply a sort of universal, commonly understood set of building blocks.

The future hides in the platonic fold.

Think of a kid's building block set with cubes, blocks, cones, archways, and columns. From these basic shapes, you can construct a wide array of larger structures. Plato's ideal forms work in a similar fashion; they are simplified building blocks of reality. But this approach of reducing reality into an idealized form leaves a hole, called the *platonic fold*. An awful lot can hide in this hole, and we get blindsided by these kinds of unexpected events.

The concept of the platonic fold, described in *The Black Swan: The Impact of the Highly Improbable* [Tal07], emphasizes that humans are really bad at trying to extrapolate future events from previous events. We assume that events form a more or less stable, linear progression, with easily defined cause and effect.

They don't. That's why we fail to predict the future in so many cases. In fact, because of our blind spots—including the platonic fold—it turns out that all consequential events in history come from the wholly *unexpected*.

That's where the book's titular "black swan" comes from. For many years, it was assumed that swans could only be white. Because no one had ever seen a black swan, its existence was thought to be impossible by the scientific community— until a black swan showed up.

Unexpected events change the game.

As a group, we tend to miss important developments because we're focused on the wrong thing or are asking the wrong questions. For example, I was cleaning my office last year when I stumbled upon a stack of magazines dating from the early to mid-1990s (I also found a 14.4 modem in the middle of a tangle of active cables, but that's another story).

The magazines made a convenient time capsule. Cover after cover fanned the ferocious debate over the most important issue of the day: who would win the desktop wars? Would the interface to conquer the desktop be based on Open Look or on Motif?

Correlation vs. Causation

Scientific studies can be easily misinterpreted; most of us are not well versed in the science of statistical analysis. One of the most popular misconceptions arises from declaring a cause and effect when there's only a correlation.

Just because two variables are correlated does not mean that either causes the other. For instance, consider reports of high incidences of leukemia for families living under power lines. The headline might even report that power lines cause cancer.

They well might, but this single correlation doesn't prove that at all. There are many other possible variables: property under power lines is cheaper, so these are poorer families, which may negatively affect diet, health care, early detection, and so on. Determining causation is a different beast than observing a correlation.

In addition, causality in the real world isn't usually as simple as "event *x* causes event *y*." Instead, it's common that *x* triggers *y*, which reinforces *x*, which then strengthens *y*, and so on. It's more a case of "both x and y" rather than "either x or y." Events can contribute to the causality in differing amounts, and they have different reinforcing properties. Even the same kind of event, observed over time, may have completely different causes in each instance.

It was the wrong question, as it turned out, and Windows—which wasn't even considered one of the contenders—took over. Then there was the middleware war; who would win? RMI or CORBA?

It was the wrong question again, because the growth of the Web largely made the issue moot. The Web was a classic black swan, an unanticipated development that changed the rules of the game completely. And on it went: pages and pages of analysis and speculation, forecasting and fretting, almost always over the wrong question. Our biases make it nearly impossible to predict the future and very difficult to navigate in the present.

As you can see, just because you "think so" doesn't make it right. Recognizing and overcoming your own cognitive bias is surely easier said than done. But here are a few suggestions that might help.

"Rarely" Doesn't Mean "Never"

"Astronomically unlikely coincidences happen daily."[6] Recently, we've witnessed all manner of devastation from 500-year floods to 100-year storms, but geologically speaking that's just a drop in the bucket—these events are not that rare. They may freak people out because they haven't happened within their memory or the memory of their parents (or even grandparents). But that doesn't mean they can't happen, and it doesn't prevent them from happening three times in a row.

In 2004, your odds of being killed by lightning in the United States were around 1 in 6,383,844.[7] That sounds like pretty good odds, right? But forty-six people died that year from lightning, despite the six-million-to-one odds. And you had sixteen times greater odds of dying from falling out of bed, although that's probably not something you'd think of as particularly dangerous. Even though it's rare, it still happens. On a more positive note, you can expect to experience a one-in-a-million miracle about once a month.[8]

The black swan cautions us not to discount unobserved or rare phenomena as impossible.

Truly random events form a mix of values that are clumped together as well as lone values; homogeneity and randomness are different things. It's perfectly valid in a completely random sample to have three Category Five hurricanes in a row, for instance.

> TIP 18
>
> Watch the outliers: "rarely" doesn't mean "never."

Look into the platonic fold, and think about what you might be missing. Any one of those minor elements that you overlooked can be the one that changes history.

Never say never.

Take time to examine the "crazy" outliers or those "impossible," astronomically unlikely events. If any of those actually did happen, what would it mean to you? What would you do differently because of it? What concerns wouldn't matter anymore, and

---

6. Michael T. Nygard in *Release It!: Design and Deploy Production-Ready Software* [Nyg07].
7. According to the National Safety Council, http://nsc.org.
8. See Littlewood's Law for the math.

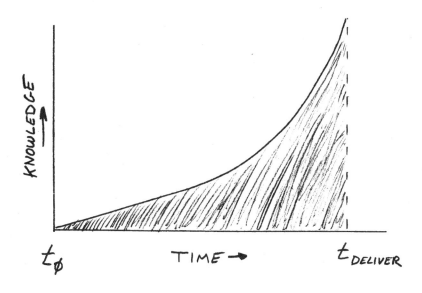

Figure 5.2: PROJECT KNOWLEDGE OVER TIME

which would become prominent? Remember, these are still unlikely events, so don't start stocking up on canned food or Hazmat suits just yet. But never say never.

Defer Closure

Our need for closure means we are driven to try to eliminate uncertainty—ready or not. But fixing on a decision prematurely reduces your options, perhaps to the point of eliminating the successful choice.

On a software project, as with an exploratory or inventive project in any discipline, it's a given that you'll learn a little bit more every day. You'll learn more about the users, the project itself, your team, and the technology, as shown in Figure 5.2.

That means you'll be at your peak of intelligence at the very end of the project and at your most ignorant at the very beginning. So, do you want to make decisions early on? No; you want to defer closure for as long as possible in order to make a better decision later. But that means critical issues may stay unsettled for a long time, which makes many people acutely uncomfortable.

Resist the pressure. Know that you will reach a decision, and the matter will be settled, just not today.

> **TIP 19**
>
> ## Be comfortable with uncertainty.

Agile software development embraces the idea of working with uncertainty. Early on, you don't know what the project end date will really be. You're not 100 percent certain which features will be present in the next iteration. You don't know how many iterations there will be. And that's perfectly OK: that's the sort of uncertainty you want to be comfortable with. You'll find answers as you go along, and by the end, everything will have been answered.

You can, of course, take some concrete steps to try to reduce uncertainty. You might talk the matter over with peers, google around for more information, or build a prototype—that sort of thing. But although these steps might help a little or a lot, they're not a cure. There will always be elements that are just plain uncertain, *and that's not a bad thing*. Chip away at it, but don't be in a rush to nail down details if it's not ready yet. Be comfortable with the fact you don't know.

Guess with explicit probabilities. For something you don't know but that *has* to be known by others, such as a go-live date, you can express it as a "target" date along with an indication of your confidence in the estimate. That is, you might report a target date such as Oct. 1, with a 37 percent chance of making that date. But be careful when reporting a date with an 80 percent probability. Folks may tend to hear that as "nearly certain" without appreciating there's a 20 percent chance it won't happen. At least you're being up front about the inherent uncertainty.

But realize that it can be really, really hard for other folks in the organization to be comfortable with these ideas. They are programmed to seek closure at all costs and will try to do so at every turn. Educate them as best you can, but be prepared for resistance.

You Can't Recall

Finally, remember that you don't remember very well. Memory is unreliable, and old memories will change over time, which just reassures you that your misconceptions and prejudices are valid. Don't rely exclusively on your memory. The Chinese proverb is correct: the palest ink is better than the best memory.

> **TIP 20**
>
> Trust ink over memory; every mental read is a write.

Instead, augment your memory with some kind of reality check. Whether it's notes that you keep or a conversation with someone else with their own memories, you need something to help keep your memories from drifting too far from reality.

Next Actions ⬇

- ☐ List the cognitive biases you recognize in yourself. We all have our favorites. Which ones are you particularly susceptible to?
- ☐ Notice how many astronomically unlikely events you have witnessed in your career. How unlikely were they in hindsight?[9]
- ☐ Start and maintain an engineer's log of notes from design meetings, coding questions and solutions, and so on. Put a mark next to older entries any time you have to go back and use it.

5.2 Recognize Your Generational Affinity

Anything that is in the world when you're born is normal and ordinary and is just a natural part of the way the world works. Anything that's invented between when you're fifteen and thirty-five is new and exciting and revolutionary and you can probably get a career in it. Anything invented after you're thirty-five is against the natural order of things.

▶ Douglas Adams, *The Salmon of Doubt*

---

9. While pondering this, remember that most of the world's data is now stored on hard drives with a ninety-day limited warranty.

We've looked at cognitive biases so far in a sort of static light. But of course, nothing is static. The biases you fell for several years ago are probably different from your current faves. But they might have a lot in common with your peers along the way, and they might differ dramatically from folks who are a little older or a little younger than you are.

As Douglas Adams points out, the biases you form change over time, and taken as a whole, the biases that drive any particular generation will be different from the biases that drive you and your peers.

Some folks value the stability of their job at the expense of any amount of abuse from their boss. Other folks will pack up and quit at the slightest perceived offense. Folks who are driven to work all hours can't understand the folks who cheerfully pack up at 5 p.m. and head home to be with their family, and vice versa.

These are more insidious forms of bias than the bugs we've looked at so far—values and attitudes that are so ingrained you wouldn't even *think* to question them. But they can dramatically affect your judgment and your perception.

Have you ever pondered why you value those things you value? Are they the values your parents instilled in you? Or are they a reaction *against* those who raised you? Did you ever sit down and deliberately decide to be liberal, conservative, libertarian, or anarchist? A workaholic or a slacker?

Consider the context. Or were you just born that way? Well, partly. We'll look at the "just born that way" factors in the next section. But remembering that context is king, let's look at you in the context of your peers and your environment.

You are a product of your times—perhaps much more so than you think. The attitudes, philosophies, and values of your parents and your *cohort* (those born about the same time as you; your peers throughout school and in the workplace; members of your generation) have a tremendous impact on your values, attitudes, and perceptions.

You and the rest of your cohort are united by shared memories, common habits, and popular styles, as well as your age and station in life at that time. For instance, the terrorist attacks of 9/11 were a major, shared global event, affecting everyone. But depending on whether you are in your 20s, your 40s, or your 60s, your reaction to those events will differ—and align more closely with everyone else who is in your similar age bracket.

How might your attitudes differ? Here are a couple of axes I can think of:

- Risk taker vs. risk adverse

- Individualism vs. teamwork

- Stability vs. freedom

- Family vs. work

Different generations inherently have different values, and your own attitudes and concerns change as you age as well.

As you and your cohort age, you begin to fulfill roles vacated by the previous generation, but you'll adapt the situation to your own outlook.

Here's a quick synopsis[10] of the last several generations in America, including the approximate birth years for each generation. These ranges are necessarily fuzzy; if you are born near one of the inflection points, you may find yourself identifying more with an adjacent bracket than with your nominal one.

And of course, these are broad generalizations at best. So, it's not to say that if you're born in these years that you have these traits, rather that taken as a whole,

These are broad generalizations.

these cohorts tend to exhibit these traits. Remember these aren't laws or set-in-stone prescriptions; these are useful abstractions to model group behavior[11] and help raise your awareness of a larger scope of context.

---

10. From several sources, including *Generations at Work: Managing the Clash of Veterans, Boomers, Xers, and Nexters in Your Workplace* [ZRF99].
11. In other words, this is a construct theory as opposed to an event theory; see the sidebar on page 14.

Kids Today

Want to see something really scary?

The Beliot Mindset List (on the Web at http://www.beloit.edu/~pubaff/mindset/) tracks interesting facts and observations about the cohort entering college in any given year.

For instance, as far as the freshman class of 2008 is concerned, MTV has never featured music videos (in case you haven't been paying attention for the last decade, it focuses on reality TV shows, celebrity gossip, and news).

Russia has always had multiple political parties. Stadiums have always been named for corporations. They've never "rolled down" a car window (let alone dialed a phone). Johnny Carson has never been on live TV; Pete Rose has never played baseball.

The Web has always been around; so has Dilbert.

GI generation, 1901–1924

All-American, get-it-done builders

Silent generation, 1925–1942

Gray-flannel conformists

Boom generation, 1943–1960

Moralistic arbiters

Generation X, 1961–1981

Free agents

Millennial generation, 1982–2005

Loyal, nonentrepreneurial

Homeland generation, 2005–???

Just being born now; half of this generation will have Millennial parents

We'll ignore the under-twenty set for the time being and take a closer look at each of the grown-up generations in turn.

The GI Generation, 1901–1924

This generation produced the first Miss America and propagated the idea of the all-American athlete. They built the suburbs and moon rockets, and they fought valiantly in World War II.

The command-and-control, rigidly hierarchical military metaphor for business—and then for software development—has its roots here.

The Silent Generation, 1925–1942

Next up, the gray-flannel conformists. This generation vastly expanded the legal system and continues a distinct focus on due process but not necessarily on decisive action.

As a possible example, consider a recent Iraq Study Group report, staffed largely by folks in this age group, which listed seventy-nine recommendations but not a single action item.

This group generated—and enjoyed—unprecedented affluence.

The Baby Boom Generation, 1943–1960

Ah, the Baby Boomers. Perhaps the most recognizable—and largest—generation, formed in the heyday of post–World War II optimism.

This group engendered a dramatic increase in crime rates, substance abuse, and risk taking in general. The tendency for this generation is to see themselves of arbiters of national values; they have always wanted to "teach the world to sing" (remember the 1970s Coca Cola commercial?).

But this inherent desire to save the world doesn't manifest itself in particularly realistic or pragmatic ways. This group is less interested in outcome and more interested in approach. Their moralizing, which reflects their all-important values, may sound preachy to other generations.

Generation X, 1961–1981

Gen X is the greatest entrepreneurial generation.

One of the best descriptions I've read of Gen X described them as being "raised by wolves." These are free agents, with an inherent distrust of institutions. They form the greatest entrepreneurial generation in U.S. history.

Fiercely individualistic, and perhaps a bit on the dark side, they'll just quit and move on if there's a problem at work. They resist being labeled at all costs. They might be viewed as undisciplined by other generations, or they might be accused of not playing by the rules.

This group is less interested in civics, believing that one-on-one involvement is more effective. They are quite pragmatic, working for a positive outcome regardless of any particular ideology or approach.

Millennial Generation, 1982–2005

In this generation, the pendulum swings away from individualism toward greater team-based work; there's a decrease in risky behaviors and a noticeably less edgy approach than their Gen X or Boomer predecessors. They are loyal to the organization and not nearly as entrepreneurial as the Gen X'ers.

Although they don't set out to save the world, they do have a greater emphasis on civics, and they expect that those in authority will fix the problem.

All Together Now

In today's culture (circa 2008 or thereabouts), we have a unique situation, one that has not happened before. We have all these generations present in the workplace at the same time, interacting with each other, getting along—and sometimes not.

While working at a large Fortune 10 company that shall remain nameless, I had the good fortune to be mentored by a older professional who took an interest in me. Even though it was early in my career, I had significant skills in Unix that my peers did not, and so this fellow saw—and adopted—a kindred spirit.

For several years we worked together; he showed me undocumented, arcane tricks and tips, and I showed him advanced theory from my then-recent degree. But the day came when I announced I was leaving that company. He basically never spoke to me again.

He was of the Silent generation that valued company loyalty— for life. My departure was an unpardonable sin to him. Although that attitude seems quaint and old-fashioned now, it was widely held at the time. I was seen by many in the organization to be a troublemaker—a disloyal maverick who wasn't playing by the rules. In fact, I was just acting as a typical X-er ready to move on, having learned what I wanted to learn and having tired of the commute.

Today, of course, the prevailing cultural attitude has shifted. It's not generally expected that you should stay with one company for more than a few years. *But that will change.* The Millennial generation may well come to embrace loyalty, favoring hierarchical, strong organizations. They will react to their collective perception that the Boomers are preachy and impractical and the X-ers are lazy and undisciplined.

> But attitudes will change.

Each generation's reaction to the perceived weakness of the immediately preceding generations creates a repeating pattern over time. In this case, the generations after the Millennials will react to their values, and the cycle repeats.

That means your generation's attitudes are somewhat predictable. And so is the next generation's. In fact, there may be only four distinct generational types.

The Four Archetypes

According to researchers Neil Howe and William Strauss,[12] if you look back through American history in the United States and Anglo-American history in Europe all the way back to the Renaissance, you'll find only four prototypical, generational *archetypes*.

---

12. See *Generations: The History of America's Future, 1584 to 2069* [SH91] and a nice summary in *The Next 20 Years: How Customer and Workforce Attitudes Will Evolve* [HS07].

Technology and Generations

A few years ago, a babysitter we had hired gazed in wonder at our kitchen phone. "Mr. Hunt, what a wonderful
idea," she said, "to tie up your phone so people won't walk
away with it! Just like the pens at the bank."

She had no idea why else you'd have a cord on a phone.
It's typical in her generation's world experience that all
phones are cordless landlines, or cell. The idea of a corded
phone as a technological necessity was alien to her.

These four types repeat over and over again, in a continuing cycle.
For the last twenty or so generations in America since the Pilgrim-
laden *Mayflower* landed here in the 1620s, there was only one
exception. Following the Civil War, one generation was so badly
damaged that they never took their place in society, and the adjoin-
ing generations (especially the older generation) filled in the gap.

These generational generalizations[13] help shed basic understanding as why people value the things they do and remind us that not
everyone shares your core values or your view of the world.

Here are the four generational archetypes and their dominant characteristics:

- *Prophet*: Vision, values
- *Nomad*: Liberty, survival, honor
- *Hero*: Community, affluence
- *Artist*: Pluralism, expertise, due process

Archetypes create
opposing archetypes.

Their research explores how each
archetypical generation can create
the next: archetypes create opposing
archetypes in a typical example of the
"generation gap." But that generation then creates one that
opposes it, and so on.

For the current generations in play, see the archetypes map shown
in Figure 5.3, on the next page.

---

13. If you can actually say that three times fast, try "unique New York."

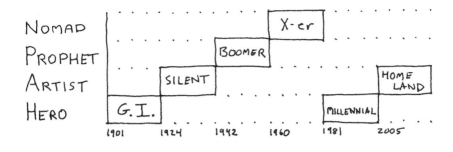

Figure 5.3: HOWE/STRAUSS GENERATIONAL ARCHETYPES

According to the Howe and Strauss model, I am among the eldest of Generation X, on the cusp of the Boomers.[14] I tend to identify with the theoretical Gen X characteristics, especially survivalism, pragmatism, and realism. And I think the most striking to me personally is to realize that *not everyone sees the world that way.*

Although I can see the Boomer's point of view on many levels, that group's ascribed lack of pragmatism—often placing their own values ahead of practicality—frustrates me. Not everyone values pragmatism; this group values ideals more so. My approach to pragmatism can be seen as "cheating," as in "You're just doing that because it works."

Well, that *is* the general idea, as far as I'm concerned. But that's my viewpoint, probably typical of my generation and probably not typical of others. Each generation faces these kinds of conflicting approaches with adjacent generations. And members of each generation will tend to defend their inherent approach above others.

How This Affects You

Not everyone shares your deep-seated values, and that doesn't mean you're right or they're wrong.

So, which approach is right? *It depends.* Context remains king; sometimes it may be more appropriate to stick to your principles regardless of consequences, as a Boomer might. In other situations

---

14. Since different researchers place these dates plus or minus a few years either way, I could be either.

it is clearly better to take a pragmatic approach, as an X-er. Command and control hierarchies have their place and can be quite effective; that's why they are popular (and not just with the GI generation). But in other circumstances, such as many commercial software development projects, a rigid hierarchy is disastrous.

Where does this influence come from?

It's likely that you will naturally prefer the approach and values favored by your generation. But realize where this influence is coming from. Perhaps your fierce individualism isn't a trait unique to yourself. Perhaps many of the characteristics you admire in other people and aspire to attain in yourself don't come from any deep reasoning or logical basis but instead from the times in which you were born.

Bear that in mind as you passionately argue for or against a topic. Are you making a logical argument, an emotional one, or just a familiar one? Is it the right argument in this particular context? Have you really considered other points of view? Rationality is often in the eye of the beholder, so you want to hedge your bets.

> **TIP 21**
>
> Hedge your bets with diversity.

The best way to keep from falling victim to your generation's particular set of biases is to embrace diversity. If you and your team all think alike, you might see your reinforced collective viewpoint as the only viable one. It's not. Just because you treasure your approach, your individualism, or your teamwork doesn't mean that younger or older folks will share that view or that it's the right answer in this context.

Next Actions ⬇

- ☐ Determine which generation you were born into. Do those characteristics resonate with you? Does a different generation resonate better?
- ☐ Determine the generations to which your co-workers belong. Do they coincide or conflict with your values?
- ☐ Think about the history of software development methodologies. Do you see a trend over time that coincides with each new generation's values?

5.3 Codifying Your Personality Tendencies

Hell is other people (L'enfer, c'est les autres).

▶ Jean Paul Sartre

Despite the influence of the fundamental attribution error we saw earlier, your own personality *does* affect your values and your perceptions, in addition to your generational affinities. This is the stuff you were born with—your own personal attitudinal context, your temperament.

You might want to think of this section in terms of buggy interfaces. It's fine if your personal interface happens to work a certain way, but it's dangerous to think that everyone conforms to that same interface. They don't. They have their own interfaces to the world and may well think yours is just as odd. So, we're going to look at major features of these interfaces and see where they might be some mismatches.

The Myers Briggs Type Indicator (MBTI) is a popular construct theory that classifies basic personality types. It's based on the work of Carl Jung and categorizes your tendencies along four independent axes.[15] According to the MBTI, you fall somewhere on the line for each dimension, and you get a letter depending on which way you lean. Again, this isn't a blueprint for behavior but an indication of preferences. These are the axes:

- *Extravert (E) vs. Introvert (I)*: Inward or outward orientation. The extravert is energized by being with people and socializing. The introvert is not; introverts are territorial and need private mental and environmental space. The introvert draws strength from solitary activities and finds social situations tiring. Seventy-five percent of the population lean to the extravert end of the scale.[16] The other twenty-five percent of us wish they'd leave us alone.

- *Sensing (S) vs. Intuition (N)*: How you obtain information. Of all the personality traits, this one axis is probably the largest source of miscommunication and misunderstanding. The sensing person emphasizes practicality and facts and

---

15. *MBTI Manual: A Guide to the Development and Use of the Myers-Briggs Type Indicator* [Mye98].

16. Statistics in this section cited in *Please Understand Me: Character and Temperament Types* [KB84].

> ### Not All Rewards Are Welcome
>
> Most companies reward teams with praise and recognition that isn't necessarily suited to all personality types. What works for extraverts, in particular, may not work with all programmers.
>
> Do you just itch at formal cake-'n'-paper-plate celebrations? For many introverts, being brought in front of the crowd, even for recognition and praise, is acutely uncomfortable. What might be a great reward for a novice probably won't be appreciated by an expert, and vice versa.
>
> Given a wide range of temperaments and skill levels, perhaps it's a good idea to have a wide range of rewards as well.

stays firmly grounded in the details of the moment. Intuitive people are very imaginative and appreciate metaphor, are very innovative, and see many possibilities—life is always around the next corner. Intuitives may skip off to a new activity without completing any. Sensors view this as flighty; intuitives view the sensors as plodding. Seventy-five percent of folks are sensing. In this book, we're trying to lean toward the minority and encourage more listening to your intuition.

- *Thinking (T) vs. Feeling (F)*: How you make decisions. Thinking people make decisions based on the rules. Feeling people evaluate the personal and emotional impact, in addition to the applicable rules. The T's strict view of the rules may seem cold-blooded to the feeling folks. The thinking folks view the F folks as "bleeding hearts." The population runs 50-50 on this axis, with a gender bias: more females tend to the F side and males to the T side.

- *Judging (J) vs. Perceiving (P)*: Your decisions are closed or left open-ended: judge quickly or keep perceiving. If you strongly favor early closure, you are a J. Js are uneasy *until* they have made a decision. Ps are uneasy when they *have* made a decision. This axis also runs about 50-50 in the general population.

Depending on which side of the fence you fall on any axis, you get that letter. The combination of the four attributes defines your *temperament*. For instance, an extraverted, sensing, feeling, perceiving personality is coded as ESFP. An introverted, intuitive, thinking, judging personality would be INTJ.

You can take a short test to determine your own MBTI score; various flavors are available on the Web and in the books cited.

The study of temperament types is most interesting when considering relationships between people. Strong Ns vs. strong Ss will generate friction when trying to work with each other. Strong Js and strong Ps probably shouldn't try to hammer out a schedule together. And so it goes.

It's probably most important to realize this: when other people react differently than you would in a given situation, they aren't crazy, lazy, or just plain difficult. And neither are you. It doesn't matter if you think the MBTI categorization is accurate or not: people operate based on different temperament types; it's almost like with a different operating system, if you will, like Windows vs. Mac or vs. Linux.

There are many ways to work out a solution and compromise. The only thing that is certain *not* to work is to try to change the other person's temperament to match

> You can't change people.

your own. That's a recipe for disaster. A bleeding-heart F type is not going to be convinced to ignore human suffering and just follow the rules, and a rigid T type is not going to be swayed by the drama and deviate from the rules. In either case, you're going against the grain. You might get your way depending on the situation, but the other person sure isn't going to like it.

This is important background information to keep in mind when collaborating with others:

They may well have a *different* set of bugs than you do.

> **TIP 22**
>
> Allow for different bugs in different people.

Think about that when constructing an argument.

Next Actions ⬇

- ☐ Take a personality test. How does that compare with your co-workers and family? Do the results resonate with you or not?
- ☐ Pretend you are the complete opposite type from yourself on each axis. What would the world look like to that kind of person? How would you interact with that person?
- ☐ If you don't already, hang out with people who have opposing personality types to yourself.

5.4 Exposing Hardware Bugs

Finally, let's look at some low-level bugs in the system—hardware bugs, if you will.

Your brain was not created all in one shot; it's been built on and built up over time. The neocortex, which is what we've largely been talking about so far, is a relatively recent addition to humankind. There are older areas of the brain that underlie these more advanced areas. And they ain't pretty.

These older areas of the brain are hardwired for more primitive, survival instinct behaviors. These areas supply the "fight or flight" response—or just a plain old emergency shutdown when the going gets really tough. This is where you'll find the roots of territorial behavior and one-upmanship.

Underneath our surprisingly thin veneer of culture and civilization, we are in fact wired very similarly to the aggressive alpha dog who marks his territory with urine. You can readily observe this behavior on the urban street corner, at the corporate boardroom, at the suburban party, and at the corporate team meeting. It's just how we are.

If you don't believe me, consider a recent report in the journal *Nature*[17] about a very modern problem—road rage. In this study, the leading predictor of a tendency for road rage was the amount of personalization on a vehicle: custom paint job, decals, bumper stickers, and so on. Even more amazing, the content of bumper stickers didn't seem to matter, just the quantity. Five "Save the

---

17. June 13, 2008. "Bumper Stickers Reveal Link to Road Rage," online at http://www.nature.com/news/2008/080613/full/news.2008.889.html.

Whales" stickers could actually prove more dangerous than one "Right to Bear Arms" sticker, for example. Why? We're marking our territory.

In 1989, Dr. Albert Bernstein originally published *Dinosaur Brains: Dealing with All Those Impossible People at Work* [Ber96], a popular, accessible exposé of the low-level wiring in our brains. He called this level of processing *lizard logic* in honor of its more primeval nature. Let's take a closer look at this level that still influences our behavior.

Lizard Logic

Dr. Bernstein describes the following aspects of the reptilian approach to dealing with life's challenges. Here's how to act like a lizard:

Fight, flight, or fright
> Whether it's a real attack, or just a perceived one, become fully aroused immediately. Be ready to start swinging or run like hell. If the situation is really bad, just freeze with fear. Maybe the bad thing will go away. This works really well when you're giving a presentation and someone asks a pointed question about your work.

Get it now
> Everything is immediate and automatic. Don't think or plan; just follow your impulses and focus on what's most exciting rather than what's most important. Use sports metaphors a lot. Answer email and IM or surf the Web; that's *always* more exciting than real work.

Be dominant
> You're the alpha dog. Claw and scratch your way to be the leader of the pack so you can abuse everyone below you. The rules apply to everyone else—but not to you. Urine marking is optional.

Defend the territory
> Sharing is for insects. Never share information, tips, tricks, or office space. Mark your territory just like a puppy, and protect your interests, no matter how trivial. If someone does something without you, cry foul and demand to know why you weren't included.

If it hurts, hiss

> Don't bother to fix the problem, but spend all your energy fixing the blame on someone instead. Cry foul, as often as you can. Let everyone know that it's just not fair.

Like me == good; not like me == bad

> Everything can be categorized into one of two buckets: good and evil. Your side is always good. Any other side is inherently evil. Explain this to your teammates often, preferably in lengthy sermons.

See anyone you know in these behaviors? A pointy-headed boss, perhaps, or arrogant co-worker?

Or worse, *yourself*?

Monkey See, Monkey Do

 As I mentioned earlier when discussing the Dreyfus model, we are natural mimics. Most of the time, that's a positive benefit, especially when learning from a mentor or other exemplar who's already proficient in that skill. But there's a downside to our natural tendency for mimicry. Emotions are contagious, just like a biological pathogen such as measles, or the flu.[18]

If you are around happy, upbeat people, it will tend to lift your mood. If you're hanging out with depressed, pessimistic people who feel like losers, you will start to feel like a depressed, pessimistic loser as well. Attitudes, beliefs, behaviors, emotions—they are all contagious.

The mob really does rule.

Acting Evolved

These lizardlike behaviors are inherent in the wiring, not in the higher-level cognitive thought processes. Thinking takes time; these actions and reactions work more quickly than that, and with less effort.

That's yet another reason why email is so pernicious.

---

18. See *Emotional Contagion* [HCR94].

A Heaven or a Hell

As we'll see later in Section 7.6, *Imagination Overrides Senses*, on page 202, you can physically rewire your brain depending on the thoughts you think. Unfortunately, that cuts both ways: negative thoughts can rewire your brain just as easily as positive thoughts.

Repeated negative thoughts form a sort of TV show—a film that you can replay in endless syndication. Each time you play *Negative Movie*, it gets more and more real and increasingly important in your psyche.

You can tell from the dialogue that this is a repeat ("You always...", "You never...") or by the characters (the Cable TV Police, the Net Police, the Legion of Idiots...). Most of these negative movies are dramas and usually far more dramatic than real.

As you start to replay one of these favorite films, try to catch yourself and remember that it's only a movie.

You can change the channel.

"The mind is its own place and, in itself, can make a Heaven of Hell, a Hell of Heaven." —John Milton, *Paradise Lost*.

In the old days of letter writing, the time it took to write longhand and the built-in delay before sending (awaiting the postal carrier) both allowed the cooler neocortex to intervene and remind you that perhaps this wasn't such a great idea.

But Internet time short-circuits the neocortex and exposes our reptilian responses. It allows you to fully vent your initial visceral reaction, whether it's in an email, a blog comment, or an IM. Although that fast, violent reaction might be a fine thing when faced with a predator in the jungle, it's less helpful when trying to collaborate on a project with co-workers, users, or vendors (well, it *might* help with predatory vendors...).

TIP 23

Act like you've evolved: breathe, don't hiss.

You know what it feels like to have that rush of intense feeling come up—when the boss sends you a snippy email or that rude driver cuts you off to exit without signaling.

Breathe out, deeply, and get rid of the stale air. Breathe in, deeply. Count to ten. Remember that *you're* the evolved one. Let the lizard reaction pass, and allow the neocortex to process the event.

Next Actions ⬇

- ☐ Notice how long it takes you to get over your initial reaction to a perceived threat. How does your reaction change once you "think about it"?
- ☐ Act on that impulse but not immediately. Plan for it; schedule it. Does it still make sense later?
- ☐ Write a new movie. If you're troubled by a given film that keeps replaying in your head, sit down and craft a new one—this time with a happy ending.
- ☐ Smile. There's some evidence that simply smiling can be as effective as antidepressant medications.[19]

5.5 Now I Don't Know What to Think

The fact that we live at the bottom of a deep gravity well, on the surface of a gas-covered planet going around a nuclear fireball 90 million miles away and think this to be normal is obviously some indication of how skewed our perspective tends to be.

▶ Douglas Adams

As we've seen earlier in the book, intuition is a powerful tool. It is the hallmark of experts. But your intuition can be dead wrong. As we've seen in this chapter, your thinking and rationality are fairly suspect as well. Our perspective is skewed all the way from our personal values to understanding our place in the cosmos, as Douglas Adams points out in this section's opening epigraph. What we think of as "normal" isn't necessarily so. You can be misled easily by your internal wiring, in addition to prejudices and biases of all sorts, and think everything is just fine.

So, where does that leave us?

---

19. Personally, I'm pretty sure chocolate is involved as well.

Remember back in the discussion on learning, when I said you want to create an $\mathcal{R}$-mode to **L**-mode flow? That is, you start off holistically and experientially and then shift to the more routine drills-and-skills to "productize" the learning.

In a similar vein, you want to lead with intuition, but follow up with provable, linear feedback.

> **TIP 24**
>
> Trust intuition, but verify.

For example, you might feel in your gut that a particular design or algorithm is the *right* way to go and that other suggestions aren't as effective. Great.

Now prove it.

It could be your expert intuition at work, or maybe it's just a cognitive bias or other bug. You need to get some feedback: create a prototype, run some unit tests, and chart some benchmarks. Do what you need to do to prove that your idea is a good one, because your intuition may have been wrong.[20]

Feedback is the key to agile software development for precisely this reason: software development depends on *people*. And as we've seen here, peo- ple have bugs, too. In short, we're all nuts—one way or another. Despite our best intentions, we need to double-check ourselves and each other.

You need unit tests for yourself, too.

Testing Yourself

When you are dead solid convinced of something, ask yourself why. *You're sure the boss is out to get you.* How do you know? *Everybody is using Java for this kind of application.* Says who? *You're a great/awful developer.* Compared to whom?

---

20. As you become more expert in a given area, you'll develop more of the capacity for accurate self-feedback, so it will become easier over time.

How do you know?

To help get a bigger picture perspective and test your understanding and mental model, ask yourself something like the following questions:[21]

- How do you know?
- Says who?
- How specifically?
- How does what I'm doing cause you to...?
- Compared to what or whom?
- Does it always happen? Can you think of an exception?
- What would happen if you did (or didn't)?
- What stops you from...?

Is there anything you can actually measure? Get hard numbers on? Any statistics?[22] What happens when you talk this over with a colleague? How about a colleague who has a very different viewpoint from your own? Do they passively agree? Is that a danger sign? Do they violently oppose the idea? Does that give it credibility? Or not?

If you think you've defined something, try to also define its opposite. This can help avoid the nominal fallacy described earlier. If all you have is a label, it's hard to pin down its opposite in any detail (and no, another label doesn't count). Contrast a behavior, an observation, a theory with its exact opposite, in detail. This action forces you to dig a little deeper and look at your "definition" with a more critical and attentive eye.

Expectations color reality.

Expectations create reality, or at least color it. If you expect the worst from people, technology, or an organization, then that's what you're primed to see. Just as with sense tuning (discussed on page 224), you'll suddenly see a lot of what you expect.

For instance, certain faux news channels have focused on such sensational, Chicken Little-esque "news" coverage that you'd think

---

21. Thanks to Don Gray for pointing out these questions from the research on NLP meta models. See *Tools of Critical Thinking: Metathoughts for Psychology* [Lev97] for more.

22. Bearing in mind Benjamin Disraeli's observation that "there are three kinds of lies: *lies*, *damned lies*, and *statistics*." Biases can be made quite convincing through the use of numbers.

the global apocalypse was scheduled for tomorrow (live coverage at 10 a.m. Eastern/7 a.m. Mountain and Pacific). It's not, but given a steady diet of their careful selection of the most heinous crimes and outrageous events, you'd easily be primed to think so.

The same phenomenon applies on a more personal note. Your expectations of your teammates, boss, or clients will bias your perceptions. And others' expectations of *you* will in turn color their perception.

Finally, to avoid the blindingly rosy glow of wishful thinking, remember that every decision is a trade-off. There ain't no free lunches. There is always a flip side, and looking closely at the trade-offs—in detail, both positive and negative—helps make sure you're evaluating the situation more fully.

It's all a trade-off.

Next Actions ⬇

- ☐ When in conflict, consider basic personality types, generational values, your own biases, others' biases, the context, and the environment. Is it easier to find a solution to the conflict with this additional awareness?
- ☐ Examine your own position carefully. How do you know what you know? What makes you think that?

It is by logic we prove; it is by intuition we discover.
   ▶ Henri Poincaré

The mind is not a vessel to be filled, but a fire to be kindled.

▶ Mestrius Plutarchos (Plutarch), 45-125 A.D.

Chapter 6

Learn Deliberately

At our current state of technology and culture, your ability to *learn* may be your most important element of success. It's what separates *getting ahead* from just *getting by*.

In this chapter, we're going to start off with a look at what learning is really all about, learn why it's suddenly so important, and explore techniques to help you learn more deliberately. We'll begin by covering how to manage goals and plan your learning over time and also focus on keeping L-mode and R-mode in balance and working effectively with each other.

With these ideas as a foundation, we'll talk about some specific techniques to help accelerate your learning, including reading techniques and mind maps, to help you work better with the material you're studying. We'll also look at some issues of learning styles and personality that might have an effect as well.

We can accelerate your learning, but first we have to talk about what learning is.

6.1 What Learning Is...and Isn't

Many HR departments haven't figured this out yet, but in reality, it's less important to know Java, Ruby, .NET, or the iPhone SDK. There's always going to be a new technology or a new version of an existing technology to be learned. The technology itself isn't as important; it's the constant learning that counts.

Historically, it hasn't always been this way; medieval farmers tilled the soil pretty much exactly as their fathers did, as did their fathers before them. Information was passed along in an oral tradition, and until recently, one could provide for one's family with minimal formal education or training.

But with the advent of the information age, that stopped being the case. It feels as though the pace of change is the fastest it has ever been, with new technology, new cultural norms, new legal challenges, and new societal problems coming at us fast. The majority of all scientific information is less than fifteen years old. In some areas of science, the amount of available information *doubles* every three years. It's quite possible that the last person to know "everything" was British philosopher John Stuart Mill—who died in 1873.[1]

We have a lot to learn, and we have to keep learning as we go. There's just no way around that. But the very word *learning* may have some unpleasant baggage, conjuring up images of youthful chalk dust torture, the mind-numbing tedium of corporate-mandated "copy machine training," or similarly ersatz educational events.

That's not what it's all about. In fact, it seems we tend to misunderstand the very meaning of the word *education*.

Education comes from the Latin word *educare*, which literally means "led out," in the sense of being drawn forth. I find that little tidbit really interesting, because we don't generally think of education in that sense—of drawing forth something from the learner.

Instead, it's far more common to see education treated as something that's done *to* the learner—as something that's poured in, not drawn out. This model is especially popular in corporate training, with a technique that's known as *sheep dip training*.

A *sheep dip* (for real) is a large tank in which you dunk the unsuspecting sheep to clean them up and rid them of parasites (see Figure 6.1, on the facing page). The sheep line up (as sheep do); you grab one and dunk in the tank for an intensive, alien, and largely toxic experience. It wears off, of course, so you have to dip them again.

Sheep dip training follows the same model. You line up unsuspecting employees, dunk them in an intensive, three-to-five-day event

---

1. Cited in *Influence: Science and Practice* [Cia01].

Figure 6.1: SHEEP DIP: ALIEN, TOXIC, AND TEMPORARY

in an alien environment, devoid of any connection to their day-to-day world, and then proclaim them to be Java developers, .NET developers, or what have you. It wears off, of course, so next year you need to have a "refresher" course—another dip.

Companies love standardized "sheep dip" training. It's easy to purchase, it's easy to schedule, and everyone fits in a nice little box afterward: you now have a nine-piece **Sheep dip training doesn't work.** box of .NET developers. It's just like fast-food chicken nuggets. There's only one drawback. This naive approach doesn't work, for several reasons:

- Learning isn't done *to* you; it's something *you* do.
- Mastering knowledge alone, without experience, isn't effective.
- A random approach, without goals and feedback, tends to give random results.

Ignite Your Own Fire

"We must encourage (each other)—once we have grasped the basic points—to interconnecting everything else on our own, to use memory to guide our original thinking, and to accept what someone else says as a starting point, a seed to be nourished and grow. For the correct analogy for the mind is not a vessel that needs filling but wood that needs igniting—no more—and then it motivates one towards originality and instills the desire for truth.

"Suppose someone were to go and ask his neighbors for fire and find a substantial blaze there, and just stay there continually warming himself: that is no different from someone who goes to someone else to get to some of his rationality, and fails to realize that he ought to ignite his own flame, his own intellect, but is happy to sit entranced by the lecture, and the words trigger only associative thinking and bring, as it were, only a flush to his cheeks and a glow to his limbs; but he has not dispelled or dispersed, in the warm light of philosophy, the internal dank gloom of his mind."

—Plutarch, Greek historian, biographer, and essayist

As Plutarch pointed out in the epigraph that opened this chapter, the mind is not a vessel to be filled but a fire to be kindled—your own fire. It's not something that someone else can do for you (see the full version of the quote in the sidebar). This is very much a do-it-yourself endeavor.

In addition, and perhaps surprisingly, simply mastering a syllabus of knowledge doesn't increase professional effectiveness.[2] It's useful, certainly, but by itself it doesn't contribute all that much to what you do in the actual, daily practice of your craft.

This has some interesting implications. Besides a continuing indictment of sheep dip training methods, it casts serious doubt on most, if not all, technology certification programs. The "body of

---

2. Klemp, G. O. "Three Factors of Success" in *Relating Work and Education* [VF77], and Eraut, M. "Identifying the Knowledge which Underpins Performance" in *Knowledge and Competence: Current Issues in Education and Training* [BW90].

knowledge" is demonstrably not the important part. The model you build in your mind, the questions you ask to build that model, and your experiences and practices built up along the way and that you use daily are far more relevant to your performance. They're the things that develop competence and expertise. Mastery of the knowledge alone isn't sufficient.

A single intense, out-of-context classroom event can only get you started in the right direction, at best. You need continuing goals, you need to get feedback to understand your progress, and you need to approach the whole thing far more deliberately than a once-a-year course in a stuffy classroom.

In the rest of this chapter, we'll look at how to make learning more effective in the real world. We'll see how to accelerate learning by approaching it more methodically and by using the best tools available for the job at hand.

To start, let's take a closer look at how to manage goals and planning by using SMART goals and the Pragmatic Investment Plan.

6.2 Target SMART Objectives

> *You got to be careful if you don't know where you're going, because you might not get there.*
>
> ▶ Yogi Berra

To get where you want to be—to learn and grow in your career and personal life—you'll need to set some goals. But goals by themselves aren't enough to guarantee your success.

Goals are great things, and you may have many of them: lose weight, find a better job, move to a bigger house (or a smaller one), write that novel, learn to play the electric guitar, write a killer Rails application, or learn all about Erlang.

But many goals never get past that stage—the lofty, generalized "I want to be better at *xyz.*" Weight loss is a prime example. Most people would like to be trimmer and fitter (especially those of us who spend a great deal of time sitting on our duffs behind a keyboard). "I want to be trim and fit" is not a very well-defined goal (although it may be a great *vision*—a long-term, desired state).

How much weight do you need to lose? How much weight do you want to bench-press? By when? Are you going to focus on limiting calories or increasing exercise? Similarly, it's a fine thing to say you want to "learn Erlang," but what does that mean? How well do you want to learn it? What do you want to be able to do with it? How will you start?

To help you focus on your goals—and be in a better position to attain them—allow me to suggest an old favorite from the consultant's bag of tricks: using SMART objectives to meet your goals.[3]

In this case, SMART stands for Specific, Measurable, Achievable, Relevant, and Time-boxed. For any goal you have in mind (losing weight, deposing your boss, conquering the world, and so on), you need to have a plan: a series of objectives that will help get to your goal. Each objective should have the SMART characteristics.

> Objectives move you to your goal.

We tend to be a bit fuzzy on the terms *goals* and *objectives*. Just to be clear: a *goal* is a desired state, usually short-term, that you're trying to reach. An *objective* is something you do to get you closer to that goal. But don't get too hung up on the terminology; different folks use these terms slightly differently.

Here's how to be SMART.

Specific

First, an objective should be *specific*. That is, it's not enough to say "I want to learn Erlang." Narrow that down to something concrete, such as "I want to be able to write a web server in Erlang that dynamically generates content."

Measurable

How do you know when you're done? That has always been one of my favorite consulting questions. To have any chance of meeting an objective, you have to be able to measure it somehow. *Measurable* goes hand-in-hand with being specific. It's hard to measure something general and abstract but much easier to measure something

---

3. Originated in *The Practice of Management* [Dru54] and widely used since then.

concrete and specific—using actual numbers. If you think you can't measure your objective, then it's probably not specific enough.

But be sure to take small bites and measure steady, incremental progress. You can't expect to lose fifty pounds in a week or learn a whole new programming language and all its libraries in a weekend. Measure your objectives, but stage them in increments.

> *"Writing a novel is like driving a car at night. You can see only as far as your headlights, but you can make the whole trip that way."*
> ▶ E.L. Doctorow

You don't have to see where you're going; you don't have to see your destination or everything you will pass along the away. You just have to see two or three feet ahead of you.

Achievable

I'd love to climb K2. It would be cool to have lunch with the Dali Lama. Oh, and establishing a lasting peace in the Middle East would be quite the accomplishment.

Ain't gonna happen.

At least, not by my hand. These are fine goals and objectives, but they aren't realistic. They are probably not attainable by me under any reasonable set of circumstances.

A goal or objective that you cannot attain is not a target; it's just a maddening, soul-sucking frustration. Some things are just not possible for most people—competing at an Olympic level, for instance. Others are possible, but at a disproportionate commitment of time and resources (say, running in a marathon).

So, be reasonable about it. You might be able to write "Hello, World!" or a simple application in a new language by next week, but you're probably not going to be able to write a complete web application framework and user interface builder with a neural net optimizer.

Make each next objective attainable from where you are *now*.

Relevant

Does this really matter to you—is it important to you, and are you passionate about it? Is it something that's even under your control?

If not, then it isn't relevant.

It needs to *matter* and be something that you have control over.

Time-Boxed

This is perhaps the most important one. It means you need to give yourself a deadline. Without deadlines, a goal will languish and be perpetually pushed aside by the more pressing exigencies of the day. It will never happen.

Again, take small bites. Give yourself frequent, small milestones. You'll be more motivated when you meet them and encouraged to rise to meet the next one.

> **Tip 25**
>
> Create SMART objectives to reach your goals.

It can help to specify your objectives personally ("I"), positively ("I will"), and in present tense or with a definite time statement ("I will do *zyzzy* by *date*").

Objectives in a Larger Context

With apologies to John Donne,[4] no objective is an island, entire of itself. Your objectives have to make sense in the larger context, which might include the following:

- Family
- Business
- Financial
- Community
- Environment

This extends the ideas of attainability and relevance. Dropping ten pounds in a week is attainable in a local sense but unwise to the whole system because of overall, long-term health concerns. Similarly, objectives that include all-nighters throughout a project might meet the project's goal and be attainable, but at disastrous cost to the developer community, their families, and eventually the business itself.[5]

---

4. Meditation XVII, 1623 A.D.
5. Thanks to Paul Oakes for suggesting this.

Goals, Objectives, and Action Plans

"So, you've decided to learn something. You've set yourself a goal. Great. Now how are you going to accomplish that goal?

"Try small specific objectives as part of an action plan. I like to take my goals and develop small—sometimes tiny—objectives to create an action plan so I can accomplish that goal.

"When I learned to play the piano, my teacher created my yearly goal and gave me specific instructions week by week to make sure I achieved that goal. Now, since I'm in charge of my own learning, I do the same.

"When I wanted to learn a new programming language, I set a goal of writing a certain number of small programs and asking for review so I could learn from my practice and from people who already knew that language. When I wanted to learn to write better, I decided to take some writing workshops and would practice specific kinds of writing each week.

"I don't have just weekly objectives to meet my goals. I am quite happy to develop very small tasks, even as small as five minutes in duration to ensure that I meet my objective so I can reach my goal. My normal size task is about a day in duration. But especially if I'm having trouble starting, I create five- or ten-minute tasks, just to get started.

"Setting yourself a goal is the first step. The next step in an action plan is to create small objectives that allow you to achieve *something* every day or so. The more small objectives you have, the more easily you'll see where you are in relation to your goal."

—*Johanna Rothman*

So in addition to looking at goals through a local lens, consider the impact they may have in the larger context of your work and life.

Next Actions ⬇

☐ Before reading on, make a list of three of your most important goals. Come up with a series of objectives for each; make sure each objective follows the SMART characteristics.

Make your SMART objective list....

6.3 Create a Pragmatic Investment Plan

Now that you have your goals well in hand, you need something like a plan to help execute them.

Back in *The Pragmatic Programmer: From Journeyman to Master* [HT00], we suggested you consider your skills and talents as a *knowledge portfolio*. That is, the skills you learn and the knowledge you master all become part of your portfolio. And like any portfolio—financial or artistic—it must be managed as time goes by.

For several years, Dave Thomas and I have presented the *Pragmatic Investment Plan* as part of our consulting practice, and I'm including a shortened version of it here for you. The *Pragmatic Investment Plan* is based on a very simple but effective idea: model your knowledge portfolio with the same care as you would manage a financial investment portfolio.

Just *having* a plan is an incredibly effective step toward achieving any goal. Too often, most of us slip into a kind of default learning schedule: you might take some time to learn a new language when you have a free moment or to look at that new library in your spare time. Unfortunately, relegating learning activities to your "free time" is a recipe for failure.

Time can't be created or destroyed, only allocated. As you soon discover, you really don't have any "free" time. Time, like closet space or disk-drive space, will get filled up much too quickly. The expression "to make time for" is a bit of a misnomer; time can't be created or destroyed. Time can only be allocated. By being deliberate about your learning, by allocating appropriate time, and by using that time wisely, you can be much more efficient in your learning.

There are several major points involved in maintaining your knowledge portfolio:

- Have a concrete plan.
- Diversify.
- Make an active, not passive, investment.
- Make a regular investment.

We'll take a look at each of these Pragmatic Investment Plan (PIP) points in turn.

PIP: Have a Concrete Plan

Just having a plan is a huge step forward. Be very specific in your plan; use the idea of SMART objectives and goals, and devise different levels of goals over time. For instance:

- Now (what's the next action you can take)
- Goals for next year
- Goals for five years out

The next action you can take might be something such as downloading a product or buying a book. Goals for next year might be specific indicators of proficiency (being able to do *xyz* in a given language or tool) or completing a specific project. Goals for five years out might be wider ranging and include things such as speaking at a conference or writing articles or a book.

This time frame is arbitrary; you might do better with now, three months out, and six months out. Or perhaps now, three years, and ten years if you're working in a slow-moving industry.

And remember what General Eisenhower advised us: the planning is far more important than the plan. The plan will change, as we'll see next. But getting in tune with your goals is invaluable.

PIP: Diversify

When choosing areas to invest in, you need to make a conscious effort to diversify your attention—don't have all your eggs in one basket. You want a good mix of languages and environments, techniques, industries, and nontechnical areas (management, public speaking, anthropology, music, art, whatever).

Part of diversification is considering the risk vs. return ratio. Any area you decide to invest in may be high or low risk and high or low return on investment. For instance, learning a popular technology such as .NET is fairly low risk—many legions of programmers are doing it, so there is plenty of support, published books, courses, job openings, and so on. But that also means it's fairly low return on investment—there are many legions of programmers doing it, so there's a lot of competition for those job openings. The fact that you do it isn't so special.

On the other hand, there are high-risk technologies. In the days when Oak first became Java, it was a high-risk choice. Maybe it would become popular, maybe not. When Java then *did* explode on the scene, those who had taken the risk were rewarded handsomely. It was a high-risk, high-reward choice.

Today, any number of technologies on the horizon are high risk and potentially high reward. They may go nowhere—that's the risk. Erlang or Haskell may be the next major language breakthrough. Or not. Ruby may be the next Java. Or not. Perhaps the iPhone will be the dominant platform.

All knowledge investments have value.

One major difference between knowledge investments and financial investments is that all knowledge investments have some value. Even if you never use a particular technology on the job, it will impact the way you think and solve problems. So, anything you learn will have value; it just may not be direct, commercial, on-the-job value. Perhaps it will help develop your R-mode or improve your R-mode to L-mode flow.

And speaking of value, don't forget that time is not the same as value. Just because you spend a lot of time doing something doesn't mean that it's adding value to your knowledge portfolio. Watching a football game or playing a video game might be relaxing and entertaining, but it doesn't add value (unless you're a quarterback or game developer).

PIP: Active, Not Passive, Investment

Another main topic from *The Pragmatic Programmer* is the idea of *feedback*. In this case, you want to always evaluate your plan in the cold light of day and realistically judge how it's going.

In the financial world, the keyword is *active* investment. You don't just sit around on your assets. You have to deliberately stop and reevaluate your portfolio. Is it performing as expected? Have key technologies or major players in the world changed since you started?

Perhaps it's time to add a few new elements that you hadn't considered previously or scrap a few plans that just aren't working out. You may have to revise your objectives or change your goals in the light of new developments.

PIP: Invest Regularly (Dollar-Cost Averaging)

Finally, you need to invest regularly. In financial terms, this lets you do *dollar-cost averaging*. That means that if you buy stock on a regular basis, sometimes you'll pay too much, and sometimes you'll get a great deal. But over the long-term, these differences smooth out, and in general you end up getting a good bargain.

It's the same here. You need to make a commitment to invest a minimum amount of time on a regular basis. Create a ritual, **Create a ritual.** if needed. Escape to your home office in the attic or down to the coffee shop that has free wi-fi. Not all your sessions will be equally productive, but by scheduling them regularly, you will win out in the long run. If instead you wait until you have time or wait for the muse, it will never happen.

To help make the most of your investment, plan what to do before you sit down at your appointed time. There's nothing more frustrating than clearing the calendar, escaping from the daily pressures of job and family, only to sit down in front of a blank screen and wonder what to do next.

Get the planning out of the way before you get there so that when you have your time, you can get right to it.

For example, if I wanted to learn the FXRuby GUI toolkit, I'd be sure to get the book first, download the components I need, and

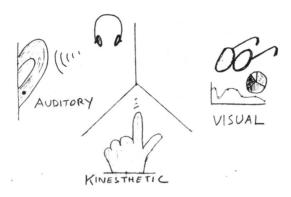

Figure 6.2: OBLIGATORY DIAGRAM FOR VISUAL LEARNERS

have an idea for something I want to write using FXRuby before sitting down and working with it in earnest. I'd also have enough time scheduled to actually dig into it; one Saturday afternoon or Tuesday night is probably not enough.

> **TIP 26**
>
> Plan your investment in learning deliberately.

Next Actions ⬇

- ☐ Write down concrete goals for now, the short-term, and long-term.
- ☐ Add two new areas that you haven't explored to help diversify your portfolio.
- ☐ Block out time each week to devote to your investment.
- ☐ Set up reminders to reevaluate your portfolio on a regular, periodic basis. What changed, and what didn't work out? What will you do now?

6.4 Use Your Primary Learning Mode

Now that you have a plan in place, we'll start talking about how to implement your deliberate learning. Because everyone is wired differently, some ways of learning will be more effective for you than others, so you need to figure out the most efficient way for you to assimilate new information.

Historically, many educators have differentiated three main types of learners: visual, auditory, and kinesthetic.

- *Visual* learners need to see the material—and the instructor. Pictures and graphs all work well for visual learners, and they will be sensitive to body language and facial expressions as well.
- *Auditory* learners have to hear the material. Lectures, seminars, and podcasts work for these folks. Tone of voice, speed, and other nuances can make a difference.
- *Kinesthetic* learners learn by moving and touching; they need to physically experience the material. This is especially appropriate for sports or arts and crafts, where you really need to *do* it to learn it.

These three modalities are very general, and as you can see, different modes may be more suitable for different activities. But it's a good starting point to consider how *you* may learn best.

Do you prefer reading to seminars or podcasts? Do podcasts annoy you because you can't see the presenter? Do you play instructional videos but not actually watch the talking head?

Take a look at Figure 6.3, on the next page. Each list of words is associated with one of the major learning modes.[6] How do you describe a learning problem? Are you "in the dark," or do you say it "looks hazy"? That might indicate you have a predominantly visual approach. if you're trying to "find the angle" and don't know how you'll "carry it forward," perhaps you have a kinesthetic approach. Listen as other folks use these words; it's a strong indication of their preferred learning style.

Multiple Intelligences

As you can see with these different learning modes, not everyone can learn best in the same manner; we are all wired a little

---

6. Thanks to Bobby G. Bodenhamer, at http://www.neurosemantics.com, for permission to reproduce this table.

Visual	Verbal	Kinesthetic
admire	announce	angle
appear	answer	beat
attractive	argue	bends
blurred	asked	bounce
bright	attune	break
clear	call	brush
cloudy	chatter	burdened
colorful	cheer	carry
conceal	complain	clumsy
dark	crescendo	comfortable
dawn	cry	concrete
disappear	deaf	crouching
display	discuss	crumble
envision	echo	exciting
exhibit	explain	feel
expose	expression	firm
eyed	growl	fits
faced	grumble	flop
flash	gurgling	force
focus	harmonize	grab
foggy	harsh	grapple
foresee	hear	grasps
form	hum	grinds
gaze	inquire	hard
glance	insult	hold
glare	lecture	hug
gleam	listen	hurt
glow	loud	impression
graphic	melodious	irritate
hazy	mention	mushy
illuminate	mumble	movement
imagine	noisy	pinch
obscure	outspoken	plush
observe	overtones	pressure
look	question	pull
peer	quiet	rub
perspective	recite	run
picture	reply	scramble
preview	request	scrape
reflect	resonance	shaky
watch	sang	skip
reveal	shout	slip
scan	shriek	smooth
see	shrill	soft
shiny	sighs	solid
show	silences	spike
sight	silent	stuffed
sightsee	sound(s)	suffer
sparkle	stammer	sweep
spy	talk	thick
staring	tell	touch
strobe	translate	trample
surface	unhearing	tremble
twinkle	utter	twist
vanish	vocal	unbudging
veil	yell	unfeeling
view		warm
visualize		wash
view		weigh
vivid		work

Figure 6.3: Representative system predicates

---

differently. That doesn't mean that a visual learner is smarter than an auditory learner, or vice versa.

In fact, the very notion of what constitutes *intelligence* has long been a matter of hot debate. Some researchers thought intelligence was a single, measurable thing. Others vehemently disagreed, pointing out that a single metric of intelligence may vary from culture to culture and that conventional testing doesn't predict performance very well. It seems that once again, context matters. Out of this debate, two theories based on cognitive context emerged: Robert Sternberg's *triarchic* theory and Howard Gardner's theory of *multiple intelligences.*

Sternberg sees a three-part mind, composed of a meta-level component that manages thought processes overall; performance-based components that do tasks, make associations, and so on; and, finally, knowledge-acquisition components that handle assimilating new information. Each part has its place, and each part is independent—one cannot be described in terms of the others. Sternberg made the point that standard IQ tests don't necessarily measure the sum total of your intelligence. He cites subjects that do very well at test taking but aren't as adept at problem solving in the real world and, conversely, folks who are great problem solvers but poor test takers.

Gardner also proposed that intelligence has many different facets and that a single measurement was insufficient. He saw intelligence as a combination of different abilities and skills and so defined seven facets of intelligence, with different talents related to each:[7]

Kinesthetic

Sports, dancing, do-it-yourself projects, woodworking, crafts, cooking

Linguistic

Verbal arguments, storytelling, reading, and writing

Logical/Mathematical

Math, numbers, sciences, taxonomies, geometry

---

7. *Frames of Mind: The Theory of Multiple Intelligences* [Gar93].

Visual/Spatial

Using diagrams/plans, sketching, painting, manipulating images

Musical

Playing music, recognizing sounds, rhythms, patterns, remembering slogans and verses

Interpersonal

Empathic; senses feelings, intentions, and motivations of others

Intrapersonal

Self-reflective; works from an understanding of inner feelings, dreams, and relations with others

Other researchers proposed additional intelligences as time went on, but even with this original set you can begin to appreciate some interesting abilities. For instance, as part of musical intelligence, there is not only the obvious musical talent but also skills such as recognizing songs and efficient recall of lyrics, slogans, verses, and other similar material.

Everyone has combinations of these different intelligences in varying amounts. Also notice that some of these abilities are geared more to L-mode or R-mode processing.

But don't use Gardner's categories as an excuse. It's easy to say "I don't have much interpersonal intelligence" or use the widespread "I'm not good at math" as an excuse to do poorly at these tasks. All this means is that those activities won't come as easily to you and will require greater effort than those that come more naturally.

How do *you* learn best? Categorizations such as Gardner's are helpful to point out all the different aspects of intelligence—you may recognize aspects of yourself that you hadn't thought about before. The important thing to recognize is that these differences mean that some ways of learning are more effective for you, and others less so. And these differences aren't necessarily cast in stone; for instance, you may find that practicing the techniques in this book changes the effectiveness of different ways of learning for you.

Personality Types

If you google around, you'll find various online surveys and quizzes that will help you identify what sort of learner you are (or at least, where your tendencies lie). You can find out whether you're an *active learner* or a *reflective learner*, visual or verbal, and so on. In fact, some methods of determining your learning style tie in to your personality, using the dimensions of personality popularized by Carl Jung and later enshrined in the Myers Briggs Type Indicator (as we saw in Section 5.3, *Codifying Your Personality Tendencies*, on page 133).

Your personality can contribute to your learning style as well. An introvert probably will be less comfortable giving an impromptu talk at a conference. An extravert might want to talk things through with a group when learning a new skill.

Beyond the Defaults

Remember that these categorizations of intelligence and personality are tendencies—not hard and fast rules or judgments. Your MBTI category, if you will, represents the *default settings* for you. You can always choose to act differently. But these are your default behaviors when no one is watching (especially when *you're* not watching.)

> Type is not destiny.

> **Tip 27**
>
> Discover how *you* learn best.

Experiment with different learning modes. To help learn a new topic, try a couple of different approaches. If you don't usually listen to podcasts or seminars, give that a shot, in addition to your usual reading or experimenting.

Next Actions ⬇

☐ Think about the intelligences you're strongest at: Which ones do you use most on the job? Are your strongest intelligences a good match for your job? Or not?

□ And which ones do you use for any hobbies? Do you have any strong intelligence that isn't being used well? Can you find a way to apply it?

□ If there's a mismatch, what can you do to make up for it? If you're a visual learner, can you start creating visuals aids for your work? If kinesthetic, would props help?

6.5 Work Together, Study Together

Studies have shown that peer study groups are very much "the real thing." The topics are chosen by the participants and so are directly relevant to your daily work. Sessions can be arranged to fit in with your schedule flexibly and conveniently; there's no expensive travel or materials required.[8] A study group is a great alternative to the alien, toxic, sheep dip experience.

Reading groups are nontoxic.

Ever since *The Pragmatic Programmer* was published, we've heard from folks using it for their own, in-company reading and study groups. It's a great book to get started with, because it's not tied to any particular technology, language, or methodology. You can start with a general book or pick something very specific and targeted to your team and your project.

You have several choices in setting up a study group, ranging from the informal to the formal. On the informal side, you can just all agree to read through a book. Maybe take turns and have team members sum up chapters on a wiki or on a mailing list or get together for lunch and discuss it.

On the more formal side, you want to take a couple of deliberate steps:[9]

Ask for proposals
See what's on everyone's mind. Get a pile of proposals, with a champion for each. Ask for a wide variety of topics: some tech-

---

8. *Improving Quality and Productivity in Training: A New Model for the High-Tech Learning Environment* [RW98].
9. For even more on this subject, see *Knowledge Hydrant: A Pattern Language for Study Groups* [Ker99].

Keys to Adult Learning

Adult learners are a different breed from either children or college students. Malcolm Knowles, in *The Adult Learner: a Neglected Species* (Kno90), identifies these characteristics of the adult learner and their learning environment:

- The adult learner is motivated to learn if learning will satisfy their own interests and needs.
- Units studied should be real-life situations, not just isolated subjects.
- Analysis of the learner's experience is the core method employed.
- Adults need self-direction; the instructor should help them engage in mutual inquiry.
- The instructor must allow for differences in style, time, place, and pace.

Notice that these ideas line up very nicely with a study/reading group made up of your peers. By its very nature, a reading group is aligned with the needs and goals of the adult learner.

nical and some on soft skills or on technology you're already using or on technology you hope to use.

Select a proposal—and a leader

You need someone to lead the study group for this particular subject. They don't have to be expert in the topic but do need to be passionate about the topic and about learning it.

Buy books

The company buys books for all participants. Most publishers (including the Pragmatic Bookshelf) provide volume discounts, so be sure to check.

Schedule lunch meetings

The company provides lunch if they can, or you can brown-bag it. Reading itself should be done on your own time, but schedule the meeting for lunch, and plan on a longish lunch of ninety minutes.

In the meeting itself, plan on spending the first half hour eating, socializing, and in informal conversation. Then, start the meeting proper. Have one person summarize the chapter or sections that everyone read. Rotate through, by topic or by chapter, so it's not always the same person. Then talk about it: ask questions, give opinions. For inspiration, you can look at questions at the end of chapters, any explicit study guide questions, or the next actions that I've provided here.

> **TIP 28**
>
> Form study groups to learn and teach.

Try to keep each group to no more than eight to ten people or so. If you have larger teams, maybe split them up into smaller groups for discussion.

Beside the incredible education benefits, it's a great way to help jell a team. The team that studies together learns together, teaches each other, and learns more effectively.

6.6 Use Enhanced Learning Techniques

Now that we've established a good framework for deliberate learning, we need to look at learning itself. In the rest of this chapter, we'll look at some specific techniques to help you learn faster and better. We'll be looking at the following:

- Better ways to *deliberately* read and summarize written material

- Using *mind maps* to explore and find patterns and relationships

- Learning by *teaching*

Any one of these techniques, by itself, can be a great help. Taken together, they can turn you into an efficient learning machine. But everyone is different, and everyone's best method of learning is different. As a result, you may find some of these techniques more effective than others—remember that one size never fits all.

6.7 Read Deliberately with SQ3R

It's an unfortunate truth that written instructions are generally considered to be the least efficient. Many of the parts of the brain and body that you want to train or

Written instruction is the least efficient.

educate aren't the parts that process language. Remember from our brain discussion that the portion of your brain that processes language is relatively small. The entire rest of your brain and body doesn't *do* language.

As a result, it seems that we learn best from observation. We are natural mimics, and the best, most effective way to learn is by observing and mimicking someone else. We'll look at this phenomenon again a little later, but in the meantime, we have a bit of a problem.

Right now, you are reading this book. Over the course of your lifetime, you've probably read a lot more books than you have attended seminars or lectures. But reading is the least effective means of learning, compared to any sort of experiential learning.

One way to make reading more effective is to approach it a little more deliberately than just picking up a book and plowing ahead. There are a number of popular techniques in use; we will look at one in detail here, but this is just one of many that work along similar lines.

This technique of studying a book or other printed matter is known as SQ3R; that's an acronym for the steps you need to take.[10]

- *Survey*: Scan the table of contents and chapter summaries for an overview.

- *Question*: Note any questions you have.

- *Read*: Read in its entirety.

- *Recite*: Summarize, take notes, and put in your own words.

- *Review*: Reread, expand notes, and discuss with colleagues.

---

10. Described in *Effective Study* [Rob70].

The first helpful aspect of this technique is that it is deliberate. Instead of randomly picking up a book, reading it, and maybe or maybe not remembering much of it, this is a much more thoughtful, conscious, and aware approach.

The Process

 To begin with, you *survey* the work in question. Look over the table of contents, chapter introductions and summaries, and any other high-level landmarks the author has left for you. You want to get a good overview of the book without delving into any details just yet.

Next, write down any *questions* you want answered. How does this technology solve this problem? Will I learn how to do this one thing, or will this point to another source? Rephrase the chapter and section heads as questions; these are all questions that you expect the book will answer.

Now you can *read* the book in its entirety. If you can, carry the book with you so you can get some reading time squeezed in while waiting for a meeting or appointment, while on a train or airplane, or wherever you may find yourself with a little spare time. Slow down on the difficult parts, and reread sections as needed if the material isn't clear.

As you go along, *recite*, recall, and rephrase the most important bits from the book in your own words. What were the key points? Take some initial notes on these ideas. Invent acronyms to help you remember lists and such. Really *play* with the information; use your $\mathcal{R}$-mode, synesthetic[11] constructs and more. What would this topic look like as a movie? A cartoon?

Finally, begin to *review* the material. Reread portions as necessary, and expand on your notes as you rediscover interesting parts (we'll look at an excellent method of taking this style of notes in Section 6.8, *Visualize Insight with Mind Maps*, on page 171).

---

11. *Crossing senses*, imagining that numbers have colors, words smell a certain way, and so on.

An Example

For example, suppose I'm reading a book on a new programming language—D, Erlang, or Ruby, for example. I'll flip through the table of contents and see where the book is going. Ah, an introduction to some syntax, a few toy projects, advanced features that I'm not interested in yet. Hmm. Is it single or multiple inheritance or mixins? I wonder what iterators look like in this language? How do you create and manage packages or modules? What's the runtime performance like? Next comes the reading itself—in large doses when I can, in small doses if needed.

Next comes recite/rephrase. It's easy to fool yourself and think, "Oh sure, I remember all of that." But it's not that easy (see the sidebar on the following page).

Try to use the information from the book: try to write a program in that language from scratch (different from any of the exercises or toy programs in the book itself). Hmm. Now how did that work again? Time to review that section or two. I'll make some notes on common bits that I know I'll have to refer to again and maybe put some sticky note flags on key tables or figures or a quick doodle on the whiteboard to help me remember what's where. Now is a good time to talk it over with friends or participate in mailing list discussions.

> **Tip 29**
>
> Read deliberately.

Does this flow of events sound at all familiar? I think it clearly echoes the $\mathcal{R}$-mode to **L**-mode shift. Like the rock-climbing experience, this starts with a holistic, shallow, but wide survey; narrows down to traditional **L**-mode activities; and broadens out with multisensory exposure (discussion, notes, pictures, metaphors, and so on).

It may be that the "normal" notes you've probably always taken are pretty tame, in terms of brain stimulus. Fortunately, a great technique can help with that and take average, boring note-taking and exploratory thinking up to a whole new level.

You need more than notes; you need a mind map.

Test-Driven Learning

Reading the same material over and over, or studying the same notes over and over, doesn't help you remember the material. Instead of studying, try testing.

Repeatedly testing yourself by trying to recall the material over and over works much better.* Deliberate, repeated attempts at retrieval consolidate learning and strengthen the connections in your brain. Repeated *input*, by itself, doesn't do you nearly as much good. Try to write a program in that new language you're studying—you'll need to retrieve the key information to do so. Try to explain key parts of that new methodology to a colleague. Keep at the retrieval—the testing of your knowledge. You might think of it as test-driven learning. And when testing yourself, you can take advantage of the *spacing effect*.

Cramming, or studying a lot of information in a short amount of time, is not very effective. We tend to forget things along an exponential curve, so spacing out your quizzing reinforces material much more effectively. For example, you might plan on retesting yourself along a 2-2-2-6 schedule: retest after two hours, two days, two weeks, and six months.

But that's not the most efficient use of your time, especially with a large amount of material. Some facts and ideas will get memorized more easily, and others will need more work. Trying to keep track of an individual memory-decay curve for each fact you're trying to memorize is too hard to do manually. But, hey, we've got this nifty computer that we can use.

Piotr Wozniak developed an algorithm to take advantage of the spacing effect, implemented in the commercial product SuperMemo (an open source implementation is available at http://www.mnemosyne-proj.org/). It's basically a souped-up flashcard program that keeps track of your performance and schedules retests according to an individual decay curve for each item.

It's a great way to take advantage of the brain's caching and archiving algorithms.

---

*. *The Critical Importance of Retrieval for Learning* (KR08). Thanks to June Kim for spotting this one.

6.8 Visualize Insight with Mind Maps

A *mind map* is a kind of a diagram that shows topics and how they are connected. Creating a mind map is a widely used creativity- and productivity-enhancing technique. Invented by British author Tony Buzan in *The Mind Map Book: How to Use Radiant Thinking to Maximize Your Brain's Untapped Potential* [BB96], similar styles of diagrams have been around since at least the third century.[12]

A modern mind map is a sort of two-dimensional, organic, and holistic outline. The rules for making a mind map are loose, but they go something like this:

1. Start with a largish piece of unlined paper.
2. Write the subject title in the center of the page, and draw an enclosing circle around it.
3. For the major subject subheadings, draw lines out from this circle, and add a title to each.
4. Recurse for additional hierarchical nodes.
5. For other individual facts or ideas, draw lines out from the appropriate heading and label them as well.

Each node should be connected (no free floaters), and the figure should be hierarchical with a single root, but in general there are few restrictions. You want to be somewhat playful with the use of colors, symbols, and anything else that has meaning for you. But trying to explain this with text doesn't really convey the result; for an example, take a look at Figure 6.4, on the next page. This figure shows the mind map I first created when studying the Dreyfus model. It's greatly reduced to fit in the book, so don't worry about trying to read the individual labels—just get a sense of the structure and flow.

A traditional outline has some subtle and troublesome limitations. For one, regular linear outlines tend to block a creative impulse; the very nature of the outline implies a hierarchy, and hierarchies tend to reinforce their own structure. So, a great idea that doesn't fit into the structure of the moment might get discarded.

---

12. Possibly beginning with the Greek philosopher Porphyry of Tyros, according to Wikipedia. Of course, cave drawings go back even further, if you don't mind bison in your mind map.

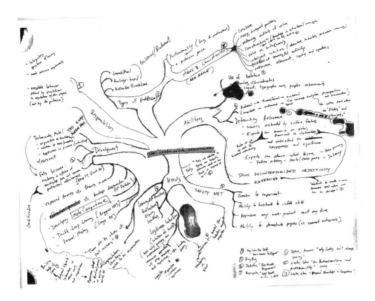

Figure 6.4: Original Dreyfus mind map—messy, organic

When creating a mind map, avoid filling in the elements in a clock-wise manner—that's just an outline going in circles.[13]

When I give lectures on this topic, I usually stop here and ask the audience whether they have ever heard of, or used, mind maps. The results are very predictable.

In the United States, I'll maybe get three or four people out of a hundred who've ever even heard of them. But in Europe, I get the opposite response—virtually everyone in the audience has used mind maps. I'm told it's a standard part of their primary educa-tion, much as making an outline or a topic sentence is here in the United States.

> **Emphasize spatial cueing and relationships.**

While mind mapping sounds like a very basic, elementary technique, it has some subtle properties. It takes advantage of the way your eye scans and reads a piece of paper. Spatial cueing conveys informa-tion to you in a way that linear words or an outline can't; the addi-tion of color and symbols adds to the richness of the representa-tion. As you go to add a new piece of information, a new thought, or

---

13. Thanks to Bert Bates for reminding me about this.

an insight to the mind map, you are faced with the question, where does this belong? You have to evaluate the *relationships* between ideas, not just the ideas themselves, and that can be a very revealing activity.

As you start to fill in the diagram, there's always room for more information. You can write smaller (without resorting to a font selection box), and you can squeeze things to the edge of the page and connect them with lines. You can draw large swoopy arrows across the page to connect remote notes that you now realize should be connected.

And then, once you've learned from this mind map, draw it again on a fresh piece of paper—perhaps fixing some of the placement issues and reflecting what you've learned since you started. Redrawing and retrieving the information from memory helps strengthen the connections and may expose additional insights in the process.

Try using different kinds of paper. Art papers may have more *tooth* than office stationary, and they offer a different tactile experience. Markers, colored pencils, and pens all offer a different feel as well. Color in particular seems to have a certain inspirational effect.

Mind Map Enhancements

Nonspecific, non-goal-oriented "playing" with information is a great way to gain insights and see hidden relationships. This sort of mental noodling is just what the $\mathcal{R}$-mode needs to be effective. But it's important to not try too hard; that's the "non-goal-oriented" part. You want to sort of let go a bit and let the answer come to you rather than consciously trying to force it. Just play with it.

You'll soon notice that the graphic enhancements are not random. They begin to add meaning. Instead of mere decoration, they help coax additional

> Use non-goal-oriented "play."

thinking and meaning from you. You're basically asking yourself "What information can I add to this relationship or object?," but you're asking your drawing side—your $\mathcal{R}$-mode—to do the enhancement.

Although many fine companies make mind-mapping software,[14] I think that a software tool is more useful for collaboration or

---

14. I use NovaMind, for Mac/Windows, at http://www.novamind.com.

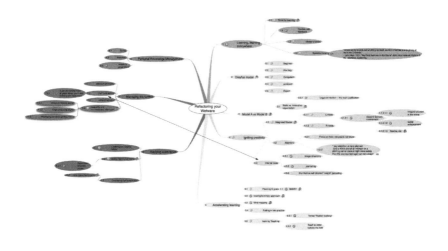

Figure 6.5: SOFTWARE TOOL MIND MAP—CLEAN AND HYPERLINKED, BUT USEFUL?

documentation—not for brainstorming, studying, or exploratory thinking. For those activities, you want to draw the mind map by hand.

> **Writing is as important as reading.**

Why is hand-drawing important? Take a look at Figure 6.5. This is a beautiful, colorful mind map I made on the Mac. It's an early form of this very book. Each node is hyperlinked to a website, PDF research paper, fragment of a note, or other important asset. But as cool as that is (and very handy for going back and finding research material), *it's not the same.*

Hand-writing is key, whether it's plain notes or a mind map. For instance, I find that taking notes during lectures really helps me retain the material—even if I never read the notes again.

The most value, I find, is to take the raw notes while listening (which helps you stay focused as you extract salient points from the lecture) and then transcribe these raw notes into "official notes." Even if I never read these notes again, the act of transcribing the raw notes is the most valuable portion of this exercise. You can do the same thing with mind maps—start with a rough messy one, and redraw it as needed. The redrawing helps form more associations in your brain.

> ⎡ Tip 30 ⎤
>
> Take notes with both *R*-mode and **L**-mode.

Try It

Here's an exercise to try:

1. Take a four-to-five-item bullet list that is of importance to you.

2. Draw a mind map for the items on the list (on paper with pen or pencil).

3. Wait a day.

4. Now spend fifteen to twenty minutes embellishing the drawing. Tart it up. Add thick lines; use color; and add little doodles, pictures, angelic cherubs from a Gothic manuscript in the corners, whatever.

5. Review the mind map a week later. Any surprises?

Using Mind Maps with SQ3R

Mind maps are most effective when you're not exactly sure what you'll find.

Taking notes from reading a book is a prime example. The next time you're reading a book (trying SQ3R, perhaps), take notes as you go in the form of a mind map. You'll have a general idea of the major topics, but as particular details emerge and as you begin to see which items are related to each other and how, the map will fill in, and a picture of your understanding will emerge.

Then, when you're in the *review* phase of SQ3R, redraw and revise your mind map according to your understanding. You'll be able to refer to the mind map to refresh your memory in a way that's much more efficient and revealing than other notes or rescanning the book itself.

Exploratory Mind Maps

Similarly, if you're working on a problem and aren't sure where you're going, mind mapping can help. Whether you are designing a new class or a system, debugging an existing one, trying to evaluate several commercial products or open source offerings, buying a new car, or writing a novel or a rock opera, try using a mind map.

Use words as titles; you don't want any lengthy prose or even full sentences. Draw icons to represent key ideas. Make important lines large and thick; more tentative associations can be spindly. Dump everything you know for now, even if you are not sure where it fits in.

Do the first iteration really, really quickly—almost like an impressionist sketch. This will help get the **L**-mode out of the way and allow the $\mathcal{R}$-mode unfettered access to the paper.

Start the mind map, and leave it handy—especially if you don't have a lot of information to add to it just yet (as we'll see a little later, just having a place to put related ideas is a great help). Fill in the facts and ideas as you get them. It doesn't have to be in one sitting. Redraw it if needed, but don't be in rush to do so. Let it be messy for a while. You're exploring a topic, after all.

Use a mind map to help clarify. If you're working in an area where you aren't even sure *what* the topic is, mind maps can be very useful to help gather your far-flung thoughts together. Jared Richardson tell us, "I use mind maps to reorganize and focus myself when writing or coding. It forces me to step back and clean up my ideas and always shows me how to move forward."

I've had the same experience; if I'm stuck in a swirling mass of ideas with no clear way forward, using a mind map is a great technique to help generate clarity and show the way.

Collaborative Mind Maps

You can extend this technique to involve a small group or the whole team. Instead of drawing a picture on paper, get everyone up at a whiteboard armed with sticky notes, as shown in Figure 6.6, on the next page.[15]

Everyone gets a handful of sticky notes and a marker. You brainstorm, write down ideas on the sticky notes, and place the notes up on the whiteboard. After a while, you can begin to coalesce common themes and cluster related notes near each other.

---

15. See *Affinity Grouping* in *Behind Closed Doors: Secrets of Great Management* [RD05] for more information on this and other fun things to do with sticky notes.

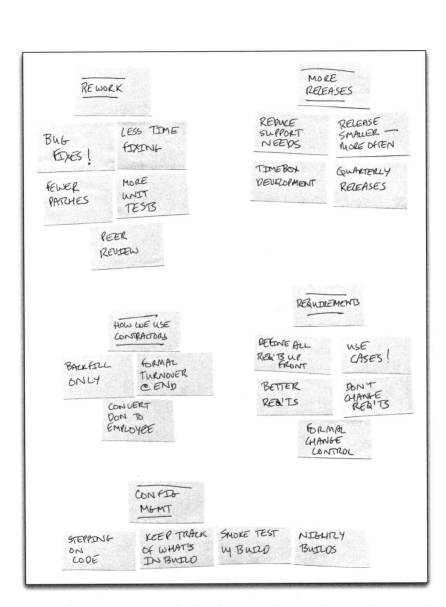

Figure 6.6: Affinity grouping in progress

Since the sticky notes let you detach and reapply, you can reposition the notes as needed.

Once things have settled out, you can draw circles around each grouping and connect them with lines. Voilà! Now you've got a mind map. Snap a digital photo of the whiteboard, and email everyone a copy.[16]

Next Actions ⬇

- ☐ Make a mind map for the next book you read.
- ☐ Make a mind map for your career and lifestyle plans or perhaps for your next vacation.
- ☐ Experiment with the effect of color; get some colored pencils, and try using color to encode meaning for individual nodes.
- ☐ Experiment with graphical annotations: doodle on your mind maps and see what happens.
- ☐ Keep iterating. After you think you're "done," go back and add just one more thing. Now do that again.

6.9 Harness the Real Power of Documenting

One of the tenets of agile software development is to avoid needless documentation. That is, if documentation doesn't provide value, don't do it: writing documentation for documentation's sake is a waste of time.

That's because it is common to waste a lot of time preparing low-level, detailed design documents that become obsolete almost immediately. Worse, these sorts of documents generally have no audience—they aren't serving any useful purpose, other than fulfilling a checkbox to prove that the team "produced documentation." Because it's such a wasteful practice, agile teams take a hard look at any documentation they are required to produce to ensure that there's a genuine need for it.

Many people interpret this as "agile developers don't do documentation," which is wrong. Agile developers *do* create documentation,

---

16. Many cell phones and laptops (and most Macs) now come with built-in cameras, so capturing just keeps getting easier.

but they use a pragmatic filter to make sure the investment in creating any documentation is really worth the effort. It has to have value.

That brings us round to this idea: what's the value in producing documentation *to the writer*? Producing low-level design documents that simply mirror the code

> Chance favors the prepared mind.

(and become obsolete almost immediately) don't provide any value to anyone. But other forms of writing documentation may prove valuable, even if there is no obvious audience for it.

Louis Pasteur once said, "Chance favors only the prepared mind," and functional MRIs and EEG tests are proving him correct. A recent study[17] suggests that mental preparation *that involves an inward focus of attention* can promote flashes of insight, even if the preparation occurs well in advance of facing any particular problem.

Turning your attention inward, as you would do when working with a mind map, sets up some condition in the brain that allows for happy flashes of insight later in the project. So, it might be that *documenting* is more important than *documentation*.

Reader and pilot Dierk Koenig sent me the following related story:

> *I noticed this phenomenon when preparing for an aerobatic routine. Sequences of aerobatic maneuvers are often preplanned and diagrammed using Aresti notation before being flown. During the flight, we should pretty much have the sequence memorized, but having a card taped up in the cockpit with the sequence drawn on it helps during brain farts.*
>
> *There are Visio add-ins that allow people to create very nice-looking Aresti cards, but I prefer to hand-draw mine, in an almost ritualistic way. I sat down to do so at the airport one day, and the owner of the school nudged another student, pointed to me, and said, "Watch this, this is cool." I had no idea why she thought so. I thought I was just drawing out my card and taking too dang much time about it.*
>
> *But apparently I was also "preparing the mind."*
>
> ▶ Dierk Koenig

---

17. *The Prepared Mind: Neural Activity Prior to Problem Presentation Predicts Subsequent Solution by Sudden Insight* [Kou06].

As I mentioned earlier (in Section 6.8, *Visualize Insight with Mind Maps*, on page 171), taking notes seems to be very important, even if you never read them again. In Dierk's case, there may be several elements at work:

- Hand-drawing the cards emphasizes R-mode processes.
- The active creation of the notes/cards helps prepare the mind for the later activity.
- Visualizing the sequences and maneuvers can help "groove" the mind (we'll talk more about this shortly in Section 7.6, *Imagination Overrides Senses*, on page 202).

> ⌐ TIP 31 ⌐
>
> Write on: documenting is more important than documentation.

You don't have to use index cards or even real paper; the back of the napkin is just fine or maybe a large whiteboard.

_____
Make a screencast.
_____

Or perhaps you might want to take an hour to create a podcast or screencast. You may find that's more productive for yourself and more engaging for the consumer of the information. It's also probably cheaper than taking a week (and a committee) to produce a lengthy document.

Screencasts are really useful to convey something dynamic: showing a user how to perform a task using your software or modeling the life cycle of an object through a complicated set of processes. It's a cheap and cheerful way to have lots of people (or remote people) look over your shoulder to see what you're talking about.

Just think of it as another way of teaching yourself the subject. Of course, another powerful learning technique lies in teaching others.

6.10 Learn by Teaching

One of the simplest and most effective techniques to learn something is to try to *teach* it. Teaching in this context doesn't necessarily mean grabbing the chalk and heading into the classroom; there are several different ways to go about it. You can begin with simple verbal "rubber ducking." In *The Pragmatic Programmer*, we described the following scenario.

You're stuck with a difficult bug. You've already spent a lot of time on it, and the deadline is looming. So, you ask a co-

Talk to the duck.

worker for help. They walk over to your screen, and you begin to explain what's going on—and what's going wrong. Before you get very far into the description, a flash of insight smacks you in the head, and you exclaim, "A-ha!" You've found the bug. Your bemused co-worker, who never had to say a word, shakes their head and walks back to their own office. To save some wear and tear on the carpet (and your co-worker), we suggest you place a surrogate—a yellow rubber duck, for instance—near your screen and, when you get stuck, just "talk to the duck."

Another useful approach is to try to explain your material to a child or someone outside your field of expertise. The trick is to do so in terms *they* can understand. This is a great opportunity to explain what you really do for a living to your great Aunt Edna, and it's a great exercise to start to see

things from your audience's point of view and to develop metaphors that will help explain and clarify the material you're working with. You may be surprised by what you learn and what insights come to you during the process.

Finally, you can reach out and try to teach a larger, more responsive audience. Start by offering to give a talk at a local user group meeting, or pen an article for a newsletter or magazine. There's nothing like the prospect of a lot of bright people picking at your every word to help clarify your thinking. And that's the real benefit to teaching in general; it clarifies your own understanding and reveals many of your underlying assumptions.

Remember the medical school mantra:

> TIP 32
> See it. Do it. Teach it.

As I mentioned earlier, constant retrieval is very effective for learning. Having to "go back to the well" while preparing to teach, and while having to think on your feet to respond to questions, all helps strengthen your neural connections.

6.11 Take It to the Streets

So far, we've seen the Dreyfus model and seen what it means to be an expert. I've shown you some of the myriad wonders of the brain, including an entire half that's probably underutilized.

In this chapter, we've taken a good look at what learning is— and what it is not. We've looked at using SMART objectives and a Pragmatic Investment Plan and some specific techniques including reading techniques, mind maps, and learning by teaching.

But all this learning is only part of the equation; next we need to look at putting learning into action and see the best ways to gain experience. We'll *play* with that in the next chapter.

In the meanwhile, it's time to begin to take it to the streets—to leave the relatively safe cloisters of the cubicle and begin to interact with the world to advance your personal learning.

Next Actions ⬇

- ☐ Take a new topic, and try to teach it to a co-worker or relative. What did you learn from teaching—and the preparation for teaching?
- ☐ If you haven't been going to a local user group, start going. Java, Ruby, and Linux groups are plentiful, but you might also find groups devoted to Delphi, agile or XP development, OOP, specific vendor products, and more.
- ☐ Listen carefully to the speakers. Make a mind map of the topic area. What would you add to it? What would you do differently? Write up a critique for the group based on your mind map.
- ☐ Contact the organizers, and offer to speak on your topic for an upcoming meeting.
- ☐ If that's not comfortable for you, then write an article on your topic or blog on it.

We should be careful to get out of an experience only the wisdom that is in it and stop there; lest we be like the cat that sits on a hot stove-lid; he will never sit on a hot stove-lid again—and that is well; but also he will never sit on a cold one anymore.

▶ Mark Twain

Chapter 7

Gain Experience

Gaining experience is key to learning and growth—we learn best by doing.

However, just "doing" alone is no guarantee of success; you have to *learn* from the doing for it to count, and it turns out that some common obstacles make this hard. You can't force it either; trying too hard can be just as bad (if not worse) than slogging through the same old motions.

In this chapter, we'll look at how to make each experience count. We'll see how to do the following:

- Build to learn, not learn to build.
- Fail efficiently with better feedback.
- Groove your neural pathways for success.

That is, we'll take a look at some key aspects to real-world learning and then see what you need to create an efficient learning environment for yourself. After that, we'll take a look at how to get better feedback—to avoid the issues of Mark Twain's overly generalizing cat (in this chapter's opening epigraph). Finally, we'll finish up with an interesting approach to gain experience virtually.

7.1 Play in Order to Learn

Your brain is designed such that you need to explore and build mental models on your own. You're not really designed to passively sit by and try to store received knowledge. There's a time and a place for both of these activities, but in the normal course of events, we get it wrong: exploring, or "playing with," the material should come before studying facts.

We seem to have a cultural tendency to put the cart before the horse: you struggle to shovel in information first and then hope to maybe use it later. That's the basis of most formal education and corporate training. But the real world doesn't work that way. For instance, imagine you were taking a dance class, only to find you had to pass a test on "dance facts" before actually dancing. Sounds absurd when I put it that way, doesn't it? Seymour Papert thinks so.

Papert is perhaps the leading expert on using technology to create new ways of learning.[1] He invented the programming language Logo: a "toy" that children could play with and, in the playing, learn deep mathematical concepts. His early work with Logo led to the LEGO Mindstorms robotic toys, named for his hugely influential book, *Mindstorms: Children, Computers, and Powerful Ideas* [Pap93]. Papert worked with world-renowned Swiss psychologist Jean Piaget and also believed that real learning—the learning that sticks with you—comes from experience and cognition, not from explicit teaching or rote practice. Their approach is called *constructivism*: we build to learn, not learn to build.

He designed the Logo language expressly to provide an environment where children could learn math concepts via direct experience by commanding a virtual "turtle" to move around and trace patterns on a virtual canvas. The young, grade-school students learned geometry, trig, and even recursive algorithms. When kids got stuck on a problem, they were told to imagine themselves as the turtle and walk through their own instructions from the turtle's perspective. By changing their viewpoint to that of the turtle, the students could leverage their existing real-world knowledge of walking, turning, and so on, to explore the microworld of the turtle. That's an important point: structuring learning so that you can build on top of existing experience.

The Meanings of *Play*

As I'm using it here, the first meaning of the word *play* is similar to what we've talked about earlier in the book, in the sense of non-goal-directed exploration. We're not really designed to just receive information but rather to explore and build mental models on our

---

1. Papert and Marvin Minsky founded the Artificial Intelligence Lab at MIT; he also was one of the founders of the famed MIT Media Lab.

own. We need to be able to poke at a problem, to explore it, or to "get used to it" (as we talked about back in Section 4.3, *Engage an R-mode to L-mode Flow*, on page 80). Playing with a problem doesn't make the problem any easier, but it gets us closer to how we're wired to learn.

Of course, in this sort of environment, you'll make mistakes. As a student, you're not being led down the garden path of the "one right answer" according to the cur-

Real life has no curriculum.

riculum. As in real life, there is no curriculum. You'll make mistakes; it will get messy. But those messes give you exactly the kind of feedback you need.

Mind maps get better the more you play with them (Section 6.8, *Visualize Insight with Mind Maps*, on page 171). With a mind map, looking for opportunities to annotate, decorate, and draw relationships helps you gain insight. This is an extension of that idea—a more active engagement, playing directly with the ideas or technology in question, not sure what you'll find, but looking to see how you can extend them, relate them, and so on.

The second sense of the word *play* introduces a sense a whimsy, or dare I say, *fun*.

I was on a business trip last week, and the flight attendant gave a little twist to the usual boring preflight speech: the *entire* speech, including the canned, legally specified parts, was set in a Dr. Seuss–style rhyme. From proper use of the seat belt to the dire warnings about disabling the smoke detector in the lavatory[2] to proper handling of the oxygen masks and life rafts, it all rhymed in a well-orchestrated meter. And for a change, people actually listened to the announcement. It was a novel presentation and was very engaging—you listened closely to see where she was headed with the talk, anticipating the stress and rhyme.

Because it was fun, the presentation was much more effective. Normally, no one pays any attention to the standard talk.

Fun is OK.

Everyone is busy reading the *Airline Catalog of Useless Merchandise* or already dozing off. But a fun speech changes the game.

---

2. Which begs the question, shouldn't there be stiff penalties for "disabling or destroying" *any* part of the aircraft, not just the smoke detector? But I digress....

Smart People and Dumb People

I think most people are a lot more capable than they give themselves credit for. Papert noted that we tend to sort people (including ourselves) into two categories: *smart* people and *dumb* people. We're confident that smart people have all the answers on a clipboard, dressed in their crisp white lab coats. Dumb people drive the car in front of us on the highway.

That's a grotesque oversimplification, of course. Remember that the Dreyfus model is a model *per skill*, not per person. The world isn't filled with smart people and dumb people; it's filled with smart lab researchers and dumb drivers, smart cooks and dumb politicians.

But regardless of any specific skill deficiencies, in general we are amazing learning machines. Consider how much a young child has to absorb in a short space of time: language, motor skills, social interaction, the effectiveness of a well-timed tantrum, and so on. We don't bombard two- or three-year-olds with vocabulary drills or make them diagram sentences to understand grammar. Instead, you just point to the toy and say "ducky," and they get it. Ducky swims. Ducky is yellow. We can grok a lot without explicit training or exercises.

One of the definitions of *fun*, according to my dictionary on the Mac, is "playful behavior."

That doesn't mean that it's easy, non-business-like, or not effective. In fact, Papert notes that his students called their work fun *because* it was hard, not *in spite of* being hard. It's hard fun: not so hard as to be insurmountable (and so not engaging) but challenging enough to maintain interest and progress at solving the problem domain.

 Working with new material or solving a problem in a playful manner makes it more enjoyable, but it also makes it easier to learn. Don't be afraid of fun.

Make a game of it—literally. Create flash cards, or invent a card or board game; use tinker-toys or Lego blocks to act out the scenario.

For example, you could create a board game that simulates visitors to a website. Where do they go next when they land on a random square? What if they never pass Go or go to Home?

I mentioned using Lego blocks for design back in Chapter 4, *Get in Your Right Mind*, on page 73 for the same reason: the idea is to engage as much of your entire being in the learning process: verbal, visual, musical, numerical, gross-motor body movement, fine-motor finger movement, and so on. All of that helps you to really play with the material and learn it more effectively.

> **TIP 33**
>
> Play more in order to learn more.

Next Actions ⬇

- ☐ On your next problem, put yourself in the picture. Anthropomorphism helps leverage experience.
- ☐ Explore and get used to a problem before diving into the facts. Come back to more exploration after absorbing the formal facts. Then go back to exploration; it's a continuous cycle.
- ☐ Play, in every sense of the word.

7.2 Leverage Existing Knowledge

Papert was careful to allow students to leverage existing knowledge in skills in their learning of new skills. We do this all the time, sometimes consciously, sometimes less so.

When faced with a sticky problem, there are a couple of classic approaches you'll probably take. First, can you break the

Try mind-size bites.

problem down into smaller, more manageable parts? This sort of functional decomposition is bread-and-butter to software developers: break things down into mind-size bites. The other very popular approach to take is to look for any similar problems you may have solved previously. Is this problem like some other? Can you use a similar solution or adapt the other solution to match this new problem?

Problem Solving with George Pólya

To solve a problem, ask yourself these questions:

- What are the unknown aspects?
- What *do* you know? What data do you have?
- What constraints and what rules apply?

Then make a plan, execute it, and review the results. Some of the techniques Pólya suggests might sound familiar:

- Try to think of a familiar problem having the same or similar unknowns.
- Draw a picture.
- Solve a related or simpler problem; drop some constraints or use a subset of the data.
- Were all the data and constraints used? If not, why not?
- Try restating the problem.
- Try working backward from the unknown toward the data.

George Pólya wrote a very influential book on concrete steps to problem solving that covers these and other classic techniques (*How to Solve It: A New Aspect of Mathematical Method* [PC85]; see the sidebar on the current page for a brief synopsis).

One of Pólya's key bits of advice is to look for similarities to previous solutions: if you don't know this, do you know how to solve something similar? Maybe the similarity is literal (this is just like a bug I saw last week), or maybe it's metaphorical (this database works just like a fistful of water). In a similar manner, Papert's students were able to leverage their existing, tacit knowledge of body mechanics, social interaction, language, and so on, to learn the turtle's microworld and learn new programming skills.

But there's a downside to looking for similarities.

You learn a new programming language relative to the concepts you knew from the last programming language. That's why in years past we saw so much C++ code that looked like C, so much Java code that looked like C++, so much Ruby code that looked like Java, and so on. It's a natural transition from one set of skills to the next.

The danger lies in not completing the transition and sticking with the hybridized approach instead of fully embracing the new skill. You need to unlearn just as much as you need to learn. Examples include moving from the horse and buggy to the automobile, from the typewriter to the computer, from procedural programming to object-oriented programming, and from single programs on the desktop to cloud computing. For each of these transitions, the new way was fundamentally different from the old way. And where they were different, you had to let go of the old way.

> **Tip 34**
> Learn from similarities; unlearn from differences.

Another danger is that your notion of a "similar" previous problem may be completely wrong. For instance, when trying to learn a functional programming language, such as Erlang or Haskell, much of what you've previously learned about programming languages will just get in the way. They aren't similar to traditional procedural languages in any way that's helpful.

Failure lurks around every corner. And that's a good thing, as we'll see next.

7.3 Embed Failing in Practice

A man's errors are his portals of discovery.
▶ James Joyce, 1882–1941

Debugging is a part of life—not just software. Lawyers have to debug the law, mechanics debug cars, and psychiatrists debug *us*.

But let's not be coy about it; we're not removing "bugs" that somehow mysteriously crept into the system when we weren't looking. *Debugging* means solving problems, generally of our own making. We're identifying errors, mistakes, and oversights, and we're correcting them. The value lies in learning from the error, which Papert sums up nicely: "Errors benefit us because they lead us to study what happened, to understand what went wrong, and, through understanding, to fix it."

Perversely enough, failure is critical to success—not just any random failure; you need well-managed failure. You need the support of a good learning environment so you can more easily gain and apply experience from both your failures and your successes.

"I don't know" is a good start.

Not all mistakes arise from things you do; others come from things you didn't do but should have done. For example, you're reading along and come across the word *rebarbative* or *horked*, and you wonder what on Earth it means. Or perhaps you see a reference to a new technology you've never heard of or a famous author in your field you've never read. Look it up. Google it. Fill in the blanks. "I don't know" is a fine answer, but don't let it end there.

We tend to think of failure or ignorance in a very negative light, as something to be avoided at all costs. But it's *not* important to get it right the first time; it's important to get it right the *last* time. In any nontrivial endeavor, you will make mistakes.

Exploration is "playing" in unfamiliar territory. You need to be able to explore freely in order to learn. But that exploration has to be relatively free from risk; you don't ever want to be held back because you're afraid to try something. You need to be able to explore even if you're not sure where you're headed. Similarly, you need to be free to invent—comfortable in the knowledge that what you create might not work out. Finally, you need to be able to apply what you've learned in your day-to-day practice. An efficient, supportive learning environment should allow you to do three things, safely: explore, invent, and apply.[3]

> **TIP 35**
>
> Explore, invent, and apply in your environment—safely.

Create an Exploratory Environment

However, you can't explore, invent, or apply ideas within the environment of practice (on the job) until you make it safe for yourself, for your team, and for your organization. You wouldn't want your heart surgeon to start your operation with, "Hmm, I'm going to try doing this *left*-handed today and see what happens."

---

3. *Explore, Invent, and Apply* [Bei91].

That wouldn't be safe; a live and unsuspecting patient is not the right context for experimentation.

You can experiment out of the line of corporate fire, for instance, at home on an open source project. That at least reduces the risk of negative consequences. But that alone is not enough to create a positive learning environment for you. Whether it's on a corporate team or a solo experiment in the dark watches of the night, you need the following:

Freedom to experiment

Few problems have a single, best solution. You could implement this next feature this way or that way; which do you choose? Both! If time is tight (and when isn't it?), try at least a prototype each way. That's experimentation, and you want to encourage it. Consider it part of "design time" when giving an estimate. You also need to make sure this experimentation doesn't adversely affect anyone else on the team.

Ability to backtrack to a stable state

Safety means that when the experiment goes awry, you can go back to the halcyon days of last Tuesday, before you started making those dreadful changes. You want to revert to a previous, known state of your source code and try again. Remember, you want to get it right the last time.

Reproduce any work product as of any time

Backtracking to a previous version of the source code isn't quite enough; you probably need to actually run the program (or work with any derivative work product) as of any point in history. Can you run a version of the program from last year or last month?

Ability to demonstrate progress

Finally, you can't get anywhere without feedback. Did this experiment or that invention work better than the alternatives? How do you know? Is the project progressing? Do more functions work this week than worked last week? Somehow, you need to demonstrate fine-grained progress—to yourself as well as to others.

In software development, it's pretty simple to set up an infrastructure to address these needs. It's what we call the Starter Kit: version control, unit testing, and project automation.[4]

- *Version control* stores every version of every file you work with. Whether you're writing source code, articles, songs or poetry, version control acts as a giant Undo button for your work.[5] Newer distributed version control systems such as Git or Mercurial are well-suited to support private experimentation.
- *Unit testing* provides you with a fine-grained set of regression tests. You can use unit test results to compare alternatives, and you can use them as a solid indication of progress.[6] In any endeavor, you need objective feedback to measure progress. This is ours.
- *Automation* ties it all together and ensures that the trivial mechanics are taken care of in a reliable, repeatable manner.[7]

This Starter Kit gives you the advantage of freedom to experiment, with comparatively little risk.

Of course, your team practices and culture have to *allow* this approach to exploration and invention. A supporting environment can make or break learning for anyone. Thich Nhat Hahn reminds us of the fundamental attribution error (described in Chapter 5, *Debug Your Mind*, on page 113); the problem is more often the environment, not the individual.

> *When you plant lettuce, if it does not grow well, you don't blame the lettuce. You look for reasons it is not doing well. It may need fertilizer or more water or less sun. You never blame the lettuce.*
>
> ▶ Thich Nhat Hahn

---

4. In fact, Dave Thomas and I felt that the idea of the Starter Kit was so important that those were the very first books we published as the Pragmatic Bookshelf.

5. See *Pragmatic Version Control using Git* [Swi08], *Pragmatic Version Control Using Subversion* [Mas06], or *Pragmatic Version Control Using CVS* [TH03] for particular systems.

6. See *Pragmatic Unit Testing In Java with JUnit* [HT03] and *Pragmatic Unit Testing In C# with NUnit, 2nd Ed.* [HwMH06].

7. See *Pragmatic Project Automation. How to Build, Deploy, and Monitor Java Applications* [Cla04] as well as *Ship It! A Practical Guide to Successful Software Projects* [RG05] for a good overview of these topics in a team context.

Next Actions ⬇

- ☐ If your software project isn't set up with a safety net (version control, unit testing, and automation), you need to get that implemented right away. Put the book down. I'll wait.
- ☐ Your personal learning projects need to have the same safety net—whether you are writing code, learning to paint, or exploring a colossal cave. Put the infrastructure and habits in place to make your project safe to explore.
- ☐ Do you know what *halcyon* means? *Anthropomorphism*? Ever hear of Nhat Hahn? Did you look them up? If not, what do you need to do to make this happen? (On the Mac, you can often Control-click [or right-click] a word and have the option to look it up in the dictionary or search using Google for that word. It's quite handy.)

7.4 Learn About the Inner Game

There are two types of failure. There are the failures that are good for us that we can learn from. But there are failures that aren't good for us. This second type of failure doesn't produce any learning: it keeps us from learning in the first place, or it shuts down our learning in mid-experience.

To recognize and overcome this second type of failure, you need to be aware of the *inner game*. Understanding the inner game will help you eliminate interference that gets in the way of learning, and it emphasizes the right kind of feedback to help you learn.

In 1974 the popular book *The Inner Game of Tennis* [Gal97] introduced a generation to a whole new level of feedback and self-awareness. It spawned a number of follow-on books including *The Inner Game of Music* [GG86] and those about skiing, golf, and more.

The Inner Game series helps further the point of learning from your own experience. In this series of books, Timothy Gallwey and other authors differentiate the obvious, "outer" game that you are engaged in and explore the subtleties of the more critical "inner" game. A big part of improving learning comes from Gallwey's idea of reducing failure-inducing interference and using feedback.

In a famous example, the author takes an older subject, a woman in her late fifties or so, who has never played tennis or indeed engaged in any significant physical activity for the past twenty years. The challenge was to teach her to play tennis in just twenty minutes. There's no way to succeed at this challenge using a traditional approach. But Tim Gallwey had a better idea—one that didn't involve any lengthy lectures or extended demonstrations.

 First, she was to just watch the ball and say out loud "Bounce" and "Hit" as Gallwey hit the ball. A minute or so of this, and it was her turn: just say "Bounce" and "Hit." Don't try to hit the ball; just say "Hit" when it seems about the right time, and swing when you feel like it. The next exercise was to *listen* to the sound of the ball hitting the racket. If you've never played, the ball makes a particularly sweet, clear sound when it hits just the right spot on the racket. This fact wasn't made explicit; our student was merely told to listen.

Next, it was time to serve. First, she was to just hum a phrase while watching Gallwey serve in order to get the rhythm of the motion. No description of the movements; just watch and hum. Next, she tried the serve—humming the same tune and focusing on the rhythm, not the motions. After twenty minutes of this sort of thing, it was time to play. She made the first point of the game and played a very respectable, lengthy set of volleys.[8]

In another example, you hit balls across the court where a chair is sitting. The idea is not to try to hit the chair but to simply note where the ball lands *in relation* to the chair. So while hitting balls, you would verbalize observations such as "Left," "Right," "Over," and so on.

We learn best by discovery, not instruction.

The Inner Game series teaches us that it can be very difficult to teach a skill by putting it into words; we learn better by discovery, not instruction. This notion is embodied in the chair example, where the learner is getting real-time feedback in the context of the situation.

---

8. See Alan Kay's videotaped lecture entitled *Doing with Images Makes Symbols: Communicating with Computers* for actual footage of the event.

Cultivate Situational Feedback

Situational feedback is the primary inner game technique that allows you to learn more efficiently by eliminating any interference. In the tennis example, the subject wasn't inundated with rules of the game; buried with minutiae of proper grip, footwork, and so on; or forced to learn "dance facts" before dancing. Instead of all those distractions, she was able to concentrate on a very simple feedback loop. Hit the ball like this, and it lands here. Hit the ball like that, and it lands over there. Follow this rhythm. It's nonverbal learning, for a nonverbal skill, with a tight feedback loop and short feedback gap.[9]

Consider an example from skiing. I've had a handful of ski lessons over the years, and invariably they turn out the same. I'm hurtling down the face with some instructor named Hans close by, issuing instructions at a frantic pace with an unidentifiable accent:

- "Keep you elbows een!"
- "Bend your knees!"
- "Tips together!"
- "Lean eento the curve!"
- "Watch your pole!"
- "Look out for the tree!"

Now I'm trying to listen to everything this guy is saying, but of course the verbal processing centers (**L**-mode) are on the *slow* side of the house. I'm back on tucking in my elbows and starting to think about my knees, and already the tree is looming close. At a certain point (and usually pretty quickly), your brain just fries with the constant barrage of instructions and stops attending. Brain freeze. It's too much to remember and keep track of all at once.

The inner game theory has the solution: instead of issuing a stream of instructions to the student, the idea is to teach the student awareness and to use that awareness to correct their performance. *Awareness* is an important tool in becoming more than a novice.

For example, in the *The Inner Game of Music* [GG86], the author relates the story of teaching a concert string bass player.

---

9. A *feedback gap* is the length of time between performing an action and receiving feedback about it.

The author had been teaching in a manner similar to the ski instructor: hold your elbow this way, your head like this, lean that way, now play comfortably. And of course, the poor student looked like a stiff pretzel.

Just be aware.

So the music teacher tried something different. He had the student play just as he was but directed him to really observe every aspect of his playing—how did it feel, where was everything positioned, what passages were difficult, and so on. Then, without explanation, he corrected the student's posture and finger placement and guided his hands through a few bars of the piece. The instruction was the same: observe all of these aspects; how does it feel now? Now go ahead and play the piece. Consistently, his students now showed great improvement after this kind of awareness exercise.

This is a key aspect to playing the inner game: don't focus on correcting individual details, but just be aware. Accept *what is* as a first step, and just be aware of it. Don't judge, don't rush in with a solution, don't criticize.

You want to try to cultivate nonjudgmental awareness: don't try to get it right, but notice when it is wrong. Then act to correct it.

> TIP 36
>
> See without judging and then act.

Going Beyond Tennis

Now you may have noticed that these examples are largely in the kinesthetic domain—they involve muscle memory and physical skills. But there is more to it than that. Performing music, for instance, has been shown by functional MRI scans to activate virtually every center in the brain.[10] From operating the instrument to reading the notes, listening to the other musicians, following the abstract principles of chord progression and such, both L-mode and $\mathcal{R}$-mode are active and cooperating along with lower-level muscle memory. So even though we're talking about skiing and playing

---

10. See *This Is Your Brain on Music: The Science of a Human Obsession* [Lev06] for more.

a string bass, the lessons can be applied to software development and other endeavors as well.

For instance, the idea of being fully aware of "what is" before acting to correct it is especially true when debugging. Too often programmers (myself included) seem to jump in to fix an apparent bug without fully evaluating what's really wrong first. Fight the urge to rush to judgment or to a potential fix prematurely. Be *fully* aware of how the system is behaving, and only then decide what part of that is "wrong" before moving on to devise a solution. In other words, don't just do something; stand there. June Kim describes the following technique to help become fully aware.

> Don't just do something; stand there.

Suppose you are doing test-first design. You added a new test and the code that will make the test pass. Thinking the test will surely pass, you click the button. What? There is a failing test that you never expected. Your heart rate goes up, your field of vision narrows, your adrenaline pumps. Breathe in deeply, and first take your hands off the keyboard. Read the error message carefully. Raise your awareness. What's happening?

Now close your eyes, and imagine where the source of the error resides in the code. Think of it like the epicenter of an earthquake. You may feel the ground shake here and over there, but the epicenter is way over *there*. What will the code look like? What about code around it? Imagine the code and its neighbors before opening your eyes.

Once you can imagine the code, now open your eyes, and navigate to the code in question. Does it look like what you expected? Is it really the cause of the error?

Now close your eyes again, and imagine a passing test. When you can imagine the test code, open your eyes, and type it in. Check whether it is the same as you imagined. Now just before you hit the test-all button, ask yourself, what will happen when I hit this button? Then click the button and see.

It may sound like a trivial exercise, but it really does make a difference. The next time you find yourself trapped in an ad hoc hack-spin-loop, try it. The idea is to raise your awareness; explicitly contrasting your imagined version of the code with the real code helps accomplish that.

And it's not just about debugging. The same is true when gathering requirements—especially when an existing system is involved. Jerry Weinberg maintains that most clients will tell you their most serious problem, and its solution, in the first five minutes you talk with them.[11] It's vital to listen to what the client has to say, instead of letting your attention wander to the cool solution you're dying to try. You can brainstorm solutions later, but first, be aware of *what is*.

The inner game ideas focus on feedback to grow expertise. You are training, and then listening to, the inner voice of experience. But that works only if you can *listen* to the inner voice of experience. Listen, listen, listen. Unfortunately, it isn't always that easy, as we'll see next.

7.5 Pressure Kills Cognition

The Inner Game series sums up this idea with the phrase, "Trying fails, awareness cures." That is, consciously *trying* generally doesn't work as well as simple awareness. In fact, trying too hard is a guarantee for failure.

The mere presence of a looming deadline can panic the mind into failure. For example, there's a well-known psychology study that was done with seminary students.[12]

> Deadlines panic the mind.

The experiment took a group of seminary students on the day of the Good Samaritan lecture. Against this backdrop of being good stewards of the earth and helping and serving your fellow man, the researchers set up an encounter. They took one set of students and explained to them that they had a critical meeting with the dean of their school right after the lecture. It was across campus, and they could not be late—their future careers depended on it. They then arranged to position an accomplice, dressed and acting as a homeless beggar, right in their path to the dean's office.

---

11. *The Secrets of Consulting* [Wei85].
12. *From Jerusalem to Jericho: A Study of Situational and Dispositional Variables in Helping Behavior* [DB73].

Pressure Hangover

You might disagree with this notion of pressure. You might think you are at your most effective when faced with an imminent deadline. While that *might* have some validity for **L**-mode activities (and I'm highly suspicious of that), it's a certain disaster for creativity and R-mode activities, according to Dr. Teresa Amabile.*

As part of a ten-year study on creativity in the workplace, Amabile and colleagues discovered just the opposite: you are the least creative when you feel time pressure.

In fact, it's even worse than that. Not only are you less creative when battling the clock, but there's a sort of after effect: a time pressure "hangover." Your creativity suffers on the day you're under the gun and remains depressed for the next two days as well.

That's why it's a good idea to end a project iteration on a Friday. That's why you really do need some down time after an unscheduled, panicked crunch.

Allow recovery time for your time-pressure hangover.

---

*. Cited in *The 6 Myths of Creativity* (Bre97). Thanks to June Kim for finding this one.

Sad but true, these devout students, under the pressure of an important meeting, practically walked *on* the beggar's head in their mad rush to get to the appointment. But a second group was told they had that same crucial meeting, only they were given some spare time between events—they weren't in a rush. The students in this second group stopped to help the beggar; they took him to the infirmary, cleaned him up, and so on.

But when the mind is pressured, it actively begins shutting things down. Your vision narrows—literally as well as figuratively. You no longer consider options. What's worse, you're shutting out most of the R-mode entirely: it's the L-mode that handles time. When you perceive time as being critical, the R-mode can't get a chance to work at all.

There goes your search engine, your creativity, and your ingenuity. The ski instructor or the bass instructor that we read about earlier can freeze up your mind in a similar fashion by unleashing a torrent of verbal instruction. Again, $\mathcal{R}$-mode is shut out.

I had an interesting experience along these lines a few years back. A couple of us attended a problem-solving workshop by Jerry Weinberg.[13] One of the exercises involved a simulation of a manufacturing operation. The group of ten to twelve people was split into workers, managers, customers, and so on; buffet tables in the conference room became the factory, and index cards tracked production, orders, and the like. Of course, in the tradition of all good simulations, it was a bit of a trap. You couldn't meet the needs of production by ordinary means. So, the pressure begins to build, and the folks in the managerial roles start making bad decisions, followed by worse decisions, followed by disastrous decisions. The participants in the worker roles begin to scratch their heads as to why their comrades are starting to act like they've had lobotomies.

Mercifully, that's about when the simulation ended. Alistair Cockburn was in the course with me, and he aptly described what we all felt: *a sort of tingling sensation* as your brain came back on line, almost as if your mind had literally gone to sleep, as an arm or leg will do when cramped in an uncomfortable position.

We need to ease up on the pressure.

Grant Permission to Fail

I said earlier that errors are important to success. The other important lesson from the Inner Game series is the idea that *permission to fail* leads to success. You don't actually need to make errors, as long as it's OK if you did. It sounds somewhat counterintuitive, but once you play with the idea, it makes a lot of sense.

> **TIP 37**
>
> Give yourself permission to fail; it's the path to success.

The bass instructor related a common problem. Many of his very talented students would simply freeze up in the spotlight and not

---

13. See *Becoming a Technical Leader: An Organic Problem-Solving Approach* [Wei86] and http://www.geraldmweinberg.com for Jerry's current offerings.

perform at their best. So, he took to a little bit of subterfuge. He'd lead the students out onto the stage, under the unforgiving glare of the spotlights, but explain that the judges weren't ready yet. They were still working on paperwork from the last candidate. The microphones weren't even on. So go ahead, he'd say, and just run through the piece once as a warm-up.

Of course, he was lying through his teeth.

The judges were, in fact, listening intently. And they were handsomely rewarded; the students performed excellently. They were free to. They were explicitly given permission to fail. For whatever reasons of cognitive or neuroscience, once you make it *OK* to fail, you won't. Perhaps, this too, helps shut down our overactive L-modes.

With the pressure off, you can be attentive. You can be comfortable and just observe—remember the first tenet, that awareness trumps trying. It's hard to just be aware and comfortable with a flawed performance under the harsh light of scrutiny or to let an idea blossom to fruition in its own time when there's a deadline looming. A "brainstorming" session where ideas get shot down as soon as they're uttered has the same debilitating effect.

Instead, it is very possible to create "failure permitted" zones on a normal software project. The key is to create an environment where the cost of failure is near zero.

> Create "failure permitted" zones.

In a brainstorming meeting, all ideas get written on the whiteboard (or whatever). There's no cost or stigma if the idea doesn't progress much further. Think about the agile practice of unit testing. Here, you're free to have a unit test fail—even encouraged. You learn from it, fix the code, and move on.

Prototyping gives you a similar freedom. Maybe it will work out, maybe not. If it doesn't work out, you can use the lessons—apply the experience—and use that in the next iteration.

On the other hand, if failure is costly, there will be no experimentation. No risk taking. No learning. Just a frozen mind, like deer in the headlights, bracing for the inevitable bloody impact.

But what if the actual environment really is risky? It's all fine and well to say you need an environment where failure is OK, but what if you're sky diving? Or running Olympic bobsled or luge? What can

you do to increase your chances of success in challenging environments such as these?

7.6 Imagination Overrides Senses

The aptly named inner game really can be played inside. In addition
to gaining experience in the real world, you can gain experience
inside your head as well.

Suppose you're sitting in the movie theater, watching the big car
chase at the climax of the movie. Your pulse is rapid, your breathing shallow, your muscles clenched.

But wait, you're not actually in the car chase. You're sitting in a
comfortable upholstered chair, in the air-conditioning, with a drink
and popcorn, watching flickering images projected on a screen. You
are not in any danger at all.[14]

Yet your body reacts as if you're in real danger. And it doesn't have
to be a movie; a book would work as well. It doesn't even have to
be happening in the present moment. Remember that really mean
bully in grade school or that awful teacher? First love? These are
just memories, but the remembering can cause appropriate physical responses. It turns out that your brain isn't very good at discriminating between input sources. Real-time sensor data, memories of past events, and even imagined circumstances that haven't
happened all result in the same physiological responses (see Figure 7.1, on the next page).

The entertainment industry is counting on it.

In fact, the situation is a little bit worse—the memory or imagining of events often overrides more accurate real-time sensor data.
This makes eyewitness reporting more than a little problematic:
you really don't see what you *think* you see.

Eggs Are White, Right?

Betty Edwards describes something similar in the phenomenon of
color constancy. That's where the brain overrides color information
received by the retina. Just as we saw earlier with the simplistic

---

14. Discounting any biohazard from that suspiciously sticky, crunchy orange
residue on the floor.

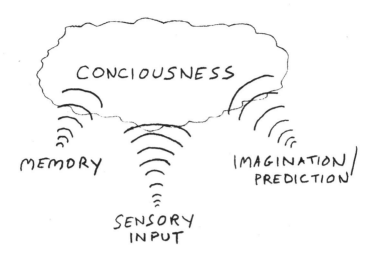

Figure 7.1: ALL INPUT IS CREATED EQUAL.

stick-figure representation, you "know" that skies are blue, clouds are white, blond hair is yellow, and trees are green with brown trunks—just like in the set of Crayola crayons.

Edwards describes an interesting test that an art teacher performed on a set of students. The teacher set up a still life consisting of white Styrofoam geometric shapes (a cube, a cylinder, and a sphere) and an egg carton of regular white-shelled eggs. He added colored floodlights to make everything in the still life a bright pinkish red and set the students to painting.

According to Edwards, every student painted the white Styrofoam objects in shades of pinkish red just as they appeared under the colored light.

But not the eggs.

The students painted the eggs white. The memorized constant that "eggs are white" overrode their actual appearance caused by the colored lights. Even more remarkably, when the teacher pointed out that the eggs were really pink, the student's didn't see it. They still insisted, "But the eggs *are* white."

Perception is based on prediction.	Much of perception is based on prediction,[15] and prediction is based on context and past experience, so much so that current, real-time input takes a backseat.

Have you ever had the experience of a friend who suddenly made a dramatic difference in their appearance? They grew or shaved a beard or changed hair style or color, and you didn't notice right away? Or even after a while?

The stereotypical story of the wife's new hairdo that the husband doesn't notice really happens: the husband "sees" based on old input. It's just how your brain works.[16]

Since this phenomenon works just as well from remembered experience and imagined experience, you can use it to your advantage.

Successful Grooving

OK, you'll need to bear with me here, because this is going to sound suspiciously like faerie dust. But, since the brain is kinda gullible with regards to its input source: imagining success is provably effective in achieving it.

You can improve your performance—whether you're playing a violin, debugging code, or designing a new architecture—by imagining that you've already done so successfully.

First, let's look at some practical examples. You may have noticed that if you're at a conference, or some sort of get-together where you're surrounded by more advanced practitioners, that your own ability increases. Maybe you can speak more articulately or argue your point a little better. Maybe the fact that you even *have* a point occurs to you.

Legendary jazz guitarist Pat Metheny takes this idea one step further and offers this advice: "Always be the worst guy in every band you're in. If you're the best guy there, you need to be in a different band. And I think that works for almost everything that's out there as well."[17]

---

15. This is a major observation in *On Intelligence* [Haw04].
16. Not, of course, that this makes for any sort of effective excuse.
17. Thanks to Chris Morris by way of Chad Fowler in *My Job Went to India: 52 Ways to Save Your Job* [Fow05].

In other words, by surrounding yourself with highly skilled people, you will increase your own skill level. Some of that is from observation and application of their practices and approaches. Some of that comes from the fact that you're conditioning your mind to perform at a higher level. You have a natural mechanism known as *mirror neurons* that help: watching someone else's behavior triggers an equivalence for you to do the same.

The Inner Game folks suggest you should pretend you are the expert, the pro, the famous soloist. They observed that sim- **We are natural mimics.** ply telling a student to "play like" someone famous in their field was enough to increase the student's performance. We are natural mimics, after all. You've heard how Miles Davis sounds; you've read Linus Torvald's code; you've read *The Pragmatic Programmer*.[18]

You can imagine writing code in your head or pretend to have that requirements conversation. You can "play" an instrument when it's not really in front of you—and you can imagine that you've got it nailed, that it's perfect.

In a similar vein, Olympic athletes do this sort of offline practicing, too. They'll envision themselves hurtling down the course, taking the turns, and reacting appropriately. By continuing this practice even off the field, the brain gets *grooved*.[19] It becomes used to the experience of doing things correctly so that when the time comes to do it in the field, success comes naturally.

> **TIP 38**
>
> Groove your mind for success.

Getting used to what "success" feels like is important enough that it's worthwhile to fake it first. That is, artificially create the conditions that you'd experience once you learn to perform at that level. You add whatever *scaffolding* is necessary to provide an approximation of the experience.

---

18. If you haven't, run, don't walk, to the bookstore and buy a copy. Seriously.
19. Edward de Bono's term.

Experience using scaffolding. Swimmers do this by being attached to a rope and pulled through the water at high speed.[20] Before a swimmer can achieve that sort of speed on their own, they get to experience what it will feel like. This isn't just a courtesy; after this experience, the swimmer's performance increases dramatically.

You can go the other way as well, by using negative scaffolding, or *unscaffolding*, if you will. That's when you make it artificially harder than it should be. Then when you're doing it for real, it seems a lot easier. Runners might tie weights to their ankles or jog through waist-deep snow. Ruby programmers might work in something like C++ for a while. C++ makes a very effective mental equivalent to heavy ankle weights; after working in C++, more dynamic languages then feel a whole lot easier by comparison. :-)

You can imagine experiences and learn from them just as effectively as if you had lived them for real. Your brain doesn't really know the difference. So, take the pressure off, become more aware of what's wrong, and pretend you've made it.

And you will.

Next Actions ⬇

- ☐ The next time you are stuck in a difficult situation, remember "Trying fails, awareness cures." Stop and become *fully aware* of the problem first.
- ☐ Plan on failing. Know that it doesn't matter and that it's OK if you make a mistake. See whether that helps take the pressure off and improves your performance.
- ☐ Be the expert. Don't just pretend, actually *play* the role of the expert. Notice how this changes your behavior.
- ☐ Consider what kind of scaffolding you might need to share in the expert experience, and see if you can arrange for that.

7.7 Learn It like an Expert

You should feel you're in a better position to take control of your own learning experiences now.

---

20. Thanks to June Kim for this example.

In this chapter, we've looked at the value of *playing* to facilitate learning and the importance of actively embedding failure as an essential part of practice. We saw the important—and by now familiar—lessons from the inner game and the tricks your brain can play on you, for better or worse.

Don't forget that as you gain experience, you'll continue to transition through the stages of the Dreyfus model. Your ongoing experience will steadily reshape your views, and you'll find yourself reinterpreting past experiences in the light of new knowledge and growing mental models.

As I noted in Section 5.1, *Meet Your Cognitive Biases*, on page 115, every read of your memory is really a write. Memory is far from inviolate; your increasing expertise will steadily add to the filters and pattern matching you employ.

That's how intuition grows: you have more patterns to draw on and apply, as well as a growing body of tacit knowledge to know what to look for and when. In other words, you'll start to see the beginnings of expert behavior.

But First, Cut the Green Wire

It seems that anytime a character in a movie is given instructions on how to defuse a bomb, they start pulling out the parts and cutting the wires in the prescribed order in earnest. And then the bomb squad corrects them, adding, "Oh, but before you do any of that, cut the *green* wire." By then, it's too late, and the ominous ticking noise reaches a crescendo. So, in the next chapter, we'll look at our "green wire," the important thing you need to do first.

I'm guessing that you're probably enthusiastic to start trying all the material in this book right away.

But then a day at work in the real world gets in the way—all the emails, the meetings, the design problems, the bugs. There's too much to do, in too little time. All the grand intentions melt away under the unforgiving crush of the exigencies of the day.

In the next chapter, we'll look at a few ways of managing the torrent of information and getting better control over the things that command your attention.

A good question is never answered. It is not a bolt to be tightened into place but a seed to be planted and to bear more seed toward the hope of greening the landscape of idea.

▶ John Anthony Ciardi

Chapter 8

Manage Focus

I don't need to tell you that we live in information-rich times. But perversely, the overabundance of information has resulted in a poverty of knowledge and attention. With so much available distraction, it's easy to lose focus. Rather than wandering around in the middle of the information highway,[1] you need to take deliberate steps to manage what you're thinking about.

Using the same approach as in Chapter 6, *Learn Deliberately*, on page 145, you'll need to manage thinking more deliberately. You need to be able to focus on the information that you want, filter the information you are bombarded with, and have the right information available to you at the right time, without being distracted by irrelevant details and without missing subtle clues that make all the difference.

In this part of the book, we are going to look at how to better manage your mind along these three axes:

- Increasing focus and attention
- Managing your knowledge
- Optimizing your current context

Attention is the act of focusing in on an area of interest. You can pay attention only to a fairly small number of things; beyond that, events and insights will escape your notice. Many, *many* things are competing for your attention in our current environment. Some of them deserve it; most do not. We'll look at ways to increase your ability to focus.

---

1. I'm picturing the old video game Frogger, with the same messy results.

Sometimes we use the words *information* and *knowledge* interchangeably, but they aren't the same thing. *Information* is raw data in a given context. For instance, the fact that Microsoft bought some company for a billion dollars is just information, and there's no shortage of information these days. *Knowledge* imparts meaning to that information. You apply your time, attention, and skill to information to produce knowledge. Looking at that particular Microsoft acquisition and knowing how it might change the market, provide new opportunities, and destroy others constitutes knowledge. We'll see a better way to organize your far-flung knowledge and insights.

Context, beyond the usage we've seen so far, is the set of stuff you are focused on at the moment. When you are debugging a program, for instance, all the variables, object interrelationships, and so on, form the current context. Think of it as the "working set" of information that you are dealing with at a given point in time.

Understanding these three interrelated topics will help you manage your mind more effectively.

The first thing you need to do is pay attention.

8.1 Increase Focus and Attention

While working on a presentation about pragmatic programming back in 2000, I came across a remarkably odd news story. There was this elderly lady in Darby, Pennsylvania, who was walking down the street to her local grocery store. A young man came running up the street and slammed into her but kept running. Fearing she had been mugged, the woman quickly felt for her purse and valuables. She was fine, but quite shaken, and proceeded on to the grocery store.

She talked to several people in the store, checked out her purchase of Oreo cookies and a newspaper, and left. It was only once she returned home that her daughter screamed as she saw the handle of a steak knife sticking out of the woman's neck.

It's amazing what you can miss when distracted. Worried at being robbed, the old lady did not particularly notice the dull pain in her neck where she had been stabbed.

If you can miss obvious things—like a knife sticking out of your neck—just think what else might be going on around you that has escaped your attention.

Attention Deficit

Your attention is in short supply. There is only so much you can pay attention to, and there are so many things that compete for your attention daily.

There's a well-known design problem in multiprocessor systems: if you're not careful, you can spend all the CPU cycles coordinating tasks with all the other CPUs and not actually get any work done. Similarly, it's easy for us humans to divide our attention fecklessly such that nothing receives our full attention and so nothing effective gets done.

Competition for your attention isn't always external, either. For instance, as we saw in Section 4.2, *Draw on the Right Side*, on page 75, your L-mode CPU has a

Beware idle-loop chatter.

sort of "idle loop" routine. If nothing more pressing is commanding your attention, your idle loop will chatter away on some low-grade worry or indolent concern, such as "What's for lunch?," or replay a traffic incident or argument. This of course then interferes with R-mode processing, and you're back to working with half a brain again.

You might hear yourself often saying, "I'd love to, but I don't have the time." Or some new task comes up at work, and you think you just don't have the time to attend to it. It's not really *time* that's the issue. As noted earlier (in Section 6.3, *Create a Pragmatic Investment Plan*, on page 154), time is just something you allocate. It's not that we're out of time; we're out of attention. So instead of saying you don't have time, it's probably more accurate to say you don't have the *bandwidth*. When you overload your bandwidth—your attentional resources—you'll miss things. You won't learn, you won't perform your work well, and your family will begin to think maybe you have a brain tumor or something.

If you're paying attention—*really* paying attention—you can accomplish marvelous things. Paul Graham, in his book *Hackers and Painters: Big Ideas from the Computer Age* [Gra04], suggests that "a navy pilot can land a 40,000 lb aircraft at 140mph on a pitching carrier deck at night more safely than the average teenager can cut a bagel."

Having been a teenager once, I can easily recall what was on my mind as I stood patiently in front of the toaster. And it had nothing to do with English muffins, bagels, toast, jam, or the buzzing appliance in front of me. The teenager's mind is easily distracted, and that doesn't seem to be one of those things that gets any better as you age.

The pilot, on the other hand, is really, seriously focused. In that situation, a moment of indecision or error, and you're spectacularly dead. We need to develop that sort of concentrated focus but without the inherent risk of incineration.

Relaxed, Concentrated Focus

Here's a simple thing to try. Sit down and take a moment. Don't think about the mistakes you made yesterday or worry about problems that might come up tomorrow. Focus on *now*. This one instant in time. Right here.

No distractions.

No chatter.

I'll wait.

It's not easy, is it? Much of meditation, yoga, and similar practices aim for the same goal: to offer some relief from that gibbering L-mode monkey voice in your head, to live in the moment, and to not divide your mental energy unnecessarily. The internal chatter knocks us off our game.

A study published in the *Public Library of Science-Biology*[2] showed that training in meditation could improve a subject's ability to pay attention throughout the day.

Their testing gauged how well subjects could allocate cognitive resources when presented with multiple stimuli, all competing for their attention at once. Sounds like a normal day at the office....

Folks who had been given substantial training in meditative techniques fared better than those who had been given only minimal

---

2. *Learning to Pay Attention* [Jon07].

training. But, most interestingly, nobody was meditating during the test itself. As the article concludes:

"So these results indicate that intensive mental training can produce lasting and significant improvements in the efficient distribution of attentional resources among competing stimuli, even when individuals are not actively using the techniques they have learned."

In other words, the benefits are with you all day long, not just when you're meditating or explicitly "paying attention." This is a huge benefit: just as with physical exercise, working out provides greater capacity and long-lasting health benefits.

See benefits 24x7.

Tip 39

Learn to pay attention.

If you want to more efficiently allocate your "attentional resources" throughout the day, you need to learn the basics of meditation.

How to Meditate

There are many forms of what we might loosely call *meditation*, ranging from the secular to the religious. We'll look at a particular form here that ought to do the trick. It originates from a Buddhist tradition, but you don't need to be a Buddhist—or anything else in particular—to use it effectively.[3]

What you want to attain here is not a trance or to fall asleep or to relax or to contemplate the Great Mystery or any of that (there are other forms of meditation

Aim for relaxed awareness.

for those particular activities). Instead, what you want is to sink into a sort of relaxed awareness where you can be aware of yourself and your environment without rendering judgment or making responses. This is known as *Vipassana meditation.* You want to catch that moment of bare attention where you first notice something but do not give it any additional thought. Let it go.

---

3. Meditation is a common theme, even if it's not explicitly stated as such. The Judeo-Christian Bible advises that we should "Be still and know that I am God." It's that "being still" part that proves difficult, regardless of one's beliefs.

In this style of meditation, "all" you have to do is pay attention to your breath. It's not as easy as it sounds, but it does have the advantage of not requiring any props or special equipment. Here's what you do:

- Find a quiet spot, free from distraction or interruption. This might be the hardest part.
- Sit in a comfortable, alert posture, with a straight back. Let your body hang off your spine like a rag doll. Take a moment to become aware of any tension that you might be holding in your body and let it go.
- Close your eyes, and focus your awareness on your breath—that small point where the air enters your body and where it exits.
- Be aware of the rhythm of your breath, the length and qualities of the inhale, the brief pause at the top of the cycle, the qualities of the exhale, and the brief pause at the bottom. Don't try to change it; just be aware of it.
- Keep your mind focused on the breath. Do not use words. Do not verbalize the breath or any thoughts you have. Do not begin a conversation with yourself. This is the *other* hard part.
- You may find yourself thinking about some topic or carrying on a conversation with yourself. Whenever your attention wanders off, just let those thoughts go and gently bring your focus back to the breath.
- Even if your mind is wandering often, the exercise of noticing that you have wandered and bringing yourself back each time is helpful.

Just as with the drawing exercise in Section 4.2, *Draw on the Right Side*, on page 75, you want to shut down the chatter. In this case, you are explicitly focusing on your breathing. In the drawing exercise, you were trying to block any words from coming. In this exercise, words can come—but you'll just let them go. Just be aware; don't judge or think. Words, feelings, thoughts, and whatever, will come up, and you'll just let them go and return your attention to the breath.

It's important to approach this exercise with the idea that you're not going to sleep. You want to relax your body and quiet your mind, but remain alert—in fact, you want to be *very* alert but to focus that awareness.

After spending some time like this, you can try deliberately controlling your breath. The *segmented breath* approach goes like this. Consider the breath to be made of air traveling in three distinct segments:

- The lower belly and abdomen
- The chest and rib cage
- The very upper chest and collar bones (but not into the throat)

Exhale fully. On the inhale, fill the lower belly first, pause ever so slightly, then fill the chest, and finally fill 'er up all the way to the collar bones. Keep your throat open and jaw relaxed. Nothing should tense up.

Pause briefly at the top, and then exhale normally.

Pause at the bottom, and then repeat.

You can also turn this around and inhale naturally and then exhale in a segmented fashion, or do both. In any case, you want to maintain awareness of the breath and the feeling of air in your lungs and then let other thoughts just slide on by.

Of course, if any of these manipulated breath activities make you anxious, short of breath, or uncomfortable in any way, return to a natural breath immediately. No one is grading or judging you on your performance; you want to do what works *for you*. Don't overdo it; try it for just a couple of minutes at first (say, three minutes).

The benefits of meditation have been widely studied. Recently,[4] researchers showed that even children—middle-school students— could benefit. Students who participated in a one-year study were found to have an increased state of restful alertness; improvement in skills indicative of emotional intelligence (self-control, self-reflection/awareness, and flexibility in emotional response); and improvement in academic performance. That's not a bad return on investment for sitting around and breathing.

Meditation might sound trivial. It's not. I strongly suggest you give it a try for awhile; paying attention is a critical skill.

---

4. *The Experience of Transcendental Meditation in Middle School Students: A Qualitative Report* [RB06].

Next Actions ⬇

- ☐ Experiment with meditation on a regular basis. Start by taking three deep relaxing "meditative" breaths at memorable times during the day: waking, at lunch, dinner, or before meetings.
- ☐ Try to build up to a set period of twenty minutes or so every day, preferably at the same time. Can you begin to quiet your inner thoughts?

Try this before reading the next section....

You need to stop reading now and try this; otherwise you'll be breathing funny while trying to read, and you won't be paying attention to the next section, which, oddly enough, is about deliberately *not* paying attention.

8.2 Defocus to Focus

Some problems yield only to a less conscious approach. And that brings up an interesting question. What counts as "work" or as "effort"?

Are you "cooking" when you're letting something marinate for twelve hours? Are you "working" when you're sitting around thinking about a problem?

Yes, is the short answer. Creativity does not function on a time clock and does not generally yield results when pressured. In fact, the situation is quite the opposite: you need to let go of the problem with your conscious mind and let the problem sit in the marinade of thought for a while.

Don't do *something*.

Tom Lutz, author of *Doing Nothing: A History of Loafers, Loungers, Slackers, and Bums in America* [Lut06], says, "It's very clear that for a lot of people the creative process includes an enormous amount of sitting around doing nothing." But to try to clarify that position, it's not the idea of not doing *anything*; it's the idea of not doing *something*.

Now this might present a problem in a post-industrial society. This kind of critical "thinking time" is generally unrecognized and unrewarded in most corporations. There's a widespread misconception that as a programmer (or other knowledge worker), if you're not typing on a keyboard, then you're not working.[5]

Handing work over to the unconscious works only if you have some data to work on. You first need to "fill up," as it were, with what facts you have.

Lutz goes on to say that everyone has their own version of the "marinade," that is, some way of letting their thoughts stew (I've always been fond of mowing the grass, for instance). We've talked about how the $\mathcal{R}$-mode needs a chance to work on the material, but there's a related idea that comes from the "multiple drafts" model of consciousness.

In *Consciousness Explained* [Den93], Dr. Daniel Dennett proposes an interesting model of consciousness. Consider that at any given moment, you have multiple rough drafts of events, thoughts, plans, and so on, constructed in your mind. Dennett defines "consciousness" as the single draft that has the most brain cells or processing activity in the brain at a single moment.

Think of the multiple drafts like different clouds of lightning bugs scattered throughout the brain.[6] Most of the different groups/clouds flash indiscriminately; a few flash together as a whole cloud. When several of the clouds flash in sync with each other, they in essence take over the brain for a brief moment. That is consciousness.

Suppose your senses register some new event. Dr. Dennett says, "Once a particular observation of some feature has been made by a specialized, localized portion of **Multiple drafts form consciousness.** the brain, the information content thus fixed does not have to be sent somewhere else to be rediscriminated by some 'master' discriminator...these spatially and temporally distributed content-fixations in the brain are precisely locatable in both space and time, but their onsets do not mark the onset of consciousness of their content."

5. As with many issues, this one may expose some generational bias as well; Millennials seem to have less of a problem with this than Boomers, for instance.
6. Thanks to Steph Thompson for suggesting this metaphor.

Procrastination vs. Marinating

How can you tell the difference between stewing thoughts in a marinade vs. time-sucking procrastination?

I've always referred to procrastination as "making paper dolls." A close friend (who shall remain nameless) had a major college exam coming up the next day. But instead of studying the night before, she was just sitting on the couch, cutting out long chains of paper dolls. That always seemed to me to be the epitome of procrastination: an unrelated, unproductive activity that blocks the real work you need to do.

But maybe I was wrong. Perhaps that wasn't procrastination at all. It was a highly tactile experience; perhaps it was her version of the marinade after all. She passed the test and went on to graduate with honors.

If the task is something you really just don't want to do, then it's likely that any diversions are simply procrastination. If you're still interested in it but feel "stuck," then the ideas are still stewing, and it's OK.

In other words, recognition has not yet reached a conscious level. He continues, "This stream of contents is only rather like a narrative because of its multiplicity; at any point in time there are multiple 'drafts' of narrative fragments at various stages of editing in various places in the brain." This flow from draft to draft creates what we perceive as narrative.

Dennett's theory is a very interesting alternative to the so-called Cartesian Theater model, where you assume there is a master center of conscious that directs the activities of the brain and hence you. It's sort of like Mike Meyers and Mini-Me or a movie theater screen where consciousness plays out.

But that's probably not the case; the multiple-draft theory supports a more distributed model of processing that's more in line with current research. There is no single source or executive monitor that's calling the shots. Instead, whichever areas are activated together right now form your consciousness. That makes consciousness a bottom-up, self-organizing, perhaps even emergent property.

Let's return to the idea of marinating; as hard as it might be to accept, you need time to allow these multiple drafts to ferment, percolate, and develop. One line of thought will be "current" and experienced as consciousness, but that doesn't mean that all the other drafts are discarded or irrelevant.

Have you heard of the consultant's Rule of Three?[7] In general, if you can't think of three ways a plan can go wrong or think of three different solutions to a problem, then you haven't thought it through enough. You can think of the multiple-drafts model in that light; let at least three alternative ideas ferment and come to consciousness. They are in there already; just let them grow and ripen.

And, yes, that might just mean sitting around and doing nothing. Feet up on the desk. Humming. Eating a crunchy snack.

> TIP 40
> ## Make thinking time.

So, now what do you do with all of this great stuff? Just as you want to go from $\mathcal{R}$-mode to $\mathbf{L}$-mode to productize learning, you want to work with knowledge in a more deliberate way.

Next Actions ⬇

- ☐ What's your favorite recipe for mental marinade? Have you tried others?
- ☐ Have you criticized others for their time spent in the mental marinade? What will you do differently now?
- ☐ Have you been criticized for marinating? How will you respond the next time it happens?

8.3 Manage Your Knowledge

Now it's time to work with your ideas, insights, raw information, and knowledge and transform the whole stewed mess into something transcendent.

But for once, what you need doesn't fit in your brain. You need to augment your processing power.

---

7. From Jerry Weinberg's *The Secrets of Consulting* [Wei85].

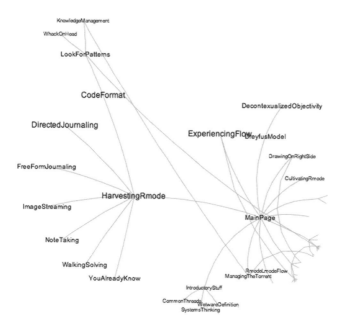

What are all these topics, and why are they all WrittenFunny? Allow me to explain...

Developing Your Exocortex

As I said in Section 3.2, *Capture Insight 24x7*, on page 51, you need to be prepared to capture information anywhere, anytime. But once you've captured it, you can't just let it sit there—that won't do you any good. You need to work with the material: organize it, develop it, coalesce disparate material, and refine and split general ideas into more specific ones.

You need a place to put your thoughts where you can work with them effectively. Thanks to modern technology, I recommend you use some sort of hyperlinked information space that allows easy self-organization and refactoring. But before we delve into the details, let me explain why this is so important.

External support is part of your mind. This is not some mere clerical activity. According to the research into *distributed cognition*, the tools you use for mental support outside your brain become part of your operating mind. As marvelous as the brain is, we can turbocharge it by providing some key external support.

Thomas Jefferson owned somewhere in the neighborhood of 10,000 books in his lifetime.[8] Jefferson was an avid reader, and these books ranged on topics from political philosophy to music to agriculture to wine making. And each book became a little part of his consciousness—probably not the whole thing; most of us don't have encyclopedic memories. It's enough to know you've read about it once and remember where to go find the details.

Albert Einstein knew this well. Supposedly he was once asked how many feet there were in a mile and replied that he wouldn't fill his brain with things that could easily be looked up. That's what reference books are for; that's an efficient use of resources.

Your own book collection, your notes, and even your favorite IDE and programming language all form part of your *exocortex*, which is any mental memory or processing component that resides outside your physical brain. As programmers and knowledge workers, we probably rely on the computer to form more of our exocortex than the general population does. But of course not all computer-based tools are created equal.

For marinating, categorizing, and developing thoughts, I find one of the most effective tools to be a personal wiki. In fact, as we'll see, by organizing your great ideas this way, *you'll get more great ideas.*

Use a Wiki

A traditional wiki (short for Wiki-Wiki-Web) is a style of website that allows anyone to edit each web page using nothing more than a regular web browser. At the bottom of every page is a link labeled *Edit This Page*, as shown in Figure 8.1, on the following page.

Clicking that link presents the contents of that page in an HTML text-editing widget. You can then edit the page and click the Save button, and your changes are now part of that web page. The markup is usually simpler than raw HTML; for instance, you can use * characters to create a bullet list, underscores for italics, and that sort of thing, as shown in Figure 8.2, on page 223. Most important, however, is the ability to link to other pages.

---

8. And donated nearly 7,000 of them to form the core of the Library of Congress in 1815.

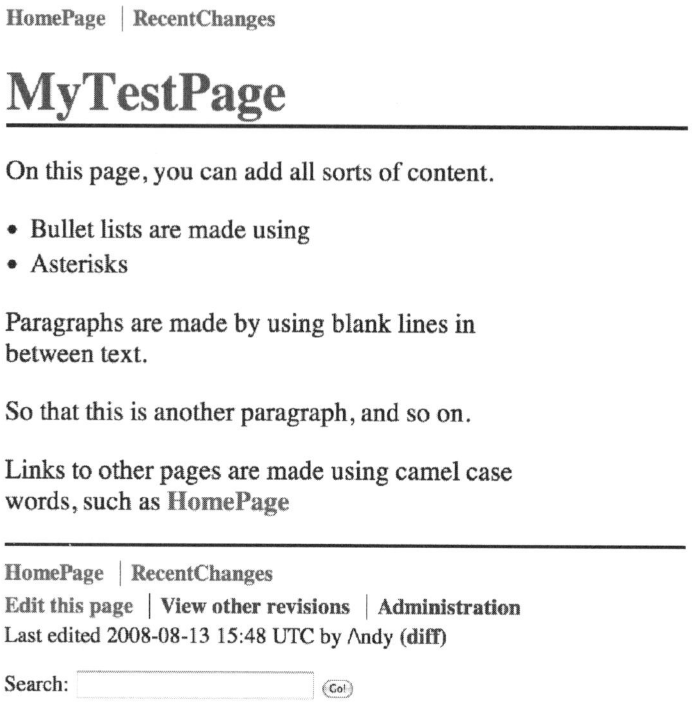

HomePage | RecentChanges

MyTestPage

On this page, you can add all sorts of content.

- Bullet lists are made using
- Asterisks

Paragraphs are made by using blank lines in between text.

So that this is another paragraph, and so on.

Links to other pages are made using camel case words, such as **HomePage**

HomePage | RecentChanges
Edit this page | **View other revisions** | **Administration**
Last edited 2008-08-13 15:48 UTC by Λndy **(diff)**

Search: [_____] (Go!)

Figure 8.1: Displaying a wiki page

You create a new page by first creating a link to it, using a *Wiki-Word*. A WikiWord is a word formed by jamming together two or more words with initial capital letters and no spaces. Once you place a WikiWord on a page, it will automatically become hyper-linked to the wiki page with that name. If one doesn't yet exist, then the first time you click it, you'll be given a blank page and the opportunity to fill it in. This makes it very easy and natural to create new pages.

Use a wiki as a text-based mind map.

But traditional wikis are web-based and have this innate separation between edit and display mode. If you need your wiki to be a web-based app for whatever reason, then that's a fine way to go. But for our purposes here, you might be better off with a slight variation on this technology.

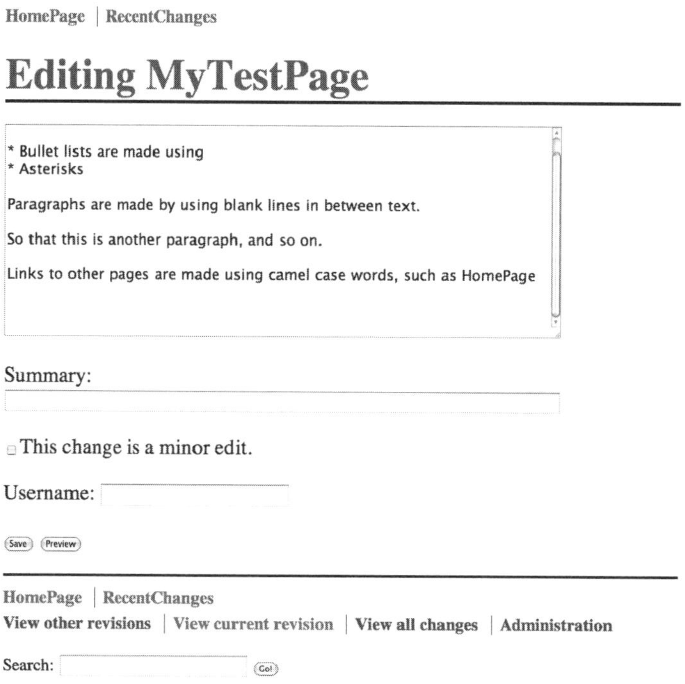

HomePage | RecentChanges

Editing MyTestPage

> * Bullet lists are made using
> * Asterisks
>
> Paragraphs are made by using blank lines in between text.
>
> So that this is another paragraph, and so on.
>
> Links to other pages are made using camel case words, such as HomePage

Summary:

☐ This change is a minor edit.

Username:

(Save) (Preview)

HomePage | RecentChanges
View other revisions | View current revision | **View all changes** | **Administration**

Search: (Go!)

Figure 8.2: EDITING A WIKI PAGE

You can use a wiki implemented in your favorite text editor—a wiki-editing mode. This gives you WikiWord hyperlinks and syntax coloring or highlights within your editor environment. I've used this feature in the vi, XEmacs, and TextMate editors to good effect. A wiki feels like a text-based mind map (and speaking of which, you might well use a mind map to help clarify and augment one section of the wiki).

One of my most successful wiki experiments was setting up a PDA as a synchronized wiki to my desktop. I used a Sharp Zaurus, a small, pocket-sized PDA with a thumb keyboard that runs Linux. I installed the vi editor and wrote some macros to give it hyperlink traversal and syntax highlighting for wiki links and so on. Then, I could synchronize the set of flat files that comprise the wiki using a version control system designed for source code (CVS, in this case).

The result is a portable wiki-in-my-pocket that is versioned and synchronized with my desktop and my laptop. Wherever I am, I have my mental wiki space with me. I can create and augment notes, work on articles or books (including this one), and so on.

While writing this book, I began to move away from the Zaurus and began using an iPod Touch, where I've got a custom Ruby-based web server that offers a more traditional, web-based wiki using this same synchronized wiki database.

You might want to investigate the same sort of thing on your laptop or PDA to free you from having to be at your desk to work your wiki. There are numerous wiki implementations to choose from. For an up-to-date list, take a look at http://en.wikipedia.org/wiki/Personal_Wiki.

> TIP 41
> ### Use a wiki to manage information and knowledge.

The real beauty of this approach is that once you have a place to put a specific bit of information, you'll notice that new, relevant bits of data suddenly start to show up out of nowhere. It's a similar phenomenon to *sense tuning*. For example, if I told you to start looking for the color red at a party, you'd suddenly start to see red everywhere. The same thing happens with a new model car. You're attuned to it, so where you may not have paid attention previously, suddenly the thing you're looking for will jump out at you.

Use sense tuning to collect more thoughts. With a wiki, you may have a random idea and write it down on your home page because you don't know what else to do with it. Some time later, you have a second idea that goes with it, and now you can move the two thoughts off together on their own new page. Now suddenly more things will come up that belong on that page—you have a place to put it, and your mind will happily oblige.

Once you have a place to put some type of thought, *you'll get more thoughts of that type*. Whether it's a wiki or a paper journal, note cards, or shoe boxes, having a place for ideas in a specific topic area or project is a major benefit of an exocortical system.

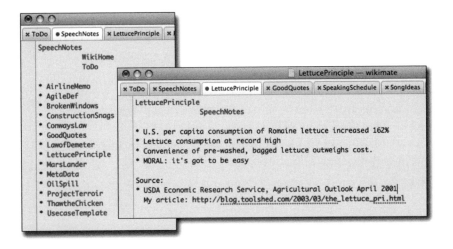

Figure 8.3: WIKI NOTES

For example, take a look at the screenshot in Figure 8.3. This shows my personal wiki format; the title of the page appears at the top of each page, then some convenient links to other wiki pages (such as ToDo) appear. WikiWords, which link to pages of the same name, are highlighted in blue—the same as regular web URLs.

I first came across a neat fact about lettuce consumption and made a page called LettucePrinciple. I heard a great joke/urban legend with the punch line "Thaw the chicken" that I thought might be useful, so I noted it in ThawTheChicken. Then NASA lost a $125M satellite because of a programming error with mismatched units, so I jotted the facts down in MarsLander.

Now that I had a couple of these kinds of thoughts floating around, I made a simple list called SpeechNotes, with the idea that I'd accumulate stuff for presentations from here. I put in ConwaysLaw, the LawofDemeter, OilSpill, and other stuff I'd used already and added a couple new ideas, such as ProjectTerroir. Now LettucePrinciple had a home, a place with similar topics, so I added it to that list. I used it as part of a presentation at a RubyConf on technology adaptation and then a blog posting.[9]

---

9.   See http://blog.toolshed.com/2003/03/the_lettuce_pri.html.

The list grew to several hundred items, which was bad. I started some *wiki gardening* and cleaned things up. I made different lists for blog posts, upcoming presentations, basic stories and research, and so on. Notes for some particular article might reference a half dozen of these pages; a book outline might pull in two dozen. But wikis are useful for more than just this kind of organization.

Transcribing your notes from their original form into the wiki (or cleaning them up in the same wiki) helps get your brain around the material. Just as transcribing notes taken in a meeting or in a class, this provides a second in-depth exposure to the material and more neural reinforcement.

And the more you work with it, the more you may start to see relationships and patterns in the material that you hadn't noticed before. And again, you can go off and mind map some of the more interesting bits to gain insight and bring that back to the wiki.

You'll be able to deliberately look for patterns.

But you want to keep your focus on what you're working on and not get distracted. In the next section, we'll see why.

8.4 Optimize Your Current Context

Context, in the sense we'll talk about it here, is the set of information that is currently loaded into your short-term memory related to the task at hand. In computer terms, it's your working set of pages that have been fetched into memory.

Computers have a distinct advantage over our mental architecture; they are built to swap context easily and naturally.

We aren't built that way. If something interrupts us, breaks our flow, or causes us to lose our focus, it's *really* expensive to drag everything back in. We call that "dragging everything back in" *context switching*. We're going to take a look at why you want to avoid that at all costs, and how to avoid distractions and manage interruptions better.

Context Switching

How much *disposable attention* do you have?[10] That is, how many things are currently demanding your attention, and how many total things can you possibly pay attention to at any given point in time? The ratio is pretty unfavorable.

You can't pay attention to as much as you think you can.

We can't pay attention to too many different things at once, because to change your focus from one item to another means you have to switch context. And unfortunately, our brains just aren't wired to support context switching very well.

Multitasking takes a heavy toll on productivity. One study[11] found that in general, multitasking can cost you 20 to 40 percent of your productivity. Right there, that cuts your eight-hour workday down to five. Other studies bump that number up closer to 50 percent, with a huge increase in errors, as well.

Just to clarify, *multitasking* here refers to performing multiple concurrent tasks at different levels of abstraction. Fixing a couple of bugs while in the same area of code doesn't count as multitasking, nor does returning several similar phone calls or cooking a multicourse meal. You get into trouble when you interrupt your code-fixing session by responding to an unrelated IM, email, or phone call or take a quick peek at a news site.

Unlike computers, our brains don't have a "save stack" or "reload stack" operation. Instead, you have to drag all the bits of memory back in, sort of one-by-one. That **It takes twenty minutes to reload context.** means that if you are deep into a task (such as debugging) and then get interrupted, it can take you an average of twenty minutes to get back into it. Twenty minutes. Consider how many interruptions you may get in a given day; if each interruption requires twenty minutes for you to recover, a good portion of your day is just plain wasted. This could explain why programmers in general hate to be interrupted—especially by nonprogrammers.

---

10. See *Flow: The Psychology of Optimal Experience* [Csi91].
11. See http://www.umich.edu/~bcalab/multitasking.html.

A Problem of Organization

You may have already experienced this problem with email: if you keep separate folders for various topics, what do you do with an email that cuts across the categories you use? Using discrete categories for filing starts to fall down after a while, and no longer is useful. In a wiki, you can get around this by cross-linking topics—it doesn't have to be strictly hierarchical. But with email, you generally can put a message only in a single folder.

Instead, it seems better to not store *any* email in folders. Instead, just have a couple of large buckets (by year or by month perhaps) and rely on some flavor of search technology to find what you need.

You might use *virtual mailboxes* if your email client supports it. This creates mailboxes on the fly based on search criteria you set up. A mail message may appear in multiple virtual mailboxes, which can help you find it when you need to.

Or, you could just use a local search engine. Something like Spotlight on the Mac or Google Desktop.

In today's digital culture, this is part of a larger, dangerous phenomenon known as *cognitive overload*. It's a cocktail of stress, too much multitasking, too many distractions, and the frequent flurry of new data to deal with. Scientists agree that trying to focus on several things at once means you'll do poorly at each of them.[12]

And if that wasn't bad enough, a controversial study done in the United Kingdom noted that if you constantly interrupt your task to check email or respond to an IM text message, your effective IQ drops ten points.

By comparison, smoking a marijuana joint drops your IQ a mere four points (see Figure 8.4, on the next page).

Whatever you do, please don't do *both*.

---

12. There are plenty of mainstream press articles on the topic, such as "Life Interrupted" [Sev04] and "Slow Down, Brave Multitasker, and Don't Read This in Traffic" [Loh07].

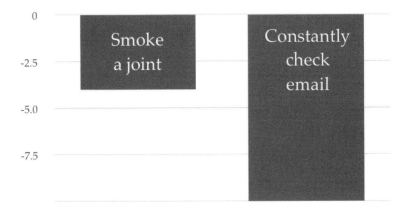

Figure 8.4: RELATIVE IQ POINT LOSS

This makes me wonder if companies should focus less on mandatory drug testing and perhaps instead concentrate on mandatory email-habit testing.[13] But of course it's not just about email and drugs; drivers conversing on cell phones cannot respond quickly to highway hazards, either. Television news channels overflow with different news stories on the main screen, small video insets, and a couple of scrolling headlines, all separated by commercials for dancing toilet paper. From a cognitive science point of view, that's just plain torture.

Given that we're *so bad* at handling multiple things at once and that we are very easily distracted by a myriad of technical marvels, let's take a look at how to avoid some common distractions and stay on task.

Avoiding Distractions

In an episode of *All Things Considered* on NPR, Paul Ford extolled the benefits of a spartan user interface.[14] Consider an early word processor such as WordStar or WordPerfect on an early text-based

---

13. Although it makes a great story, the underpinnings of this study were questionable. See http://itre.cis.upenn.edu/~myl/languagelog/archives/002493.html.
14. "Distracted No More: Going Back to Basics" by Paul Ford, *All Things Considered*, November 23, 2005.

> ### Deliberate Switching
>
> One way to help fight this is to approach context switching more deliberately (notice a trend here?). Instead of just jumping over to an IM or email, make it a deliberate act. Close down what you're working on. Take a couple of deep breaths (we'll talk more about the importance of breathing and email apnea in just a bit). Muster up some curiosity and interest in the new activity. Face it full on and well-armed.

operating system (CP/M, MS-DOS, et al). There were no windows. No mouse. No email, no games. A working setup that is so bland, it turns out to be inspiring. Or more precisely, it's a setup that helps you maintain your focus on the task at hand.

One of my favorite tools for portable writing is my Sharp Zaurus. Toward the end of its life, I ended up taking everything off of it except the vi editor. I took off the wireless card and synchronized it using only the CF memory card. This left me with a device with very few distractions; there is literally nothing else to do on it except write. No games, no email, no Web—just the chapters and bits of text on which you're working. It's spartan but effective.

On a more full-featured system, you can run a specialized application to hide everything except the one application you're currently using. For instance, on the Mac you can use Think![15] to black out every application other than the one that has focus, or DeskTopple,[16] which can hide your desktop icons, replace your wallpaper, and autohide application windows on a timer.

Single-Task Interfaces

Under Mac OS X, you can use the utility QuickSilver to set up globally accessible keystroke-based commands. It reminds me of the terminate-and-stay-resident program SideKick on those early systems.

---

15. Available from http://freeverse.com/apps/app/?id=7013.
16. See http://foggynoggin.com/desktopple.

For instance, I have it rigged so that with just a few keystrokes I can send a one-line email message to someone in my address book. Now on the surface of it, this doesn't sound like much. However, being able to send an email message without bringing up all of Mail is a huge advantage.

Say you're in the middle of some other task. You get the sudden thought that you have to send an email to someone. Perhaps you're in the middle of debugging an application and you realize you will be late for a lunch appointment. You press a few keys, send off the mail, and get back to debugging.

Now compare that to the usual experience.

You're in the middle of debugging, and you realize you have to send an e-mail. You context switch to the Mail application, bring it up, start to send the email, and notice several new emails have come into your inbox, and now the distraction is right in front of you. You will quickly become ensnared by the new email messages and lose your train of debugging thought. Context blown.

In a similar vein, I have Quicksilver rigged so that I can add a line to my to-do list with just a few keystrokes. Otherwise, you run the same risk as with email. You have to turn your context to the to-do list, and as soon as you're there to type in your new entry, you see all the other things you're supposed to be doing, and once again you are distracted.

You can do the same sort of thing in Linux by keeping a small terminal window open with a shell script that will add to your to-do list.

When you have a thought, it's much better to send it to where it belongs—whether that's the to-do list or email—and then get right back to what you're doing.

Organize and Process Tasks Efficiently

While we're talking about streamlining your interface and work habits, we'll have to take an obligatory tangent to discuss GTD.

David Allen's *Getting Things Done: The Art of Stress-Free Productivity* [All02], known by the acronym GTD, is a hugely popular book/method/cult aimed at helping you organize, prioritize, and effectively complete your work.

232 ▶ CHAPTER 8. MANAGE FOCUS

He supplies a methodology and a lot of tips and tricks (who knew a labeler could be so much fun) to help you be more efficient at plowing through tasks.

In terms of the ideas we've looked at here, Allen makes three critical points. The first two have to do with processing email or other inbox-related piles, the last is a more general note:

1. *Scan the input queue only once*: Whatever input queue you are dealing with, be it in an email inbox, voicemail, or paper inbox, don't use the arrival box as a storage device. Go through and sort the new arrivals into whatever piles are necessary, but don't keep rescanning the same old stuff in the input queue. If it's something that can be dispatched in less than two minutes, then do it and get it over with, or pawn it off on someone else entirely if you can (aka delegation). Constantly reviewing the same 1,000 inbox messages to work on the last 20 important ones just wastes your time and mental energy.

2. *Process each pile of work in order*: Once you have your piles, work them. Stay on task, and avoid context switching. As we saw earlier, switching to another task will blow your mental stack, and you'll lose more time as you get back into the task. We programmer types are highly susceptible to being distracted by shiny things. Stick to your pile.

3. *Don't keep lists in your head*: Allen spots another important aspect of maintaining an exocortex. Dynamic refresh of mental lists is *very* expensive. Instead, keep to-do lists and such somewhere in your exocortex—on a sticky note, in a wiki, in a calendaring or dedicated to-do list tool, or in something similar.

The GTD method has a lot of fans, and if effective prioritizing and task organization are the sort of thing you have trouble with, GTD might help.

8.5 Manage Interruptions Deliberately

Even the best organized to-do lists and daily plans will not help insulate you from distractions, however. Everyone is subject to distractions, but these days we have a wider selection of distractions than ever.

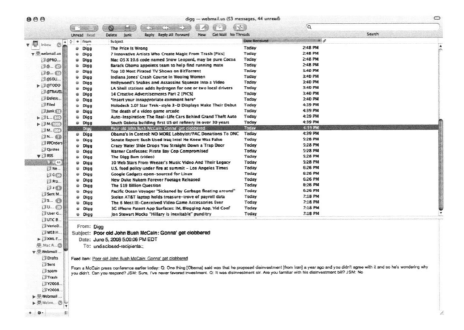

Figure 8.5: A MAZE OF TWISTY LITTLE PASSAGES, ALL ALIKE

The Net offers the widest assortment of distraction in history. Everything from the usual disgust at greedy, rapacious spammers to a cool how-to make your own snow-making-machine video on YouTube; inflammatory Digg postings about yet more election fraud or thieving politicians (as shown in Figure 8.5); a couple of IMs from your closest friends; and a dozen new Wikipedia articles—all there to entice, inform, and distract you.

Here are some suggestions to help cut down on interruptions from your team, your communication channels, and yourself.

Set Project Rules of Engagement

When is it OK to interrupt your teammates with a question, to ask for help tracking down a bug, or to request an impromptu code review? When is it OK for them to interrupt you? How about emergencies from your manager?

These are all valid questions, and the best way to manage them is to provide answers up front—before the project begins. Set up certain

Can't All Be Winners

Not every day will be a productive day. If events turn chaotic, it might be more effective to acknowledge that and realize you're just not going to get in the groove. Fight the fires, enjoy the pizza at your desk, and hope for a better tomorrow.

times of the day as work sessions where you are not to be interrupted. Set up other times for collaboration, daily stand-up meetings,[17] and the usual assortment of unanticipated contingencies.

Maybe you are freshest in the mornings or perhaps late in the day. However you manage to work it out, at least you'll have one portion of the day where you can actually be productive. I've heard from teams who have created email-free afternoons or entire days: no email, no phone calls, no interruptions. The developers involved said these were the most productive, happiest times of the week.

> ### Tip 42
> Establish rules of engagement to manage interruptions.

So establish the rules of engagement (really, the rules of interruption) for your team early in the project.

Rein in Email

But not everyone plays by the rules. Your teammates in close proximity will honor the rules you've set up, but what about co-workers in remote offices or all the people you might deal with from other companies, customers, and all the rest of the sea of humanity that's on the other end of an email, IM, or phone call?

You can't get the whole world to play by your schedule.

Or can you?

---

17. See *Practices of an Agile Developer: Working in the Real World* [SH06].

Beware of Email Apnea

In February 2008, Linda Stone coined the term *email apnea*. One morning, she noticed, "I've just opened my email, and there's nothing out of the ordinary there. It's the usual daily flood of schedule, project, travel, information, and junk mail. Then I notice...I'm holding my breath."

email apnea: a temporary absence or suspension of breathing, or shallow breathing, while doing email.*

Shallow breathing, hyperventilating, or holding your breath altogether are not just mere inconveniences or odd side effects; not breathing normally and deeply can be seriously damaging to your health. Bad breathing contributes to stress-related diseases, fires up parts of your flight-or-fright response, dumps glucose into your bloodstream, and has a host of other unfortunate effects.

Does the anticipatory stress of email affect your breathing? How about a program crash or tracing through a debugger? Or any other common scenario on the computer?

If you find any of these affect your breathing, just sit back and take a deep breath. Every time.

---

*. See http://www.huffingtonpost.com/linda-stone/just-breathe-building-th_b_85651.html.

You are more in charge of email than you think; it's up to you as to how often you pick up and respond to email. Here's something to try: limit your email handling to specific, scheduled times during the day—probably not first thing, though. Set a time, pick up and prioritize your email, and time-box it. Move on to real work after some fixed time. It can be a hard discipline to maintain, but I have some tips that might help.

First, fix your email announcement. A bouncing icon is irresistible; it begs to be clicked. So too is an endless stream of unreasonably chipper "You've got mail" pronouncements. If you can, turn it all off. At a minimum, play a sound only on important messages, such as those from your spouse or boss.

Second, bump up the polling interval. Don't poll for mail every minute or sit there like a lab rat constantly clicking the Get Mail button in hopes of a treat.[18]

Next, be aware that you are setting the expectation on reply speed and email quantity. Remember the Golden Rule of Email:

TIP 43

Send less email, and you'll receive less email.

On top of that, remember that you're in control of the pace; you can set the tempo:

TIP 44

Choose your own tempo for an email conversation.

Your email reply speed sets the tempo for the conversation. That is, the faster you reply, the faster you are expected to reply in the future. Send fewer emails, less often, and you'll take the frantic pace down to a more reasonable level.

Finally, the best advice for email is *out of sight, out of mind.* Exit your email client when not in use.

Context-Friendly Breaks

So, you've been plugging away for awhile, and you feel you're getting stuck or bored or just need a break. You have a couple of choices.

You can turn away from the computer and start idly doodling on a blank piece of paper. This is a distraction but a minor one. You can go for a walk—as long as you don't encounter anyone else who starts a conversation, then just walking by itself remains pretty context-friendly.

Or you could check out what's on the front page at CNN, Digg, or Slashdot, and so on. That's a major distraction. Or worse, you might check your email. Now you're guaranteed to lose your train

---

18. Actually, that isn't so far-fetched, according to some studies. Whether it's a pellet or a good email, you'll keep hitting the button. It's called *intermittent variable reward reinforcement,* and we fall for it just like the pigeons and lab rats.

of thought and a minimum of twenty to thirty minutes lost productivity once you try to get back into it, *if* you even get a chance to get back to it today.

One way to try to keep in context is to raise the *physical* cost of entry and exit to help remind you of the hidden *mental* cost. For instance, if you can easily flip open and close your laptop, constantly slipping in and out of context, then you will. But if it's a pain to leave your environment and then come back to it, maybe you'll be less tempted.

Make the cost obvious.

My office is set up such that there are many light switches that I go around and turn on. I take a few minutes to pick something fun to listen to while I'm working. Having made this investment, set everything up, and sort of settled myself in, I'm less likely to jump up on a whim, turn everything off, leave, come back, and do it all over again. Once I'm installed, I'm there for a while.

The laptop works the same way—if I just flip it open on battery power for a few minutes, I'm not likely to stay there long. If I set up with a power cord, laptop chiller pad, and so on, I've made a bit more commitment. It's not a lot, granted, but it does help remind me of the cost of entry and exit.

Enable Maskable Interrupts

In CPU terms, interrupts come in two flavors: *maskable* and *nonmaskable*. A *maskable interrupt* can be ignored. Those are the sort we want to emulate.

> **TIP 45**
>
> Mask interrupts to maintain focus.

There's a reason your phone is equipped with voicemail and possibly a Do Not Disturb (DND) button. Folks have let phone calls roll over to voicemail (or answering machines) ever since 1935, for good reason.

IM follows the same dynamic—don't answer if you're busy. Call them back when *you* are ready so you don't lose all the context you've laboriously assembled.

Put a sign on your cube during a debugging session, or close the door if you have one.

Save Your Stack

Possibly the best thing you can do if you think you're going to get interrupted is to *prepare* to be interrupted. There's a lot of interest in the scientific community on task interruption and resumption. There are two time periods of interest: the *interruption lag* and the *resumption lag.*

Prepare to be interrupted. Once you've started a task, you proceed along until some interrupt comes in. This is the *alert* that you'll soon need to start a secondary task. The time between the alert and the start of the next task is the interruption lag. Now you proceed on the new task for a while and at some point switch back to the original task. The time it takes you to get back up to speed is the resumption lag.

When the alert first comes in, you know you're being interrupted. You have a precious few seconds before the interruption takes hold, before you have to answer the phone or respond to the person in your doorway. In those few seconds, you need to leave some "bread-crumbs" for yourself. That is, you want to leave cues that you can pick up on once you get back to resuming the task.

For instance, suppose I'm writing an email message or writing an article. I'm in the middle of expressing some thought, and I get interrupted. I will often quickly jam out a couple of words—not a full sentence—just to remind myself of the thought I was working on. It seems to help, and there's a lot of research on this sort of cue preparation.[19,20]

Further, if you assume you can get interrupted at just about any point, you can begin to make a habit of constantly leaving little reminders of where you are.

---

19. *Preparing to Resume an Interrupted Task: Effects of Prospective Goal Encoding and Retrospective Rehearsal* [TABM03].
20. *Task Interruption: Resumption Lag and the Role of Cues* [AT04].

8.6 Keep a Big Enough Context

The more you can keep information in context, the better. Personally, this is why I tend to have a lot of piles on or near my office desk. I call that context. The cleaners call it "a mess."

But often "out of sight" means "out of mind." I need the pertinent things that I'm working on close at hand—in my mental *working set*, if you will, out on the desk where I can see them all at a glance, easily.

And in fact, keeping task-related items in context can be a huge benefit. You can instantly realize productivity gains of 20 to 30 percent just by getting yourself a second monitor, regardless of how you measure productivity.[21]

> Get an instant productivity gain of 20 to 30 percent.

Why is that?

Instead of the *desktop* metaphor, what you really have is closer to the *crowded airline seat* metaphor as decried by Frederick Brooks years ago. On a nice big desktop, you can spread out your work and see what you're doing—all at once. In a crowded airline seat, you don't have enough room to see more than one document (or one portion of a document) at once. You have to shuffle papers back and forth constantly.

I dare you to go to Staples or Office Depot and find an office desk that measure 17 inches diagonally. You can't, because that's a ludicrously small dimension for an office desk. And yet, most monitors are in the 17-to-21-inch range. And that's where we do all of our work. On a small screen, you have to switch between active windows and applications all the time because you can't keep enough context in such a small space.

Do you know what Alt-Tab (or Command-Tab on Mac) is called? It's a *context switch*. And as we've seen, context switching kills productivity. Even a small action like using Alt-Tab to switch between windows that aren't all visible takes time and requires short-term memory and energy.

---

21. According to a Jon Peddie Research survey, "Whether you measure productivty in facts researched, alien spaceships vaporized, or articles written," quoted in *The Virtues of a Second Screen* [Ber06].

Task vs. Topic

Think about the applications you write. Do you organize the UI and architecture by task or by topic? What would happen if you reorganized the UI by task? Would your users be deliriously happy?

 There are many tasks I can still manage on the laptop, but there are some tasks that I simply *have* to do on my dual-head, 23-inch displays. It's important that the two monitors are the same size and brand; you don't want to be distracted by having to refocus on a smaller monitor or adjust to a different color temperature.

Many of the more progressive companies I've visited lately not only offer free snacks and sodas but have also standardized on multi-monitor setups.

TIP 46

Use multiple monitors to avoid context switching.

Maintain Task Focus

With all that screen real estate, it's easy to open a bazillion applications and once again get lost in the clutter.

On most modern OSs, you can use a *virtual desktop* switcher. This allows you to have a number of different screens set up such that you can then switch between them using a special keystroke. Each screen is independent of the others and is called a *workspace*. The secret is in how you divvy up applications among the workspaces.

Use virtual desktops.

At first, I organized it by application: I had all my browser windows in one workspace, all my terminals in another, and so on. When I realized that this arrangement caused even *more* switching around than before, I then reorganized it according to task.

Figure 8.6: MAC OS X SPACES

Just as an example, here is how I usually have my workspaces set up now (see Figure 8.6):

Communications: I use this workspace for any communication, scheduling, or planning-related task, with the following windows. Because this contains the most disruptive apps, I try really hard not to let these "leak out" to other workspaces.

- Email
- To-do list
- Chat
- Calendar
- Project status dashboards—current author status, book production schedule, and so on

Writing: When I'm writing, I don't want to be distracted by email and such, so I keep this workspace populated solely with writing tools.

- TextMate (editor)
- Dictionary/Thesaurus
- OmniGraffle (diagram editor)
- Acrobat Reader (for proofing)

Coding: This is the same idea as writing but with different tools. This workspace usually has a fair number of terminal windows open; I usually start with a couple in different aspect ratios:

- One normal one
- One normal height but really wide
- One normal width but really tall

Starting with these windows already open just saves a little time; when you need it, it's there for you. The contents of this workspace will vary considerably depending on the language and environment you're writing for, but you'd at least have your code editor or IDE, perhaps a unit testing GUI, various browser windows for the app or related documentation, terminal windows with log files, make or ant processes, and so on.

Surfing: I keep one whole workspace for surfing (aka "research"), including any helper-apps that might pop up.

- Browser windows
- Acrobat, QuickTime, RealPlayer, and so on

Music: And of course, man does not live by business alone. You gotta have some tunes when you're coding, answering emails, or whatever.

Controlling the music needs to be transparent: you want to control volume, play/pause, and so on, instantly when the phone rings or someone comes in the office. Some keyboards now have built-in music controls, or you can set up hotkeys.

Sometimes I use an external control surface (having dedicated buttons instead of Ctrl-Alt-Shift-Meta-F13 for pause is a real luxury and incredibly convenient). You can use a MacBook remote as well.

This is also the workspace where I leave all my music hobby apps (that's the reason for the availability of a control surface). That way they aren't right in front of me to tempt me away from work, but I can jump in quickly and play when I finally get a spare moment. If you're into gaming, this might the workspace where you leave a game open.

> **TIP 47**
>
> Optimize your personal workflow to maximize context.

8.7 How to Stay Sharp

In this chapter, we've looked at a lot of issues around the idea of focus and attention. I have encouraged you to pursue meditation as a tool for mental sharpness and clarity, extolled the virtues of maintaining an exocortex, and warned against the dangers of distraction.

So, what does it take to stay sharp? The biggest thing is self-awareness—remembering that you need to deliberately work at staying sharp. Left to our own devices, our default settings aren't ideal for programming and knowledge work.

If nothing else, remember to do these three things:

1. Learn to quiet your chattering **L**-mode.

2. Deliberately work with and add to thoughts in progress, even if they aren't "done" yet.

3. Be aware of just how expensive context switching can be, and avoid it in all its myriad forms.

If you start trying to tackle at least these areas, you will be well on your way to managing your focus and taking control of your attention.

Next Actions ⬇

- ☐ Think of routine things that you need to do that tend to distract you. Is there any way to streamline them to get them done without exposing additional distractions?
- ☐ Figure out when your most productive coding time occurs, and arrange to limit distractions during that time.
- ☐ Keep track of "down" vs. "thinking" time; take care not to confuse the two.
- ☐ How easy is it for you to get pulled away—or to pull yourself away—from your work? Can you make it harder to pull away so you can stay focused more easily?
- ☐ Observe experts, if there are any on your team, and see what they do to avoid distraction.

The real voyage of discovery consists not in seeking new landscapes, but in having new eyes.
▶ Marcel Proust

Chapter 9

Beyond Expertise

Thank you for taking this journey with me. Some of you have heard this material in talks, presentations, and keynotes over the past few years. I don't profess to be an expert in any of these subjects, but maybe if I stick with it awhile, I'll progress beyond competence.

So now what?

You've read through my various observations and occasional insights, you've been jazzed by a few good ideas and maybe confused by others, but I hope you've gotten "new eyes" and somewhere have the germ of an intention—of what you want to do next. But like everything we've looked at here, you need to approach this deliberately. So, let me suggest a few things that might help you achieve change, take a look at where to start, and, finally, see what lies beyond expertise.

9.1 Effective Change

Your brain is not necessarily going to cooperate with us on this venture. While your mind has an intention to learn, your physical brain is trying to keep things, well, lean. Like an overactive housekeeper, if the brain doesn't think this is emotionally charged content, valuable to your survival, out it goes. It's relegated to the same pile as the morning drive to work that we talked about earlier. So, you have to convince your brain that this is important. You have to *care*. Now that we have your attention....

Practice makes permanent.

Change is always harder than it looks—that's a physical reality, not just an aphorism. An old, ingrained habit makes the equivalent of a neural highway in your brain. These old habits don't go away. You can make new neural highways alongside, going a different route and making shortcuts, but the old highways remain. They are always there for you to revert to—to fall back on. Practice may not make perfect, but it sure makes permanent.

Realize that these old habits will remain, and if you revert to one, don't be too hard on yourself. It's how you're wired. Just acknowledge the lapse, and move on with your new intention. It will surely happen again; just be aware of when it does, and get back on the right path again. It's the same thing whether you're changing your learning habits, quitting smoking, or losing weight.

The topic of change, be it personal or organizational, is huge and complex.[1] Appreciate that it's not easy, but it does yield to consistent effort. Here are just a couple of suggestions to help you manage effective change:

Start with a plan.

Block out some time, and fight for it. Keep track of what you've accomplished, and review your accomplishments when you feel you haven't done enough. You've probably come further than you think. This is a great use of your exocortex: use a journal, a wiki, or a web app to track your progress.

Inaction is the enemy, not error.

Remember the danger doesn't lie in doing something wrong; it lies in doing nothing at all. Don't be afraid to make mistakes.

New habits take time.

It takes something like a minimum of three weeks of performing a new activity before it becomes habit. Maybe longer. Give it a fair chance.

Belief is real.

As we've seen throughout, your thoughts will physically alter the wiring in your brain and your brain chemistry. You have

---

1. For more on effective organizational change patterns, see *Fearless Change: Patterns for Introducing New Ideas* [MR05].

to believe that change is possible. If you think you'll fail, you'll be correct.

Take small, next steps.

Start with the low-hanging fruit. Set up a small, achievable goal, and reward yourself for reaching it. "Rinse and repeat": set up the next small step. Take one step at a time, keeping your big goal in mind but not trying to map out *all* the steps it takes to get there. Just the next one. Learn what you need to know for the goals further out once you get closer to them.

9.2 What to Do Tomorrow Morning

In any new venture, there's a certain amount of inertia. As an object at rest, I have a tendency to remain there. Moving in a new direction means I have to overcome inertial resistance.

> *Whatever you can do, or dream you can do, begin it. Boldness has genius, power, and magic in it. Begin it now*
>
> ▶ *Faust*, Johann Wolfgang von Goethe

Just start! It doesn't particularly matter what you choose to start with, but start something from this book deliberately, first thing tomorrow morning.

Here's a suggested checklist of some possible first steps:

- ☐ Start taking responsibility; don't be afraid to ask "why?" or "how do you know?" or "how do I know?" or to answer "I don't know—yet."
- ☐ Pick two things that will help you maintain context and avoid interruption, and start doing them right away.
- ☐ Create a Pragmatic Investment Plan, and set up SMART goals.
- ☐ Figure out where you are on the novice-to-expert spectrum in your chosen profession and what you might need to progress. Be honest. Do you need more recipes or more context? More rules or more intuition?
- ☐ Practice. Having trouble with a piece of code? Write it five different ways.
- ☐ Plan on making more mistakes—mistakes are good. Learn from them.

☐ Keep a notebook on you (unlined paper, preferably). Doodle. Mind map. Take notes. Keep your thoughts loose and flowing.

☐ Open up your mind to aesthetics and additional sensory input. Whether it's your cubicle, your desktop, or your code, pay attention to how "pleasing" it is.

☐ Start your personal wiki on things you find interesting.

☐ Start blogging. Comment on the books you've read.[2] Read more books, and you'll have more to write about. Use SQ3R and mind maps.

☐ Make thoughtful walking a part of your day.

☐ Start a book-reading group.

☐ Get a second monitor, and start using a virtual desktop.

☐ Go through the "next actions" for each chapter and try them.

I've barely scratched the surface on a variety of really interesting topics, and researchers are discovering new things and disproving old ideas all the time. If anything I've suggested here doesn't work out for you, don't worry about it, and move on. There's plenty more to try.

9.3 Beyond Expertise

Finally, after all this talk about expertise and becoming more expert, what lies *beyond* the expert? In an oddly circular way, the most sought-after thing you want to achieve after becoming an expert is...the beginner's mind.

> *In the beginner's mind there are many possibilities, but in the expert's there are few.*
> ▶ Shunryo Suzuki-Roshi

The professional kiss of death for an expert is to *act* like one. Once you believe in your own expertness, you close your mind to possibilities. You stop acting on curiosity. You may begin to resist change in your field for fear of losing authority on a subject you've spent so long mastering. Your own judgment and views, instead of supporting you, can imprison you.

---

2. And of course, I'd really appreciate it if you mentioned this book. Please use this link if you do: http://pragprog.com/titles/ahptl. Thanks in advance.

I've seen a lot of this over the years. Folks invest heavily in some language, say, Java, or C++ before it.[3] They get all the certifications; they memorize the fifteen lineal feet of books on the API and related tools. Then some new language comes around that lets them write programs much more concisely and more intuitively, test more thoroughly, achieve greater concurrency more easily, and so on. And they don't want any part of it. They'll spend more energy deriding the newcomer than in seriously evaluating it for their needs.

That's not the kind of expert you want to become.

Instead, always keep a "beginner's" mind. Ask "what if?" You want to emulate a child's insatiable curiosity, full of wonder and amazement. Maybe this new language is really cool. Or maybe this other, newer language is. Maybe I can learn something from this cool object-oriented operating system, even if I never intend to use it.

Approach learning without preconceived notions, prior judgment, or a fixed viewpoint. See things exactly as they are—just as a child would.

Wow. This is cool. I wonder how it works? What *is* it?

Be aware of your own reaction to new technology, new ideas, or things you don't know about. Self-awareness is key to becoming an expert—and beyond—but it falls prey to the "old-habit-neural-highway" problem.

Be aware of yourself, of the present moment, and of the context in which you're operating. I think the biggest rea-

Be aware.

son that any of us fail is that we have a tendency to put things on autopilot. Unless we sense some new and novel attribute, we zone out. Leonardo da Vinci complained about this 600 years ago: "People look without seeing, hear without listening, eat without awareness of taste, touch without feeling, and talk without thinking." We remain guilty of this all the time: we scoff down a hurried meal on the go without actually tasting or savoring it;

---

3. I'd mention C programmers, except that they all *stayed* C programmers through the years.

we hear users or sponsors tell us precisely what they want in a product, but we don't listen. We look all the time without seeing. We presume we already know.

In the novel *The Girl with the Pearl Earring*, the author describes a fictional account of the painter Vermeer and a serving girl who may have inspired one of Vermeer's most well-known paintings (and the title of the book). In the story, Vermeer takes to teaching the girl how to paint. He asks her to describe the dress a young lady is wearing. She replies that it is yellow. Vermeer feigns amazement: is it really? She looks again, a little more carefully, and then says, well, it has some brown flecks as well. Is that all you see? asks Vermeer. Now the girl studies the dress more intently. No, she says, it has flecks of green and brown, a bit of silver on the edge from a nearby reflection, specks of black where openness of the weave shows the garment underneath, darker yellow where the shadows of the folds of the dress fall, and so on.

When the girl first sees the dress, she reports merely that it is "yellow." Vermeer challenges the girl to see the world as he sees it: full of marvelous complexity and rich, subtle nuances. That's the challenge we all face—to see the world that way and to continue to see that world—and ourselves—fully.

> *"Eternal vigilance is the price of liberty."*
> ▶ Popular phrase after John Philpot Curran, 1790

Not only is eternal vigilance the price of liberty, but it's the price of awareness as well. As soon as you go on autopilot, you're not steering anymore. Maybe that's OK on a long straight highway, but life more often resembles a twisty, narrow road like the Road to Hana in Maui. You need to con-stantly reevaluate yourself and your condition, lest habits and past wisdom blind you to the reality in front of you.

Tip 48

Grab the wheel. You can't steer on autopilot.

Go ahead and grab the wheel. You have everything you need: the same brain as Einstein, Jefferson, Poincaré, or Shakespeare. You have more facts, fictions, and viewpoints at your fingertips than at any other time in history.

Best of luck, and let me know how it goes.

My email address is andy@pragprog.com. Let me know what worked really well for you and what fell flat. Point me to your new blog or that great open source project you've started. Scan and email me that cool mind map you made. Post to the forums at forums.pragprog.com. This is just the beginning.

Thanks,

Photo Credits

Portrait of a wizard, 1977, marker on cardboard by Michael C. Hunt.

Man with hat, 2007, pen and ink by Michael C. Hunt.

Portrait of Henri Poincaré, public domain image courtesy of Wikipedia.com.

Portrait of John Stuart Mill, public domain image courtesy of Wikipedia.com.

Photo of labyrinth at Grace Cathedral copyright Karol Gray, reprinted with permission.

Photo of labyrinth etched in marble copyright Don Joski, reprinted with permission.

Photo of plunge sheep dip copyright 1951 C. Goodwin, reprinted under the terms of Creative Commons Attribution 3.0.

Photo of Mark II engineer's log courtesy of the U.S. Naval Historical Center.

Screen shot of PocketMod courtesy of Chad Adams, reprinted with permission.

Diagram of affinity grouping copyright Johanna Rothman and Esther Derby, reprinted with permission.

Figure of representational system predicates courtesy of Bobby G. Bodenhamer, at www.neurosemantics.com, reprinted with permission.

Pencil illustrations by the author.

Except as noted, remaining photographs courtesy of iStockPhoto.com.

Appendix B

Bibliography

[AIT99]   F. G. Ashby, A. M. Isen, and A. U. Turken. A neuro-psychological theory of positive affect and its influence on cognition. *Psychological Review*, (106):529–550, 1999.

[All02]   David Allen. *Getting Things Done: The Art of Stress-Free Productivity.* Simon and Schuster, New York, 2002.

[Ari08]   Dan Ariely. *Predictably Irrational: The Hidden Forces That Shape Our Decisions.* HarperCollins, New York, 2008.

[AT04]   Erik M. Altmann and J. Gregory Trafton. Task interruption: Resumption lag and the role of cues. *Proceedings of the 26th Annual Conference of the Cognitive Science Society*, 2004.

[BB96]   Tony Buzan and Barry Buzan. *The Mind Map Book: How to Use Radiant Thinking to Maximize Your Brain's Untapped Potential.* Plume, New York, 1996.

[Bec00]   Kent Beck. *Extreme Programming Explained: Embrace Change.* Addison-Wesley, Reading, MA, 2000.

[Bei91]   Paul C. Beisenherz. Explore, invent, and apply. *Science and Children*, 28(4):30–32, Jan 1991.

[Ben01]   Patricia Benner. *From Novice to Expert: Excellence and Power in Clinical Nursing Practice.* Prentice Hall, Englewood Cliffs, NJ, commemorative edition, 2001.

[Ber96]   Albert J. Bernstein. *Dinosaur Brains: Dealing with All Those Impossible People at Work.* Ballantine Books, New York, 1996.

[Ber06]   Ivan Berger. The virtues of a second screen. *New York Times*, April 20 2006.

[Bre97]   Bill Breen. The 6 myths of creativity. *Fast Company*, Dec 19 1997.

[Bro86]   Frederick Brooks. No silver bullet—essence and accident in software engineering. *Proceedings of the IFIP Tenth World Computing Conference*, 1986.

[BS85]   Benjamin Samuel Bloom and Lauren A. Sosniak. *Developing Talent in Young People.* Ballantine Books, New York, 1st edition, 1985.

[BW90]   H. Black and A. Wolf. Knowledge and competence: Current issues in education and training. *Careers and Occupational Information Centre*, 1990.

[Cam02]   Julia Cameron. *The Artist's Way.* Tarcher, New York, 2002.

[CAS06]   Mark M. Churchland, Afsheen Afshar, and Krishna V. Shenoy. A central source of movement variability. *Neuron*, 52:1085–1096, Dec 2006.

[Cia01]   Robert B. Cialdini. *Influence: Science and Practice.* Allyn and Bacon, Boston, MA, 4th ed edition, 2001.

[Cla00]   Guy Claxton. *Hare Brain, Tortoise Mind: How Intelligence Increases When You Think Less.* Harper Perennial, New York, 2000.

[Cla04]   Mike Clark. *Pragmatic Project Automation. How to Build, Deploy, and Monitor Java Applications.* The Pragmatic Programmers, LLC, Raleigh, NC, and Dallas, TX, 2004.

[Con01]   Hans Conkel. *How to Open Locks with Improvised Tools.* Level Four, Reno, NV, 2001.

[Csi91]   Mihaly Csikszentmihalyi. *Flow: The Psychology of Optimal Experience.* Harper Perennial, New York, NY, 1991.

[Dan94]   M. Danesi. The neuroscientific perspective in second language acquisition research. *International Review of Applied Linguistics*, (22):201–228, 1994.

[DB72]   Edward De Bono. *PO: a Device for Successful Thinking*. Simon and Schuster, New York, 1972.

[DB73]   J. M. Darley and C. D. Batson. From jerusalem to jericho: A study of situational and dispositional variables in helping behavior. *Journal of Personality and Social Psychology*, (27):100–108, 1973.

[DD79]   Hubert Dreyfus and Stuart Dreyfus. The scope, limits, and training implications of three models of aircraft pilot emergency response behavior. *Unpublished*, 1979.

[DD86]   Hubert Dreyfus and Stuart Dreyfus. *Mind Over Machine: The Power of Human Intuition and Expertise in the Era of the Computer*. Free Press, New York, 1986.

[Den93]   Daniel C. Dennett. *Consciousness Explained*. Penguin Books Ltd, New York, NY, 1993.

[Doi07]   Norman Doidge. *The Brain That Changes Itself: Stories of Personal Triumph from the Frontiers of Brain Science*. Viking, New York, 2007.

[Dru54]   Peter F. Drucker. *The Practice of Management*. Perennial Library, New York, 1st perennial library ed edition, 1954.

[DSZ07]   Rosemary D'Alesio, Maureen T. Scalia, and Renee Zabel. Improving vocabulary acquisition with multisensory instruction. Master's thesis, Saint Xavier University, Chicago, 2007.

[Dwe08]   Carol S. Dweck. *Mindset: The New Psychology of Success*. Ballantine Books, New York, 2008 ballantine books trade pbk. ed edition, 2008.

[Edw01]   Betty Edwards. *The New Drawing on the Right Side of the Brain*. HarperCollins, New York, 2001.

[FCF07]   Fitzsimons, Chartrand, and Fitzsimons. Automatic effects of brand exposure on motivated behavior: How apple makes you "think different". http://faculty.fuqua.duke.edu/%7Egavan/GJF_articles/brand_exposure_JCR_inpress.pdf, 2007.

[Fow05] Chad Fowler. *My Job Went To India: 52 Ways to Save Your Job*. The Pragmatic Programmers, LLC, Raleigh, NC, and Dallas, TX, 2005.

[Gal97] W. Timothy Gallwey. *The Inner Game of Tennis*. Random House, New York, rev. ed edition, 1997.

[Gar93] Howard Gardner. *Frames of Mind: The Theory of Multiple Intelligences*. BasicBooks, New York, NY, 10th anniversary ed edition, 1993.

[GG86] Barry Green and W. Timothy Gallwey. *The Inner Game of Music*. Anchor Press/Doubleday, Garden City, NY, 1st edition, 1986.

[GHJV95] Erich Gamma, Richard Helm, Ralph Johnson, and John Vlissides. *Design Patterns: Elements of Reusable Object-Oriented Software*. Addison-Wesley, Reading, MA, 1995.

[GP81] William J. J. Gordon and Tony Poze. Conscious/subconscious interaction in a creative act. *The Journal of Creative Behavior*, 15(1), 1981.

[Gra04] Paul Graham. *Hackers and Painters: Big Ideas from the Computer Age*. O'Reilly & Associates, Inc, Sebastopol, CA, 2004.

[Haw04] Jeff Hawkins. *On Intelligence*. Times Books, New York, 2004.

[Hay81] John R. Hayes. *The Complete Problem Solver*. Franklin Institute Press, Philadelphia, Pa., 1981.

[HCR94] Elaine Hatfield, John T. Cacioppo, and Richard L. Rapson. *Emotional Contagion*. Cambridge University Press, Cambridge, 1994.

[HS97] J. T. Hackos and D. M. Stevens. *Standards for Online Communication*. John Wiley and Sons, Inc., New York, 1997.

[HS07] Neil Howe and William Strauss. The next 20 years: How customer and workforce attitudes will evolve. *Harvard Business Review*, July 2007.

[HT00]   Andrew Hunt and David Thomas. *The Pragmatic Pro-
            grammer: From Journeyman to Master.* Addison-Wesley,
            Reading, MA, 2000.

[HT03]   Andrew Hunt and David Thomas. *Pragmatic Unit Test-
            ing In Java with JUnit.* The Pragmatic Programmers,
            LLC, Raleigh, NC, and Dallas, TX, 2003.

[HT04]   Andrew Hunt and David Thomas. Imaginate. *Software
            Construction,* 21(5):96–97, Sep-Oct 2004.

[HwMH06]   Andrew Hunt and David Thomas with Matt Hargett.
            Pragmatic Unit Testing In C# with NUnit, 2nd Ed. The
            Pragmatic Programmers, LLC, Raleigh, NC, and Dallas,
            TX, 2006.

[Jon07]   Rachel Jones. Learning to pay attention. *Public Library
            of Science: Biology,* 5(6):166, June 2007.

[KB84]   David Keirsey and Marilyn M. Bates. *Please Understand
            Me: Character and Temperament Types.* Distributed by
            Prometheus Nemesis Book Co., Del Mar, CA, 5th ed edi-
            tion, 1984.

[KD99]   Justin Kruger and David Dunning. "unskilled and
            unaware of it: How difficulties in recognizing one's own
            incompetence lead to inflated self-assessments". *Jour-
            nal of Personality and Social Psychology,* 77(6):1121–
            1134, 1999.

[Ker99]   Joshua Kerievsky. Knowledge hydrant: a pattern lan-
            guage for study groups. http://www.industriallogic.com/
            papers/khdraft.pdf, 1999.

[KK95]   M. Kurosu and K. Kashimura. Apparent usability vs.
            inherent usability: Experimental analysis on the deter-
            minants of the apparent usability. *Conference compan-
            ion on Human factors in computing systems,* pages 292–
            293, May 7-11 1995.

[Kle04]   Gary Klein. *The Power of Intuition: How to Use Your Gut
            Feelings to Make Better Decisions at Work.* Doubleday
            Business, 2004.

[Kno90]   Malcolm S Knowles. *The Adult Learner: a Neglected Species.* Building blocks of human potential. Gulf Pub. Co, Houston, 4th ed edition, 1990.

[Kou06]   John Kounios. The prepared mind: Neural activity prior to problem presentation predicts subsequent solution by sudden insight. *Psychological Science,* 17(10):882–890, 2006.

[KR08]   Jeffrey D. Karpicke and Henry L. Roediger, III. The critical importance of retrieval for learning. *Science,* 319(5865):966 – 968, Feb 2008.

[Lak87]   George Lakoff. *Women, Fire, and Dangerous Things: What Categories Reveal About the Mind.* University of Chicago Press, Chicago, 1987.

[Lev97]   David A. Levy. *Tools of Critical Thinking: Metathoughts for Psychology.* Allyn and Bacon, Boston, 1997.

[Lev06]   Daniel J. Levitin. *This Is Your Brain on Music: The Science of a Human Obsession.* Dutton, New York, NY, 2006.

[Lew88]   Pawel Lewicki. Acquisition of procedural knowledge about a pattern of stimuli that cannot be articulated. *Cognitive Psychology,* 20(1):24–37, Jan 1988.

[Loh07]   Steve Lohr. Slow down, brave multitasker, and don't read this in traffic. *The New York Times,* Mar 25 2007.

[Lut06]   Tom Lutz. *Doing Nothing: A History of Loafers, Loungers, Slackers, and Bums in America.* Farrar, Straus and Giroux, New York, 1st edition, 2006.

[Mac00]   Michael Macrone. *Brush Up Your Shakespeare!* Harper-Resource, New York, 1st harperresource ed edition, 2000.

[Mas06]   Mike Mason. *Pragmatic Version Control Using Subversion.* The Pragmatic Programmers, LLC, Raleigh, NC, and Dallas, TX, second edition, 2006.

[MR05]   Mary Lynn Manns and Linda Rising. *Fearless Change: Patterns for Introducing New Ideas.* Addison-Wesley, Boston, 2005.

[Mye98]   Isabel Briggs Myers. *MBTI Manual: A Guide to the Development and Use of the Myers-Briggs Type Indicator*. Consulting Psychologists Press, Palo Alto, Calif., 3rd ed edition, 1998.

[Neg94]   Nicholas Negroponte. Don't dissect the frog, build it. *Wired*, 2.07, July 1994.

[Nor04]   Donald A Norman. *Emotional Design: Why We Love (or Hate) Everyday Things*. Basic Books, New York, 2004.

[Nyg07]   Michael T. Nygard. *Release It!: Design and Deploy Production-Ready Software*. The Pragmatic Programmers, LLC, Raleigh, NC, and Dallas, TX, 2007.

[Pap93]   Seymour Papert. *Mindstorms: Children, Computers, and Powerful Ideas*. Basic Books, New York, 2nd ed. edition, 1993.

[PC85]   George Pólya and John Horton Conway. *How to Solve It: A New Aspect of Mathematical Method*. Princeton University Press, Princeton, expanded princeton science library ed edition, 1985.

[Pie81]   Paul Pietsch. *Shufflebrain: The Quest for the Hologramic Mind*. Houghton Mifflin, Boston, 1981.

[Pin05]   Daniel H. Pink. *A Whole New Mind: Moving from the Information Age to the Conceptual Age*. Penguin Group, New York, 2005.

[Pol58]   M. Polanyi. *Personal Knowledge*. Routledge and Kegan Paul, London, 1958.

[Pre02]   Steven Pressfield. *The War of Art: Break Through the Blocks and Win Your Inner Creative Battles*. Warner Books, New York, warner books ed edition, 2002.

[Raw76]   G. E. Rawlinson. *The Significance of Letter Position in Word Recognition*. PhD thesis, University of Nottingham, Nottingham UK, 1976.

[Raw99]   G. E. Rawlinson. Reibadailty. *New Scientist*, (162):55, 1999.

[RB06]   C. Rosaen and R. Benn. The experience of transcenden-
          tal meditation in middle school students: A qualitative
          report. *Explore*, 2(5):422–5, Sep-Oct 2006.

[RD05]   Johanna Rothman and Esther Derby. *Behind Closed
          Doors: Secrets of Great Management*. The Pragmatic Pro-
          grammers, LLC, Raleigh, NC, and Dallas, TX, 2005.

[Rey08]   Garr Reynolds. *Presentation Zen: Simple Ideas on Pre-
          sentation Design and Delivery*. New Riders, Berkeley,
          CA, 2008.

[RG05]   Jared Richardson and Will Gwaltney. *Ship It! A Practical
          Guide to Successful Software Projects*. The Pragmatic
          Programmers, LLC, Raleigh, NC, and Dallas, TX, 2005.

[RH76]   Albert Rothenberg and Carl R. Hausman. *The Creativity
          Question*. Duke University Press, Durham, N.C., 1976.

[Rob70]   Francis Pleasent Robinson. *Effective Study*. Harper-
          collins College, New York, NY, fourth edition, 1970.

[RW98]   Linda S. Rising and Jack E. Watson. Improving quality
          and productivity in training: A new model for the high-
          tech learning environment. *Bell Labs Technical Journal*,
          Jan 1998.

[Sac68]   Sackman. Exploratory experimental studies comparing
          online and offline. *Communications of the ACM*, pages
          3–11, Jan 1968.

[SB72]   G. Spencer-Brown. *Laws of Form*. Julian Press, New
          York, 1972.

[Sch95]   Daniel L. Schwartz. The emergence of abstract rep-
          resentations in dyad problem solving. *Journal of the
          Learning Sciences*, (4):321–354, 1995.

[Sen90]   Peter Senge. *The Fifth Discipline: The Art and Practice of
          the Learning Organization*. Currency/Doubleday, New
          York, 1990.

[SES90]   Jonathan Schooler and Tonya Engstler-Schooler. Ver-
          bal overshadowing of visual memories; some things are
          better left unsaid. *Cognitive Psychology*, 22, 1990.

[Sev04]   Richard Seven. Life interrupted. *Seattle Times*, Nov 28 2004.

[SH91]   William Strauss and Neil Howe. *Generations: The History of America's Future, 1584 to 2069*. Morrow, New York, 1st edition, 1991.

[SH06]   Venkat Subramaniam and Andy Hunt. *Practices of an Agile Developer: Working in the Real World*. The Pragmatic Programmers, LLC, Raleigh, NC, and Dallas, TX, 2006.

[Smi04]   David Livingston Smith. *Why We Lie: The Evolutionary Roots of Deception and the Unconscious Mind*. St. Martin's Press, New York, 1st edition, 2004.

[SMLR90]   C. Stasz, D. McArthur, M. Lewis, and K. Ramsey. Teaching and learning generic skills for the workplace. *RAND and the National Center for Research in Vocational Education*, November 1990.

[SO04]   H. Singh and M. W. O'Boyle. Interhemispheric interaction during global/local processing in mathematically gifted adolescents, average ability youth and college students. *Neuropsychology*, 18(2), 2004.

[SQU84]   Edwin A. Abbott (A. SQUARE). *Flatland: A Romance of Many Dimensions*. Dover 2007 Reprint, New York, 1884.

[Swi08]   Travis Swicegood. *Pragmatic Version Control using Git*. The Pragmatic Programmers, LLC, Raleigh, NC, and Dallas, TX, 2008.

[TABM03]   J. Gregory Trafton, Erik M. Altmann, Derek P. Brock, and Farilee E. Mintz. Preparing to resume an interrupted task: Effects of prospective goal encoding and retrospective rehearsal. *International Journal Human-Computer Studies*, (58), 2003.

[Tal07]   Nassim Nicholas Taleb. *The Black Swan: The Impact of the Highly Improbable*. Random House, New York, 2007.

[TH03]   David Thomas and Andrew Hunt. *Pragmatic Version Control Using CVS*. The Pragmatic Programmers, LLC, Raleigh, NC, and Dallas, TX, 2003.

[Tra97]   N. Tractinsky.   Aesthetics and apparent usability: Empirically assessing cultural and methodological issues. *CHI 97 Electronic Publications: Papers*, 1997.

[VF77]   Dyckman W. Vermilye and William Ferris. *Relating Work and Education*, volume 1977 of *The Jossey-Bass series in higher education*. Jossey-Bass Publishers, San Francisco, 1st edition, 1977.

[vO98]   Roger von Oech. *A Whack on the Side of the Head*. Warner Business Books, New York, 1998.

[Wei85]   Gerald M. Weinberg. *The Secrets of Consulting*. Dorset House, New York, 1985.

[Wei86]   Gerald M. Weinberg. *Becoming a Technical Leader: An Organic Problem-Solving Approach*. Dorset House, New York, 1986.

[Wei06]   Gerald M. Weinberg. *Weinberg on Writing: The Fieldstone Method*. Dorset House Pub., New York, 2006.

[Whi58]   T. H. White. *The Once and Future King*. Putnam, New York, 1958.

[WN99]   Charles Weir and James Noble.   Process patterns for personal practice: How to succeed in development without really trying. http://www.charlesweir.com/papers/ProcessPatterns.pdf, 1999.

[WP96]   Win Wenger and Richard Poe. *The Einstein Factor: A Proven New Method for Increasing Your Intelligence*. Prima Pub., Rocklin, CA, 1996.

[ZRF99]   Ron Zemke, Claire Raines, and Bob Filipczak. *Generations at Work: Managing the Clash of Veterans, Boomers, Xers, and Nexters in Your Workplace*. AMACOM, New York, 1999.

Index

A

Achievability, in goal-setting, 151
Adams, Douglas, 140
The Adult Learner: A Neglected Species (Knowles), 164
Advanced beginners, 20–21
Aesthetics, 64–66, 103
Affinity groups, 177f
Agile methods, described, 4
Allen, David, 232
Amabile, Teresa, 199
Anchoring, 115
Archetypes, 129, 130, 131f
Armstrong, Louis, 36
Artist, 130
The Artist's Way (Cameron), 98
Attention, 209, 211
    see also Focus
Attractiveness and usefulness, 66–68
Auditory learners, 159, 160f
Automation, 192
Awareness, 196, 249

B

Baby Boomers, 127
Backtracking, 191
Ball bearings technique, 98
Bandwidth, 211
Beck, Kent, 89
Beginner's mind, 248–251
Beginners, advanced, 20–21
Beliot Mindset List, 126
Bernstein, Albert, 136
Bias, *see* Cognitive bias
Bird by Bird: Some Instructions on Writing and Life (Lamott), 84
Bisociation, 87

The Black Swan: The Impact of the Highly Improbable (Taleb), 118
Blogging, 96, 97
Bono, Edward de, 87
Brains, 45–72
    activities for, 72
    change and, 109, 245–247
    as dual-CPU, 46f, 46–51
    exocortex, 221–222, 233
    grooving, 205
    input sources, 202, 203f
    insight and, 51–54, 55f
    left vs. right side of, 58
    linear vs. rich characteristics, 57f, 61f, 55–63
    neurogenesis and, 67
    neuroplasticity, 70–71
    overview of, 45–46
    pattern matching, 68–70
    patterns and, 102–110
    primitive aspects of, 136
    rich mode and, 63–68, 75–80
    sensory input, 73–77
    synchronization, 80–91
    verbalization delay, 51
    see also Debugging; Experts; Focus; Learning
Breaks, 237
Broken Windows theory, 67
Brooks, Frederick, 2, 240
Brown, George Spencer, 102
Bus, 47–51
Buzan, Tony, 171

C

Change, 109, 245–247
Claxton, Guy, 58
Closure, 116, 121
Cockburn, Alistair, 200

Coding workspace, 243
Cognition, pressure and, 198–202
Cognitive biases, 115–123
Cognitive interference, 76
Cognitive overload, 229
Collaborative mind maps, 176
Color constancy, 202
Colvin, Geoffrey, 37
Communications workspace, 242
Competency, 21–22
Confirmation bias, 116
Consciousness, 51
Consciousness Explained (Dennett), 218
Construct theory vs. event theory, 14
Constructivism, 184
Context
  consideration of, 5–6
  focus and, 210, 227–233, 240–243
  generations and, 124
  goals and, 152
  importance of, 22, 41–43
  for neurogenesis, 67
Context switching, 227, 228, 240
Corn muffin recipe, 19f
Correlation vs. causation, 119
Cramming vs. spacing, 170
Creativity, 217
Cross-sensory feedback, 74

D

da Vinci, Leonardo, 249
Darwin, Charles, 26
de Bono, Edward, 87
Debugging, 113–143, 189
  cognitive biases, 115–123
  exposing bugs, 136–140
  generational affinities, 124–132
  intuition and, 140
  overview of, 114f, 113–115
  personality tendencies, 133–136
Decontextualized objectivity, 42
Deliberate learning, see Learning
Deliberate switching, 231
Dennett, Daniel, 218
Design Patterns: Elements of
  Reusable Object-Oriented
  Software (Gamma, et al.), 23
Design, importance of, 68

Dinosaur Brains: Dealing with All
  Those Impossible People at Work
  (Bernstein), 137
Distractions, 230
Distributed cognition, 221
Diversity, 132
Diversity, in learning, 156
Documenting, 178–180
Doing Nothing: A History of Loafers,
  Loungers, Slackers, and Bums
  in America (Lutz), 217
Dollar-cost averaging, 157
Don't Dissect the Frog, Build It
  (Negroponte), 62
Don't Repeat Yourself, see DRY
  principle
Donne, John, 152
Drawing, 75, 76, 174
Drawing on the Right Side of the
  Brain (Edwards), 76
Dreyfus mind map, 172f
Dreyfus Model, 13, 14
  application of, 25–32, 43–44
  effectiveness of, 31–38
  rate yourself, 44
  skill acquisition and, 29f
  stages of, 17–26
DRY principle, 23
Dual-CPU mode, of brain, 46–51
Dweck, Carol, 71

E

Edison, Thomas, 98
Education, 146
  see also Learning
Edwards, Betty, 58, 76, 202
Einstein, Albert, 222
Eisenhower, 155
Email, 229, 230f, 235
Email apnea, 236
Enhanced learning techniques, 166
Eno, Brian, 108
Environment, 191
Ericsson, K. Anderson, 32
Event theory vs. construct theory, 14
Exocortex, 221–222, 233
Experience, 183–207
  failing and, 189–192
  imagination and, 202–206
  inner game and, 193–198
  learning and, 183–187

leveraging knowledge, 187–189
overview of, 206–207
pressure and, 198–202
see also Experts; Learning
Experimentation, 191
Experts, 13–44
beginner's mind, 248–251
communication of, 16
context and, 41–43
Dreyfus model and, 17–26, 43–44
Dreyfus model, application of,
31–38
environment for, 36–38
vs. novices, 15–17, 28
overview of, 13–15
pattern matching and, 68
rules and, 25–32
skill distribution and, 29, 30f
stage of, 24–26
as teachers, 31
time required to become, 32
tool trap of, 39–41
as wizards, 15f
see also Experience; Focus;
Learning
Exploration, 190
Exploratory mind maps, 175
Exposure effect, 116
Extravert, 133
Extreme programming, 84
Extreme Programming Explained:
Embrace Change (Beck), 89

F

Failure, learning from, 189–198, 200
False memory, 116
Feedback, 74, 141, 157, 195
Feeling, 134
The Fifth Discipline: The Art and
Practice of the Learning
Organization (Senge), 6
First drafts, 84
Focus, 103, 209–244
context and, 227–233
improving, 210–216
interruptions and, 233–239
knowledge management and,
220–229
overview of, 209–210
rest and, 217–220
self-awareness and, 244

tasks in context, 240–243
Ford, Paul, 230
Forest vs. trees, 68–70
Four archetypes, 129
Free time, 155
Free-form journaling, 96
From Novice to Expert: Excellence and
Power in Clinical Nursing
Practice (Benner), 28
Functional shift, 108
Fundamental attribution error, 115

G

Galin, David, 83
Gallwey, W. Timothy, 193, 194
Gardner, Howard, 161, 162
Generation X, 128
Generational affinities, 124–132
Getting Things Done: The Art of
Stress-Free Productivity (Allen),
232
GI Generation, 127
The Girl with the Pearl Earring
(Chevalier), 250
Goals, 149–154
Gordon, Deborah, 39
Gould, Elizabeth, 67
Grace Cathedral (San Francisco),
100f
Graham, Paul, 211
Group work, 164–166, 176

H

Hackers and Painters: Big Ideas from
the Computer Age (Graham),
211
Hahn, Thich Nhat, 192
Handwriting, 174
Hare Brain, Tortoise Mind: How
Intelligence Increases When You
Think Less (Claxton), 58
Harstock, Shawn, 49
Harvesting patterns, 102–110
Hawthorne effect, 116
Hero, 130
Hierarchical pattern, 69
Holographic memory, 48
Howe, Elias, 93, 94f, 95
Howe, Neil, 129, 131f
Humor, 90, 91

I

Ideas, *see* Brains; Insight
Ignorance, 26
Image streaming, 95–96
Imagination, 202–206
Index cards, 52
Infinite regression, 20, 40
Information, 210
Inner game, 193–198
The Inner Game of Music (Green & Gallwey), 193, 196
The Inner Game of Tennis (Gallwey), 193
Input, 202, 203f
Insight, 51–54, 55f, 179
Intelligence, 161
Interference, 97, 195
Interruption lag, 239
Interruptions, managing, 233–239
Introvert, 133
Intuition, 25, 27, 133
    errors in, 140
    mode for, 47
    rich mode and, 62
Investment, in learning, 157

J

Jefferson, Thomas, 222
Journaling, 96
Judging vs. perceiving, 134
Jung, Carl, 133
Just Write technique, 99

K

Kahn, Louis, 68
Ki-Chun, 103
Kim, June, 103, 197
Kinesthetic learners, 159, 160f
Knowledge, 220–229
    leveraging, 187–189
Knowledge portfolio, 154
Knowles, Malcolm, 164
Koenig, Dierk, 85, 104, 179
Koestler, Arthur, 87

L

Labyrinths, 99, 100f, 101
Lakoff, George, 87
Lamott, Anne, 84
Laws of Form (Brown), 102

Learning, 3
    defining, 145–149
    among disciplines, 6
    diversity in, 156
    do-it-yourself approach to, 148
    documenting and, 178–180
    enhanced techniques for, 166
    groups and, 164–166
    investing in, 154–158
    knowledge management and, 220–229
    mind maps for, 172f, 174f, 177f, 171–178
    over time, 121f
    play and, 183–187
    SMART goals and, 149–154
    SQ3R, 167–169, 175
    styles of, 158f, 160f, 159–164
    success and, 145
    synthesis and, 62
    by teaching, 181–182
    test-driven, 170
    see also Brains; Experts; Focus; Skills
Lemon juice man, 26
Levy, Jerre, 56, 76
Linear mode, 47–51
    characteristics, 57f, 55–63
    pattern matching and, 68–70
Lists, 233
Lizard logic, 137
Logo, 184
Lozanov, George, 82
Lutz, Robert A., 63
Lutz, Tom, 217

M

Malicious obedience, 28
Marinating, *see* Focus; Problem solving
Martial arts, 103
Maskable interruptions, 238
Maxims, 22
Measurability, in goal-setting, 150
Meditation, 212–216
Memory
    bus contention and, 47–51
    dynamic nature of, 49
    false, 116
    holographic, 48
Mental whacks, 105

Metacognitive abilities, 30
Metaphors, 86, 87, 89, 91
Metheny, Pat, 204
Mill, John Stuart, 146
Millennial Generation, 128
Mimicry, 138
Mims, Forrest M. III, 11
*The Mind Map Book: How to Use
    Radiant Thinking to Maximize
    Your Brain's Untapped Potential*
    (Buzan), 171
Mind maps, 172f, 174f, 177f,
    171–178, 185
    see also Wikis
*Mind Over Machine: The Power of
    Human Intuition and Expertise
    in the Era of the Computer*
    (Dreyfus & Dreyfus), 13
*Mindset: The New Psychology of
    Success* (Dweck), 71
*Mindstorms: Children, Computers,
    and Powerful Ideas* (Papert),
    184
Mirror neurons, 205
Moleskine notebooks, 53, 54
Morning pages, 98
Multiple intelligences, 161
Multitasking, 228
Myers Briggs Type Indicator, 133,
    163

N

Negroponte, Nicholas, 62
Neurogenesis, 67
Neuroplasticity, 70–71
*The New Drawing on the Right Side
    of the Brain* (Edwards), 58
Next actions, 10
"No Silver Bullet-Essence and
    Accident in Software
    Engineering" (Brooks), 2
Noble, James, 114
Nomad, 130
Nominal fallacy, 117
Notepad, 51
Novices
    Dreyfus model of, 18–20
    vs. experts, 15–17, 28

O

Objectives, *see* Goals

Oblique strategies, 108
Odds, 120
The Once and Future King (White),
    107
Oracles, 107
Oracular whack, 107
Outliers, 120

P

Pair programming, 84
Papert, Seymour, 184, 186, 187, 189
Parity rule, 85
Pasteur, Louis, 179
Pattern matching, 31, 68, 95,
    102–110, 227
PDA, 52
Perceiving vs. judging, 134
Perception, 204
Perfectionism, 84
Personality tendencies, 133–136
Personality types, 163
Piaget, Jean, 184
Picasso, Pablo, 59
Pink, Dan, 58, 64
Platonic fold, 118
Play, learning and, 183–187
Plutarch, 148
Po technique, 87
Pocket Mod, 52, 53f
Podcast, 180
Poincaré, Henri, 101
Practice, 32
*Practices of an Agile Developer:
    Working in the Real World*
    (Subramaniam & Hunt), 24
Pragmatic Investment Plan (PIP),
    154–158
*The Pragmatic Programmer: From
    Journeyman to Master* (Hunt &
    Thomas), 4, 23, 32, 89, 154,
    157, 181
Predictions, 117–119, 204
*Presentation Zen: Simple Ideas on
    Presentation Design and
    Delivery* (Reynolds), 3
Pressure, 198–202
Problem solving, 1, 21, 92, 187
    image streaming, 95–96
    mode for, 47
    see also Image streaming
Procrastination, 219

Proficiency, 22–24
Programming
  awareness in, 197
  code patterns and, 103
  errors and bugs in, 2
  failure permitted zones and, 201
  interruptions and, 234–239
  learning and, 3
  multitasking and productivity, 228
  organizing tasks, 232
  pair, 84
  problem solving and, 1
  safely, 191
  version control and, 192
Prophet, 130
Proposals, 164
Pólya, George, 188

Q

Questions, reading and, 168
QuickSilver, 231, 232

R

Random juxtaposition, 88
Reading deliberately, 167–169
Recipes, for novices, 18, 19f
Recite, reading and, 168
Relevance, goal-setting and, 151
Resistance, 97
Responsibility, 34–36
Resumption lag, 239
Review, reading and, 168
Rewards, 134
Rich mode, 47
  characteristics, 57f, 61f, 55–63
  encouraging, 92–103
  exercise for, 80
  insight and, 51–54
  memory and, 47–51
  pattern matching and, 68–70
  pressure and, 199
  rise of, 63–68
  synchronization of, 80–91
  tapping into, 75–80
Richardson, Jared, 176
Rising, Linda, 77
Rituals, 157
Road rage, 136
Role-playing, 77
Rothman, Johanna, 77, 153

Rubber ducking, 181
Rule of Three, 220

S

Scaffolding, 206
Schmidt, Peter, 108
Screencast, 180
The Sea of Cortez (Steinbeck), 42
Seance, 82
Selection, 68
Self-awareness, 244, 249
Self-serving bias, 115
Senge, Peter, 6
Sense tuning, 225
Sensing, 133
Sensory Input, 73–77
Sewing machine invention, 93, 94f
Shakespeare, William, 108
Sheep dip, 146, 147f
Shu Ha Ri, 36
Silent Generation, 127
Single-task interfaces, 231
Situational feedback, 195
Skills
  acquisition of, 13, 17–26, 29f
  distribution of, 29, 30f
  learning, 3
  most important, 3
SMART goals, 149–154
Software design, 2
Spacing vs. cramming, 170
Spatial cueing, 172
Specificity, in goal-setting, 150
Sperry, Roger W., 56
Split-brain studies, 56, 57f
SQ3R, 167–169, 175
Steinbeck, John, 42
Sternberg, Robert, 161
Stone, Linda, 236
Strauss, William, 129, 131f
Study groups, 165
SuperMemo, 170
Survey, reading and, 168
Symbolic reduction fallacy, 117
Synthesis, 62
System metaphor, 89

T

Tactile enhancement, 74
Teachers, 31
Teaching, 181–182

Temperaments, *see* Personality
    tendencies
Terry, Clark, 36
Test-driven learning, 170
Think!, 231
Thinking vs. feeling, 134
Thomas, Dave, 23, 105, 154
Time, 155, 211
Timed-boxed, goals and, 152
Tool trap, 39–41
Training, *see* Learning
Triarchic theory, 161

U

Uncertainty, 122
Unit testing, 192
Unix wizard, 15f
Unmaskable interruptions, 238
"Unskilled and Unaware of It: How
    Difficulties in Recognizing
    One's Own Incompetence Lead
    to Inflated Self-Assessments"
    Kruger & Dunning, 26, 30

V

Values, 125
Version control, 192
Vipassana meditation, 214
Virtual desktop switcher, 241
Virtual mailboxes, 229
Vision, 149
Visual learners, 158f, 159, 160f

Visual voicemail, 52
Voice memos, 52
von Oech, Roger, 106

W

Walking, 99
Weinberg, Jerry, 197, 200
Weir, Charles, 114
Wetware, defined, 1, 5
A Whack on the Side of the Head
    (von Oech), 106
Whack, mental, 105
Whack, oracular, 107
White, T.H., 107
A Whole New Mind: Moving from the
    Information Age to the
    Conceptual Age, 58, 64
Wikis, 223f, 224f, 226f, 222–229
WikiWord, 223
Women, Fire, and Dangerous Things:
    What Categories Reveal About
    the Mind (Lakoff), 87
Work environment, 36–38
Work to rule, 28
Workspaces, 242, 242f
Wozniak, Piotr, 170
Wright, Steven, 91
Writing, 99, 174, 178
Writing workspace, 242

Y

Youngman, Henny, 91

Also by Andy Hunt

Practices of an Agile Developer

Agility is all about using feedback to respond to change. Learn how to • apply the principles of agility throughout the software development process • establish and maintain an agile working environment • deliver what users really want • use personal agile techniques for better coding and debugging • use effective collaborative techniques for better teamwork • move to an agile approach

Practices of an Agile Developer:
Working in the Real World
Venkat Subramaniam and Andy Hunt
(189 pages) ISBN: 0-9745140-8-X. $29.95
http://pragprog.com/titles/pad

Pragmatic Unit Testing

You don't test a bridge by driving a single car over it right down the middle lane on a clear, calm day. Yet many programmers approach testing that same way-one pass right down the middle and they call it "tested." Pragmatic programmers can do better than that! With this book, you will:

• Discover the best hiding places where bugs breed
• Learn how to think of all the things that could go wrong • Test pieces of code without using the whole project • Test effectively with the whole team.

Available in both **C#** and **Java** editions.

Pragmatic Unit Testing in C#, 2nd Ed.
Andy Hunt and Dave Thomas with Matt Hargett
(240 pages) ISBN: 978-0-9776166-7-1. $29.95
http://pragprog.com/titles/utc2

More on Agile Projects

Agile Retrospectives

Mine the experience of your software development team continually throughout the life of the project. Rather than waiting until the end of the project—as with a traditional retrospective, when it's too late to help—agile retrospectives help you adjust to change *today*.

The tools and recipes in this book will help you uncover and solve hidden (and not-so-hidden) problems with your technology, your methodology, and those difficult "people issues" on your team.

Agile Retrospectives: Making Good Teams Great
Esther Derby and Diana Larsen
(170 pages) ISBN: 0-9776166-4-9. $29.95
http://pragprog.com/titles/dlret

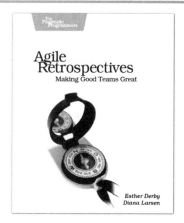

Manage It!

Manage It! is an award-winning, risk-based guide to making good decisions about how to plan and guide your projects. Author Johanna Rothman shows you how to beg, borrow, and steal from the best methodologies to fit your particular project. You'll find what works best for *you*.

• Learn all about different project lifecycles • See how to organize a project • Compare sample project dashboards • See how to staff a project • Know when you're done—and what that means.

Your Guide to Modern, Pragmatic Project Management
Johanna Rothman
(360 pages) ISBN: 0-9787392-4-8. $34.95
http://pragprog.com/titles/jrpm

The Pragmatic Bookshelf

The Pragmatic Bookshelf features books written by developers for developers. The titles continue the well-known Pragmatic Programmer style and continue to garner awards and rave reviews. As development gets more and more difficult, the Pragmatic Programmers will be there with more titles and products to help you stay on top of your game.

Visit Us Online

Pragmatic Thinking and Learning's Home Page
http://pragprog.com/titles/ahptl
Source code from this book, errata, and other resources. Come give us feedback, too!

Register for Updates
http://pragprog.com/updates
Be notified when updates and new books become available.

Join the Community
http://pragprog.com/community
Read our weblogs, join our online discussions, participate in our mailing list, interact with our wiki, and benefit from the experience of other Pragmatic Programmers.

New and Noteworthy
http://pragprog.com/news
Check out the latest pragmatic developments in the news.

Save on the PDF

Save on the PDF version of this book. Owning the paper version of this book entitles you to purchase the PDF version at a terrific discount. The PDF is great for carrying around on your laptop. It's hyperlinked, has color, and is fully searchable.

Buy it now at pragprog.com/coupon.

Contact Us

Phone Orders:	1-800-699-PROG (+1 919 847 3884)
Online Orders:	www.pragprog.com/catalog
Customer Service:	orders@pragprog.com
Non-English Versions:	translations@pragprog.com
Pragmatic Teaching:	academic@pragprog.com
Author Proposals:	proposals@pragprog.com

Pragmatic Thinking and Learning

This card summarizes the tips from
Pragmatic Thinking and Learning:
Refactoring Your Wetware
(ISBN 978-1-9343560-5-0)
by Andy Hunt.

For more information about THE PRAGMATIC BOOKSHELF please visit
www.pragprog.com.

TIPS 1 TO 20

1. **Always consider the context.**
(pg. 6)

2. **Use rules for novices, intuition for experts.**
(pg. 28)

3. **Know what you don't know.**
(pg. 30)

4. **Learn by watching and imitating.**
(pg. 35)

5. **Keep practicing in order to remain expert.**
(pg. 38)

6. **Avoid formal methods if you need creativity, intuition, or inventiveness.**
(pg. 41)

7. **Learn the skill of learning.**
(pg. 44)

8. **Capture all ideas to get more of them.**
(pg. 53)

9. **Learn by synthesis as well as by analysis.**
(pg. 63)

10. **Strive for good design; it really works better.**
(pg. 68)

11. **Rewire your brain with belief and constant practice.**
(pg. 71)

12. **Add sensory experience to engage more of your brain.**
(pg. 74)

13. **Lead with $\mathcal{R}$-mode; follow with L-mode.**
(pg. 82)

14. **Use metaphor as the meeting place between L-mode and $\mathcal{R}$-mode.**
(pg. 86)

15. **Cultivate humor to build stronger metaphors.**
(pg. 91)

16. **Step away from the keyboard to solve hard problems.**
(pg. 102)

17. **Change your viewpoint to solve the problem.**
(pg. 106)

18. **Watch the outliers: "rarely" doesn't mean "never."**
(pg. 120)

19. **Be comfortable with uncertainty.**
(pg. 122)

20. **Trust ink over memory; every mental read is a write.**
(pg. 123)

21. **Hedge your bets with diversity.**
(pg. 132)

22. **Allow for different bugs in different people.**
(pg. 135)

23. **Act like you've evolved: breathe, don't hiss.**
(pg. 139)

24. **Trust intuition, but verify.**
(pg. 141)

25. **Create SMART objectives to reach your goals.**
(pg. 152)

26. **Plan your investment in learning deliberately.**
(pg. 158)

27. **Discover how *you* learn best.**
(pg. 163)

28. **Form study groups to learn and teach.**
(pg. 166)

29. **Read deliberately.**
(pg. 169)

30. **Take notes with both $\mathcal{R}$-mode and L-mode.**
(pg. 175)

31. **Write on: documenting is more important than documentation.**
(pg. 180)

32. **See it. Do it. Teach it.**
(pg. 181)

33. **Play more in order to learn more.**
(pg. 187)

34. **Learn from similarities; unlearn from differences.**
(pg. 189)

35. **Explore, invent, and apply in your environment—safely.**
(pg. 190)

36. **See without judging and then act.**
(pg. 196)

37. **Give yourself permission to fail; it's the path to success.**
(pg. 200)

38. **Groove your mind for success.**
(pg. 205)

39. **Learn to pay attention.**
(pg. 213)

40. **Make thinking time.**
(pg. 219)

41. **Use a wiki to manage information and knowledge.**
(pg. 224)

42. **Establish rules of engagement to manage interruptions.**
(pg. 234)

43. **Send less email, and you'll receive less email.**
(pg. 236)

44. **Choose your own tempo for an email conversation.**
(pg. 236)

45. **Mask interrupts to maintain focus.**
(pg. 237)

46. **Use multiple monitors to avoid context switching.**
(pg. 240)

47. **Optimize your personal workflow to maximize context.**
(pg. 242)

48. **Grab the wheel. You can't steer on autopilot.**
(pg. 250)

CONTEXT MATTERS.
www.PragProg.com/titles/ahptl